$\mathcal{D}$EVOTIONS FOR A NEW BEGINNING

HAL M. HELMS

PARACLETE PRESS
BREWSTER, MASSACHUSETTS

Devotions for a New Beginning

2006 First Printing this Edition

© 1999 by Creative Joys, Inc.;
Revised edition ©2006 by Paraclete Press, Inc.

Originally published in 1984 under two separate titles: *A New Beginning* and *The Heart of the Matter.*

ISBN: 1-55725-239-4

Unless otherwise designated, Scripture quotations are taken from the Revised Standard Version of the Bible, copyright 1946, 1952, 1971 by the Division of Christian Education of the National Council of the Churches of Christ in the USA. Used by permission.
Scripture quotations designated KJV are taken from the King James Version of the Bible.

Library of Congress Cataloging–in–Publication Data
Helms, Hal McElwaine.
    Devotions for a new beginning / Hal M. Helms.—Rev. ed.
        p. cm.
    Rev. ed. of: A new beginning ; The heart of the matter. 1984.
    ISBN 1–55725–239–4
    1. Catholic Church—Prayer-books and devotions—English.
2. Bible—Devotional literature. I. Helms, Hal McElwaine. New beginning. II Helms, Hal McElwaine. Heart of the matter. III. Title.
BX2110.H46 2006
242—dc22   2005037489

10 9 8 7 6 5 4 3 2 1

Published by Paraclete Press
Brewster, Massachusetts
www.paracletepress.com

Printed in the United States of America.

Cover Photo: Roderick Chen/Superstock

Contents

Introduction

This is not your ordinary devotional. Yes, each entry begins with a recommended Bible reading, followed by a reflection on it, a closing prayer, and questions that help you to carry these thoughts throughout your day. However, these devotions are not simply uplifting; they also probe deeply into the struggles of daily living. They will help you in facing life's difficulties head-on, with God's help. There are no easy answers, here, but instead, you will discover God's assurance that you are on a spiritual journey, even when it doesn't "feel" like you are.

The devotions are organized thematically, around such issues as the Lordship of Christ, Why Discipline?, God's Will or My Will?, and more. Each of the scriptures, meditations, and questions are carefully chosen and presented in such a way that you may find God at work uniquely in your life, in your particular circumstances.

As you prayerfully read through these daily reflections and answer the probing questions for yourself, many emotions, conflicts, and struggles will surface. That is good! Don't be afraid of the process; it will draw you to seek the guidance of the Holy Spirit and develop your relationship deeply with him.

There are twenty-four chapters, or weeks, of devotions and, as mentioned earlier, they are not in random order—their placement is deliberate. This devotional is meant to challenge, encourage, and motivate you in your journey. It is meant to mature the life of Jesus in you.

You might consider doing these devotions with a friend, a spouse, or a small group.

During the first twelve weeks, you will see that some basics are being stressed and deepened in your heart. The themes of these first twelve weeks address vital issues common to all of us: the blessings of obedience, the importance of facing your feelings realistically, and battling your thought life. They also lay important groundwork for the second twelve weeks of material.

The latter twelve weeks deal with the roadblocks that prevent growth and maturity. Unknowingly, we can spend years on detours or be broken down in some of life's ditches, because we allow unrecognizable roadblocks (unforgiveness, anger, control, vindictiveness, misplaced faith) into our lives. Great freedom results when these blocks are identified and we forsake lifelong patterns; this freedom comes from God and brings incredible joy!   —Hal Helms

A NOTE FROM THE PUBLISHER
In the thirty-plus years that these devotions have been in use in various forms, thousands of people have found them to be the very words that have started a fresh work of God in their lives. God desires to heal us and make us whole. *Devotions for a New Beginning* promises to be a faithful friend, a challenge, and a support on your spiritual journey.

We would love to hear from you, and to receive your reactions to the devotions in this book. Please write to us at:

Paraclete Press
Attn: Devotions for a New Beginning
P.O. Box 1568
Orleans, MA 02653

newbeginning@paracletepress.com

THE LORDSHIP OF CHRIST

God has highly
exalted him . . .
that at the
name of Jesus
every knee should bow . . .
and every tongue
confess that
Jesus Christ is Lord,
to the
glory of God the Father.

Philippians 2:9–11

ONE

Jesus is Lord
Daily Reading: Acts 2:22–24, 32–42

"Let all the house of Israel therefore know assuredly that God has made him both Lord and Christ, this Jesus whom you crucified." (v. 36)

The word slips too easily from our tongues: "Lord!" But when Peter preached this sermon on the Day of Pentecost, it was no glib profession for him. The word *Kurios* had a very special meaning in that day. This was the term used for the emperor and for the "gods" which people worshiped in that time. It meant, "authority and power," and an individual was responsible to be obedient to his "lord."

Herein lies the heart of the problem for most of us as Christians. How glad we were, "when all was sin and shame," to welcome Jesus as Christ, Messiah, Anointed Savior, who came to us in our need, bound up our wounds, and forgave and cleansed us by his own sacrificial offering on the cross! Words can never describe what that reality means to anyone who has been convicted of sin by the Holy Spirit and has found the glorious freedom of forgiveness.

But where we have the trouble is in translating the genuine sense and knowledge of how much we owe him for his love, into daily obedience to him as Lord. Here we need help!

"Not everyone who says to me, Lord, Lord, shall enter the kingdom of heaven, but he who does the will of my Father who is in heaven" (Matthew 7:21).

A Prayer: Father, forgive me that I have failed so often to do the good that I knew and have done the evil that I hate. Heal me, body, soul, and spirit, that my life may show forth your

praise and glory. You have become my Savior. By your grace, I choose this day to make you Lord of all my life, including ——————— , ——————— , *and* ———————.
In the Name of Jesus. Amen.

Behold a sinner, dearest Lord
Encouraged by thy gracious word
Would venture near to seek the bread
By which thy children here are fed.
    (Anon.)

Ruler of All Nature
Daily Reading: Mark 4:35–41

"Who is this, that even wind and sea obey him?" (v. 41)

Our Lord is a mighty God! At his command seas are quiet and winds are still. His will and his word are greater than all the forces of nature, for by his will they exist and are.

"Worthy art thou, our Lord and God, to receive glory and honor and power, for thou didst create all things, and by thy will they existed and were created" (Revelation 4:11).

It is important for me to recognize that Jesus is the Lord and Ruler of my universe. As I move about this day, I would see him at work, and see the expression of his will and wisdom in the ordinary things as well as the big things. Not only in the stormy sea, but in the rustling grass, in the songs of birds, the passing of clouds or sunshine, I would see his creative and providential hand.

Fairest Lord Jesus, Ruler of all nature,
O thou of God and man the Son,
Thee would I cherish, thee would I honor
Thou my soul's glory, joy, and crown.

Most of us make God smaller than he really is, by our limited faith. Like the people of Nazareth, whose lack of faith kept Jesus from doing many mighty works among them, we limit him. Low vision, low aim, little faith, little results.

As I set out on this course of discipline, I would take high aim, heed the upward call, and keep my eyes on him who is Ruler of all!

A Prayer: We praise you, O Lord! We praise you in your sanctuary. We praise you in your mighty firmament! We praise you for your mighty deeds; we praise you for your excellent greatness! Not only with our lips, O Lord, but in our lives, by giving up ourselves to your service. In Jesus' Name. Amen.

1. How can you keep your vision of the Lord a large vision and still be aware of him in the little things of your life?
2. What is the greatest and most loving thing God has done for you?

Lord of the Commonplace
Daily Reading: 1 Kings 20:26–30

Because the Syrians have said, "The Lord is a god of the hills but he is not a god of the valleys," therefore I will give all this great multitude into your hand, and you shall know that I am the Lord. (v. 28)

Syria made a big mistake by tl [...]
the valley! Apparently she respec [...]
but thought she could get away wit [...]
it came to fighting in the valleys. [...]

To me, the valley symbolizes the [...]
no grand visions, no far horizons. Ju [...]
commonplace. How easy it is to get [...]
we saw when our hearts were lifted up [...]
inspiration. Now the vision has faded [...]
reality.

Is he the Lord of the commonplace, [...]
you must *absolutely* let the necessity of [...] you to him.
For he is Lord of the commonplace, else the whole structure
falls and great is the ruin of it!

Writing about Carl Sandburg's life, Ben Hecht says, "The
commonplace is the nightingale that sings in his poetry. Out
of him the ordinary look of life spoke with sudden, vivid
meanings, as if someone had washed the staleness from its
face and uncovered its deeply human gleams."

Jesus does that with our commonplaceness, the ordinary
tasks, relationships, worries, concerns and hopes that make
up our lives.

In these weeks, we need to know Jesus in the common
places. He is there, and he is Lord. Don't fail to seek him!

*A Prayer: Grant us, O Lord, to pass this day in gladness and
in peace, without stumbling and without sin that, reaching the
eventide victorious over all temptation, we may praise thee,
the eternal God, who art blessed and dost govern all things,
world without end. Amen.*

(Mozarabic Liturgy)

1. What can you do to become more aware of Jesus in the ordinary tasks of your day?

2. How have you discovered Jesus' care in your commonplace activities?

Lord of the Mountains
Daily Reading: Isaiah 49:8–13

"And I will make all my mountains a way." (v. 11a)

Mountains not only symbolize inspiration, such as the Mount of Transfiguration, but also that which is impossible and impassible for us. We all have our mountains of difficulties!

But stop and think! The mountain you face, which seems so hard to climb, is "his mountain." "I will make all *my* mountains a way," says the Lord. Whatever the difficult circumstance in your life at this moment, God in his great mercy and love for you has made that his circumstance. If it were yours alone, you would have reason to feel discouraged. But it is not yours alone. "For the Lord has comforted his people, and will have compassion on his afflicted."

Although you may long for greater ease, less demanding tasks, a more level road, this mountain way he calls you to walk is his way. Not only does he call you to it, but he promises to be with you.

The way may seem hard, even dreary. But look up! Keep plodding onward. The heavenly company is cheering you on, and Jesus himself, "the pioneer and perfector of our faith" supplies you with secret strength against all temptations *when you abandon all for him.*

We need the mountain way. No other way leads to the fulfillment and fullness of the life he offers.

> I know not where the road will lead
> I follow day by day,
> Or where it ends, I only know I walk the King's highway!
> I know not if the way is long, and no one else can say;
> But rough or smooth, up hill or down, I walk the King's highway.
> *(Evelyn Atwater Cummins)*

A Prayer: O God, who has commanded us to be perfect as thou art perfect, put into my heart, I pray thee, a continual desire to obey thy holy will. Teach me day by day what thou wouldest have me to do, and give me grace and power to fulfill the same. May I never from love of ease, decline the path which thou pointest out, nor, for fear of shame, turn away from it. Amen.

(Henry Alford, 1810–1871)

1. When the way is smooth and easy, whose strength do we usually rely on? Why?

2. When the way gets hard, Jesus often becomes more real to us. Why?

Lord of Our Relationships
Daily Reading: Colossians 3:12–16

If any one has a complaint against another, forgiving each other as the Lord has forgiven you. (v. 13)

In the Lord's prayer we are taught to pray, "Forgive us our trespasses (or sins) as we forgive those who trespass (or sin) against us." This is the acid test of our sincerity before a holy and all-seeing God. Before him, the secrets of all hearts are open, and we cannot hide even that which is hidden from us. Yet every time we pray in the words Jesus taught us, we ask God to forgive us *only* as we forgive others. A frightening thought!

Many of us have learned to bury and hide our negative and unforgiving feelings toward others. We know these feelings are wrong, and so we bury them away, like a dog burying a bone in the backyard. After a while, we may even have a hard time remembering what it was. But it lies there, unresolved and unforgiven, unless from the heart, we truly forgive.

Our buried resentments, often going back to the early days of our lives, can be the unconscious and hidden source of many difficulties—including the way we feel about ourselves, the way we worry about how others feel about us, and on and on. Only the Spirit of Truth can unearth that which we have so carefully hidden, and bring it to light, that real healing and forgiveness can happen.

Ask the Spirit of Truth to bring up the hidden resentments and take them to the Cross of Jesus. There, seeing how greatly you have wronged and sinned against a loving and holy God, do not refuse to forgive those who have hurt and wronged you! You cannot truly be free unless you let him be the Lord of your relationships.

A Prayer: That it may please thee to forgive our enemies, persecutors, and slanderers, and to turn their hearts: we beseech thee to hear us, good Lord . . . . That is may please thee to give us true repentance, to forgive us all our sins, negligences, and ignorances; and to endue us with the grace of thy Holy Spirit to amend our lives according to thy Holy Word: we beseech thee to hear us, good Lord.

from the Litany, Book of Common Prayer

1. Make a list of the people who have influenced your life. Ask yourself the question, "Do I hold anything against anyone on this list?"

Lord of Our Thought Life
Daily Reading: 2 Corinthians 10:1–6

We destroy arguments and every proud obstacle to the knowledge of God, and take every thought captive to obey Christ. (v. 5)

Who is in control of your thought life, the secret things that fill your mind? Is Jesus Lord of your thought life?

The mind is the battleground where Satan attacks God's children. He uses every subtlety, every temptation, every imagination he can in order to lure and distract God's children away from the path of obedience and life.

He especially uses our *rightness* and *guilt*. On the one hand, the object is to keep us from confessing our wrongness that we might be cleansed and set free, and on the other hand, the guilt is meant to paralyze and enervate us.

If in our thoughts we harbor jealousies, envyings, resentments, and the like, we will eventually act out of those thoughts. For out of the heart are the issues of life.

Jesus wants to be Lord of your thought life—let him! Let him begin to take control of your thoughts by bringing them to him in confession and repentance whenever you realize that you have gotten into darkness. Don't despair, but allow him to "take them captive" into obedience to him.

Fenelon, counseling one who was entertaining imaginary conversations, said, "When you perceive that your imagination is beginning to work, be satisfied with turning to God, without directly combating these fancies. Let them drop, occupying yourselves in some useful way." (*The Royal Way of the Cross*, p.49)

Give thanks, knowing that God is working with you to bring your thoughts under the Lordship of Christ!

A Prayer: *God be in my head, and in my understanding.*
God be in my eyes, and in my looking.
God be in my mouth, and in my speaking.
God be in my heart and in my thinking.
God be at my end, and at my departing".
(Old Sarun Primer, 1558, Salisbury, England)

1. What thoughts do you find to be the most distracting for you?

King of Kings and Lord of Lords
Daily Reading: Philippians 2:1–11

Therefore God has highly exalted him and bestowed on him the name which is above every name. (v. 9)

Let us think today about that Name. It was not always so exalted and honored! Even today, sadly, it is used in blasphemy and cursing, often taken in vain!

But it is the Name above every name. In the beginning, the Word dwelt with God and was God. The Son, who is in the bosom of the Father, knew the worship of all the heavenly host.

But though he was "in the form of God" (v. 6), he did not hold on to his divine glory and privileges, but emptied himself and took the "form of a servant." He gave up what was his by right and became what we are, sin excepted.

In that form, lowly, unnoticed, the Carpenter of Nazareth grew up, the son of Mary. But obedience to the Father's will took him into Jerusalem, and all the countryside, and after a brief ministry, the authorities arrested him on a false charge, beat him almost to death, and then crucified him between two thieves outside the walls of the city. His Name was in total shame. "He was numbered among the transgressors."

But that Name, the human name, Jesus, has been borne with total faithfulness to the Father's will. He had allowed no shame, no rejection, no pain or failure to keep him from doing his Father's will. And that life of perfect obedience is now offered to God willingly as a sacrifice, for the salvation of all those who were lost in disobedience. Moreover, he has now set them free from their life-long bondage, and given them a new possibility, a new freedom to obey from the heart, by the power of his Spirit. He even allows them to be called by his name—*Christians*.

Having walked this same path that we walk, he is able to strengthen and help those whom he calls brethren. "For because he himself has suffered and been tempted, he is able to help those who are tempted" (Hebrews 2:18). That means you—today.

A Prayer: Lord Jesus Christ, Keeper and Preserver of all things, let thy right hand guard us by day and by night when we sit at home, and when we walk abroad, when we lie down and when we rise up, that we may be kept from all evil and have mercy upon us sinners. Amen.

(St. Nerses of Clajes, fourth century)

1. Jesus gave up his rights. What rights, opinions and demands do you have that keep him from being Lord of your life?

2. As you look at your own life, where do you recognize you prefer to be served rather than be a servant? Why?

Chapter Review

There is a scripture in John 4 which states that "my food is to do the will of God." Are you, to the best of your ability, trying to do the will of God? Then you will be blessed.

1. In the Daily Devotional, which day that talked about the Lordship of Christ did you find most meaningful?

2. Where did you recognize that Jesus Christ was not the Lord of your life?

3. What one strong opinion do you have that you know God would like you to give up?

WHY DISCIPLINE?

For the moment
all discipline
seems painful
rather than
pleasant; later
it yields the
peaceful fruit of
righteousness
to those who
have been trained
by it.

Hebrews 12:11

TWO

Those Who Have Been Trained by It
Daily Reading: Hebrews 12:1–11

For the moment all discipline seems painful . . . later it yields the peaceful fruit of righteousness to those who have been trained by it. (v. 11)

To those who have been trained by it. We have a choice in anything that anyone says to us or anything that happens to us, either to let it work for us, or to refuse to let it work for us.

Pressure can turn us into something hard and bitter, or it can break us and make us soft and merciful. It depends on whether or not we *have been trained by it.*

A word of correction spoken by a husband, wife, parent, employer, or friend can either be a cause of anger and stored-up resentment, or we can let it work for us, and be trained by it.

The choice is *ours.* The person who would become an athlete must undergo *painful* discipline to get into shape. Ask anyone who has. The person who would become a musician must sacrifice hours and hours of practice, day after day. Sometimes it is inwardly very painful. But it must be done if the goal is to be achieved. There could be no army without discipline!

We Christians cannot afford to be soft on ourselves if we would become the praises of God's glory. We cannot afford to go on undisciplined, living by the whim and feeling of the moment if we would grow in Christ. The disciplines we face are only tools to help us become better soldiers, disciples, followers of Jesus. The goal is well worth the effort. The discipline may not be pleasant at the moment but keep your eye on the goal—and on the Leader. He has already endured his discipline!

A Prayer: Lord, open my eyes to see how your disciplines are being worked in my life, and give me grace to cooperate with you, so that I may be trained by them to become what you want me to be. I ask this in the Name of Jesus Christ my Lord. Amen.

1. How can you cooperate with God so that he can turn pressure into a blessing in your life?

2. As you look at your life, are there areas where you are demanding your own way and are unwilling to face the discipline that you need in order to grow? List these areas.

Let Us Rejoice in Our Sufferings
Daily Reading: Romans 5:1–11

More than that, let us rejoice in our sufferings, knowing that suffering produces endurance, and endurance produces character, and character produces hope, and hope does not disappoint us. . . . (vv. 3–5a)

Ours is not a "suffering" religion. There is no glorification of suffering for its own sake. Jesus says to his followers, "I will not leave you desolate," (John 14:18); "Peace I leave with you," (John 14:27); "These things I have spoken to you, that my joy may be in you, and that your joy may be full," (John 15:11). Joy is a keynote of his life and whenever he is present "there is fullness of joy!"

What, then, can Paul mean about rejoicing in our sufferings?

First, we can rejoice, knowing that God is *using* the suffering for our good, and it is not "going to waste"!

Second, we can rejoice in knowing the presence of Jesus in ways we cannot know it when everything is bright and pleasant. Stars can be seen only at night and many hidden things of God we can receive only in and through our suffering. As we suffer out of whatever it is which brings us pain, we know him in a deeper and more intimate way.

"The love of Jesus, what it is
None but his loved ones know."

Finally, we can rejoice, as Jesus did, "for the joy set before him." The Cross was not an easy thing for him. Neither is our cross an easy thing for us. But the joy set before him—the hope that beyond the suffering there was a new reality waiting—carried him through!

A Prayer: O loving Jesus, help me to set aside all self-pity and false ideas about how hard my lot in life is! I look at what you suffered and am ashamed of how little I am willing to suffer and how easily I say "Enough!" Give me grace to share the joy you offer me even in the midst of my sufferings. I thank you for it, Lord Jesus. Amen.

1. How can self-pity take away all the constructive value of suffering and turn it into a destructive experience?

2. How can you cooperate with God so that he can turn suffering into a blessing in your life?

Adding to Your Faith
Daily Reading: 2 Peter 1:1–11

If these things are yours and abound, they keep you from being ineffective or unfruitful in the knowledge of the Lord Jesus Christ. (v. 8)

Salvation is a free gift! We come to the Lord in our helplessness and need, and he saves us by his own grace and through the sacrifice of his own life on the cross! It stands forever as the great, unfathomable mystery of our faith. It is the eternal Good News. Catherine Hankey's familiar gospel song says it well:

I love to tell the story,
'Twill be my theme in glory
To tell the old, old story
Of Jesus and his love.

It remains the touchstone against which everything else must be measured. Our Hope and our Salvation is in Who he is and what he has done for us!

The apostle here, however, gives us an important reminder that even in this knowledge of his love we may become ineffective and unfruitful—unless we do our part. Paul referred to himself and Apollos as "God's fellow workers." Peter here challenges us to "add to your faith." The list of virtues is impressive, even staggering: "Virtue, knowledge, self-control, steadfastness, godliness, brotherly affection, and love." It shows us where the inner battles are to be fought and where our work as Christian men and women truly lies—for most of us have far to go before achieving all these qualities.

Let God speak to you about where you need to pay closer attention to one or more of these areas in your life. Do not let disappointment in yourself or discouragement rob you of eventual victory!

A Prayer: Merciful and gracious God! Let thy grace strengthen my faith, awaken my love, and maintain my hope. Let thy grace be my joy and glory, my comfort and life. Let thy grace create meekness, humility, patience, devotion, and prayer in me, for thy grace works all good within me. Amen.

(Johann Arndt, 1551–1621)

1. How can you keep from letting discouragement or disappointment in yourself rob you of eventual victory?

As a Man Disciplines His Son
Daily Reading: Deuteronomy 8:5–16

"Know then in your heart, as a man disciplines his son, the Lord your God disciplines you." (v. 5)

Israel was taught to see God's love and God's training as the great realities of her life. God had set his love on her, but she was by nature a rebellious people. Yet God did not cease to love her!

"Sons I have reared and brought up, but they have rebelled against me. The ox knows its owner, and the ass its master's crib; but Israel does not know, my people do not understand." (Isaiah 1:2b-3)

In this Deuteronomy passage, we are reminded of the forty-year wilderness experience Israel had before reaching the Promised Land. They were being led out of bondage. But the way led "through the great and terrible wilderness, with its fiery serpents and scorpions and thirsty ground where there was no water. . . ." And the reason for all this was "that he might humble and test (or prove) you, *to do you good in the end*" (vv. 15-16). God's love and God's discipline.

Without discipline we become presumptuous, and take his love and grace for granted. With discipline, we can enter into a loving relationship as those who have learned both their own need of it and the amazing love behind it. See discipline as from One whose will is "to do you good in the end."

A Prayer: Your steadfast love, O Lord, never ceases. Your mercies never come to an end. They are new every morning. Great is your faithfulness. The Lord is my portion; therefore I will find hope in him. Amen.

(Adapted from Lamentations 3:22–24)

1. How do you come to really know that God's discipline is his love?

2. Where do you see God's Fatherly discipline in your life?

As a Good Soldier
Daily Reading: 2 Timothy 2:1–11

Take your share of suffering as a good soldier of Christ Jesus. (v. 3)

Take your share. What is your share of suffering? Does it seem that you have been allotted more than your share? Have you ever wondered if the Christians in the Colosseum with the lions thought they were being asked to take more than their share, or those who were used to light the roads leading to Rome, human torches, under the wicked Nero? Or what the soldiers in the Battle of Hastings, or at Valley Forge or in the swamps of Vietnam felt? Take your share! We are in a spiritual battle, and it will not be won by those who give in to self-pity, self-indulgence, or self-justifying rationalizations.

As a good soldier of Christ Jesus, we are enlisted under the banner of the Cross. We have heard the call in our hearts, we have received the amazing love and forgiveness he offered us in our need. Now he says, "Behold, I send you. . ." and we find ourselves in a battle. Many Christians are surprised to find it so! Our daily disciplines are battles to be fought and won to train us for battles yet to be encountered. But remember Jesus Christ *risen from the dead!* He has won the victory!

Must I be carried to the skies
On flowery beds of ease,
While others fought to win the prize
And sailed through bloody seas!

No! I must fight if I would reign!
Increase my courage, Lord.
I'll bear the cross, endure the pain,
Supported by thy Word.

A Prayer: Lord Jesus Christ: You are the Savior and Captain of my soul. I am yours, and I desire to be yours this day and always. Take from me, all that hinders my service to you, and give me grace to be a loyal and faithful soldier to my life's end. In your holy Name. Amen.

1. What spiritual battles have you fought this week?

2. What hindrances do you see in your life that keep you from victory?

Ready, Aim, Fire!
Daily Reading: 1 Timothy 6:11–16

Fight the good fight of faith; take hold of the eternal life to which you were called when you made the good confession in the presence of many witnesses. (v. 12)

In this passage, young Timothy was urged to "aim at right-eousness, godliness, faith, love, steadfastness, gentleness" (v. 11). He would not always hit the target, but he was to keep on aiming! There is no place for discouragement and no *reason* for it in the Christian life. If we get discouraged, it is because we have put too much faith in *ourselves* and too little in Jesus. It is because we have underestimated the seriousness of our condition and how radical a change following Jesus truly requires. It is because we would rather give in than fight against ourselves.

So away with discouragement! *Eternal life*, life in all its fullness and contentment is ours by the gift of God's grace in Jesus Christ. But we must constantly "lay hold" or "take hold" of that life, and that process means fighting the good fight against "the world, the flesh and the devil."

One of the devil's chief weapons is discouragement, and we overcome by keeping alive our remembrance of who we are and who Jesus is. We are rescued and he is the Savior! So, take aim!

Fight the good fight with all thy might,
Christ is thy strength and Christ thy right;
Lay hold on life, and it shall be
Thy joy and crown eternally.

Cast care aside, lean on thy Guide;
His boundless mercy will provide;
Trust, and thy trusting soul shall prove
Christ is its life and Christ its love.
       (J. S. B. Monsell, 1863)

A Prayer: In your strength I will fight. By your grace I shall stand. In your Name I will win. Amen.

1. Are there areas in your life where you'd rather give in than to fight yourself? What are they?

2. If you've been discouraged about anything this week, how did you handle it?

Discipline and Preparedness
Daily Reading: Matthew 25:1–13

"But the wise took flasks of oil with their lamps." (v. 4)

What has discipline to do with preparedness? Today's scripture ties them together, because to be disciplined is to be in a state of readiness. As we fight against self-love, self-indulgence, and carelessness, we are "tuned-up" for whatever comes. If our prayer life, our reading of God's Word, our personal habits or our obligations are slovenly, we are like soldiers who are not prepared for the call to battle. The enemy may find us unaware!

The Lord, too, bids us to be ready for his appearing. Not only at the Second Coming, or at the hour of death, but wherever he appears in our lives. Are we in a state of readiness for him? Are we prepared to hear his Word of truth, to see his hand, to minister to "one of these little ones" in his name? All this has to do with discipline, to prepare us for whatever he has for us to do. Usually, this will be nothing great or spectacular. It may not even be religious or spiritual in the narrower sense. But if it is done "as unto the Lord," it will not lose its reward.

Let us be with the wise, who "took flasks of oil with their lamps," and be ready.

A Prayer When Tempted:
  Jesus, you know the temptations I feel.
  You are acquainted with all my way.
  You know my heart, my thoughts, my wants and desires.
  O Jesus, whose will was one with the Father's, by your grace, make my will one with yours.
  I offer it to you now, Lord. Have mercy on me and come to my assistance!
  I claim the Name of Jesus as the sign of victory over these thoughts that beset me.
  Jesus is Victor! Hallelujah!

1. Are you slovenly about some personal habits or obligations in your life? What are they?

2. What can you do to begin to change?

Chapter Review

This week the emphasis was on discipline. It has been amazing to realize how many of us see discipline as a negative thing. We cannot understand how it could be a freeing tool of God—and yet we find it to be exactly that. The more disciplined we are, the freer we feel. It certainly is a paradox.

1. What disciplines do you find easiest to follow?

2. What disciplines have you found hardest?

3. What specific discipline do you want to work harder on this week?

GOD'S WILL OR MY WILL?

*"Nevertheless
not my will but
thine be done."*

Luke 22:42

THREE

"I Seek Not My Own Will"
Daily Reading: John 5:30–44

"I seek not my own will, but the will of him who sent me."
(v. 30b)

Long before Jesus was born, the Psalmist prophetically spoke of him by the Spirit, saying, "Lo, I come; in the roll of the book it is written of me: I delight to do thy will, O my God; thy law is within my heart." (Psalm 40:7-8) Of him it could be said, and of no other, "His will was one with the Father's will."

But this does not mean Jesus was never tempted. Even though his human nature was sinless, he nevertheless was fully human, and therefore subject to the same temptation that Adam and Eve experienced. They succumbed to the lies and seductions of Satan, but Jesus, when tempted, confronted Satan with the truth, and kept his will in complete oneness with the Father.

O wisest love! That flesh and blood
Which did in Adam fail
Should strive afresh against the foe—
Should strive and should prevail!
(John Henry Newman)

Jesus has been tempted, and has prevailed. He knows what it means to face temptation, and *therefore* can help us when we flee to him. He it is who can help us, and he will help us if we, like him, will say, "I seek not my own will. Not my will, but thine be done!"

A Prayer: Lord, our wills are two yet one with yours. We struggle to keep them for our own, yet we have heard your call and we have seen the fruit of yielding up our own way. Take my will and make it thine, this very day. In Jesus' Name. Amen

1. There is a wise saying which goes like this: "I can't stop the birds from flying over my head, but I can stop them from nesting in my hair." How can this be applied to the experience of temptation?

2. Why is it wise to "nip temptation in the bud"?

Teach Me To Do Thy Will
Daily Reading: Psalm 143

The psalmist wrote in a situation of deep trouble. Such phrases as "crushed to the ground," "my spirit faints within me," and "he has made me sit in darkness," give some indication of the seriousness of his plight. In a situation like that, it would be very tempting to wallow in self-pity and to think dark, vindictive thoughts against "the enemy." In fact, some of the psalms are very free in expressing that kind of emotional release, and we all need it at times. God seems to be saying, through the Psalms, that it is all right to recognize and express these feelings to God! After all, he knows they are there even better than we know it ourselves.

But here in this psalm, there is something more. "I have fled to thee for refuge!" (verse 9). The place to go in our struggles against the enemy is to the place of refuge. But it is not just a passive, peaceful place, where we will be patted on the head and told that everything will be all right. The very next verse says it: "Teach me to do thy will, for thou art my God!" To remain in the place of refuge, and to know the peace we all long to have inwardly, we must seek to know and to do the will of God.

"My thoughts are not your thoughts, neither are your ways my ways, says the LORD" (Isaiah 55:8). Because this is so, we need to be taught his ways and his will.

He teaches us his will in many ways, and even though we may not find his disciplines easy, there is a tremendous fulfillment in following them. We are learning as we follow. Our prayer is being answered even as we pray.

A Prayer: Father, teach us to come to you by the one and living Way, Jesus Christ. Keep us humble and gentle, self-denying, firm and patient, active, wise to know your will and to discern the truth; loving, that we may learn to resemble you and our Savior, Jesus Christ, in whose Name we pray. Amen. (Adapted)

1. We learned today that we need to be taught his will and his ways. How are we taught his will and his ways?

2. David in the Psalms is very free in expressing his feelings. Why is this good?

Say or Doing?
Daily Reading: Matthew 21:23–46

"Which of the two did the will of his father?" (v. 31a)

Jesus told the story of the two sons who were told to go and work in their father's vineyard. The first said, "I will not," but changed his mind afterward, and went. The second answered,

"I go, sir," but did not go. And then Jesus poses the question: "Which of the two did the will of his father?"

Profession is easy. The promises we make with our lips are not costly, unless we are prepared to follow through. Sometimes such a force of resistance and rebellion, that the first word out of our hearts is "No! I will not!" But then, by the grace of God, we begin to look at the foolish and hurtful thing we have done. We begin to repent of that within us which resists doing God's will. We may pray. There may even be tears of repentance. But the most important thing is, we begin to see how wrong we are! And, like the first son, we repent and do what God has required of us. We may not like it. We may not enjoy doing it. But we do it anyway!

On the other hand, the most dangerous spiritual condition is the self-deception that lurks in this story. Because the second son was pleasant, because he did not outwardly oppose his father, he may even have counted himself to be a good and obedient son. Certainly most of us have done something similar, and it may take us some time to come to the realization that we are not obedient just because we think of ourselves as good Christians. We may generously overlook our own faults, but Jesus is saying here that more than lip service, more than promises, more than "Yes, I go," are required. Sooner or later, we must do the will of the Father. Better sooner than later. Better now than tomorrow. Better deeds than words.

A Prayer. Give us such an awareness of your mercies, that with truly thankful hearts we may show forth your praise, not only with our lips, but in our lives, by giving up ourselves to your service, and by walking before you in holiness and righteousness

all our days; through Jesus Christ our Lord. Amen.
(Adapted from Morning Prayer service, Book of Common
prayer, 1979)

1. Which son are you like?

2. What does repentance mean to you?

Not Everyone Who Says, Lord, Lord
Daily Reading: Matthew 7:15–28

"Not every one who says to me, 'Lord, Lord', shall enter the
kingdom of heaven, but he who does the will of my Father
who is in heaven." (v. 21)

As Christians, we live between what we have been and what
we are to become. Our lives are in process of changing. It may
seem as though we are never going to change in this or that
area, but in point of fact, we are changing; we are becoming.

What are we becoming! That depends on the direction and
aim of our hearts. If they are "toward the Lord," then the
changes, however slow and painful, are moving toward
becoming conformed to the will of God. If our hearts are set
on doing our own will, following our own course, then we are
changing in a negative way. Look at older people, and you can
see that they show in clearer, less hidden ways what they have
been becoming for many decades. It can be encouraging, it
can serve as a warning!

In another place we are told that it is not God's will that any
should perish, but that all should come to eternal life. His will
is life-abundant, for all. Therefore to begin doing the will of
God is not to fulfill some hard, rigid task. "For my yoke is

easy, and my burden is light," Jesus said (Matthew 11:30). God's will is fulfilled as we leave our own ways, recognize our own inadequacy and sin, and begin to walk in his ways. It is not some new legalism, where all we do is to follow the new rules. It is walking by the Spirit, being guided both by inward impulse and by outward circumstances, with the help and fellowship of others, along a path of life. It is a path of LIFE, a movement from where we have been to where we are going. At times we are discouraged; at other times, we are exalted and full of joy. But we keep on moving, seeking more and more to "do the will of our Father in heaven."

Let this truth penetrate your thoughts and flood you with new zeal and hope!

A Prayer: Thy kingdom come—in me today, O Lord. Thy will be done—in me today, O Lord, as it is by those who are perfected in the heavenly kingdom. For thine is the kingdom I seek. Thine is the power to accomplish it. Thine is the glory, for ever and ever. Amen.

1. Where have you found that the will of God is not hard and rigid?

2. What specifically is God's will for you today?

If Any Man's Will Is to Do His Will...
Daily Reading: John 7:14–31

"If any man's will is to do his will, he shall know whether this teaching is from God or whether I am speaking on my own authority." (v. 17)

With all the different doctrines, ideas and teachings that one can hear or read, it is no wonder that people feel confused. Maybe you are one who has felt this confusion, and have asked yourself the question, "How can I know? How can I be sure?" Jesus here is saying that there is a definite connection between our willingness to do God's will and our ability to know truth from falsehood. Unless there is in us a deep, underlying desire to find and do the will of God, we can be tossed about by all kinds of half-truths, quarter-truths, or downright falsehoods. Look at the evidence all around us.

This does not mean that we always *like* doing the will of God, or that we always succeed in carrying out his will. Paul is a good example of this, when, as we know, he gave up everything to follow Christ, suffered many things—beaten, stoned, shipwrecked, rejected—and yet, writing from prison, he says, "Not that I have already obtained this (his goal), or am already perfect, but I press on to make it my own. . . ." (Philippians 3:12a). His *will* was set to go on with Jesus. That is basic to everything. If we would know him and his power in our lives, we must set our wills, like a ship set on course, or a rocket pointed for the moon—*to do his will*. In that condition, he promises that we will *know*.

When that is not our heart's desire, when there is a mixture of wanting his will and wanting our own, we can be confused. We may waver about which course to take. But when we put down our own will and choose his, in spite of all the fightings that may go on within us, then we are on the way! We do not have to stay locked in uncertainty, if we will but set our wills, over and over again, *to do his will*.

A Prayer: Heavenly Father, send your Holy Spirit into our heart to direct and rule us, according to your will, to comfort

us in all our afflictions, to defend us from all error, and to lead us into all truth through Jesus Christ our Lord. Amen.
(Book of Common Prayer, 1979)

Today's teaching talks about setting our wills to do the will of God.

1. Why is doing God's will not always easy?

2. Give an example from your own life to illustrate your answer.

When the Will Is Defective
Daily Reading: Romans 7:13–25

I can will what is right, but I cannot do it. (v. 18b)

Has that ever been your experience? It has been mine over and over again. What it shows us is that there is much about us that we do not understand. We act out of hidden, unrecognized motivations that lie deeply buried within us. It has been the sobering experience of Christians in all ages that we can desire, but that we cannot always accomplish what is right. We need help! It seems as though we should be able to summon strength to do the will of God perfectly, but in actual experience, there is still too much of the old carnal (fleshy) nature alive in us. We are not yet sanctified and mature in Christ. So there are times when we are under the rulership of Jesus and there are times when we give expression to the old nature. One commentator says, "There is no believer, however advanced in holiness, who cannot adopt the language used here by the apostle. . . . Everyone feels that he cannot do the things he would, yet is sensible that he is guilty for not doing them. Let any man test his power by the requirement to love God perfectly at all times. Alas! How entire our inability! Yet how deep our self-loathing and self-condemnation !"(Jamison, Fausett and Brown, Commentary.)

Confronted with the defectiveness of our wills, we turn for help, not only in prayer to the Lord, but to others. By exposing our need, by giving others permission to speak truth to us, by being willing to listen to the Word of God through our sisters and our brothers in Christ, we can realize his help in a greater way. He helps us, not only through the inward grace he gives, but through the ministry of others in the body of Christ, making us members of a body instead of soloists in the spiritual battle. Thanks be to God for his merciful provision!

A Prayer: O God, I thank you for my fellow members in Christ's Body, who are willing to help me in my battle against the habits and the bondage of my old carnal nature. Amen.

Today's lesson talks of exposing our need.
1. To whom could you expose your need?

2. Why is it hard for you to expose our need?

Living by the Will of God
Daily Reading: 1 Peter 4:1–19

Arm yourselves . . . so as to live for the rest of the time in the flesh no longer by human passions, but by the will of God (v. 1b-2). Therefore let those who suffer according to God's will do right and entrust their souls to a faithful creator. (v. 19)

I heard a preacher say once that when he was a child, the only time he heard about "the will of God" was when someone died. People would stand around and say in a hushed voice, "It was God's will." So, said he, when he became a man, and someone happened to mention "the will of God," he would think, "Has it come to *that*?"

How many of us, when we struggle with our own wills against his will, actually think that God's will is wrong, unkind, hard, or unfair! The one-talent man in Jesus' parable said to his master, "Master, I knew you to be a hard man, reaping where you did not sow, and gathering where you did not winnow; so I was afraid. . . . Too often, when we want what he does not will, we hurl the same kind of accusations at God—consciously or unconsciously. And then we struggle to make his will conform to ours.

If we insist too long and too hard, God may give us up to our own wills. He often does that. But he is not obligated to make things turn out the way we thought they would or hoped they would. If we insist on our own way, we have to live with the consequences.

Living by the will of God may be a real struggle—it is for most of us. But he promises that in his will we will be cared for and blessed. We may not have all the details just the way we want them, but we will find that our wants and his will can more and more become one. Did living by our feelings (our passions) bring us freedom and peace? Why not then choose to live by his will?

A Prayer: O Almighty and most merciful God, of thy bountiful goodness keep us, we beseech thee, from all things that may hurt us; that we, being ready both in body and soul, may cheerfully accomplish those things which thou commandest; through Jesus Christ our Lord. Amen.

1. Where have you seen that living by the will of God may be a real struggle but in the long run it always brings blessings?

2. Where have you seen that insisting on having your own way leads to disaster or disappointment?

Chapter Review

1. Do you feel you know how to find the will of God in little things easily _____ occasionally _____ with difficulty _____ ?

Do you feel you know how to find the will of God in big things easily _____ occasionally_____ with difficulty _____ ?

2. How have this week's readings helped you in this regard?

LEARNING TO LISTEN

*But he who
listens to me
will dwell secure
and will be at
ease, without
dread of evil.*

Proverbs 1:33

FOUR

God Speaks in Many Ways
Daily Reading: Hebrews 1

In many and various ways God spoke of old to our fathers by the prophets. (v. 1)

We believe in a God who speaks! "He is There and He is Not Silent" is the title of a book which has had wide popularity in Christian circles. This means that we have fellowship with him, not only in what we say to him, but in listening to what he has to say to us.

In this week's devotions and Bible study, we are thinking about the various ways God speaks. It is an important lesson for every earnest Christian to learn. Otherwise, we may end up trying to live our lives like deaf runners, who have only the distant goal in mind, but no fellowship or instruction along the way. He has not left us so bereft!

From the beginning of the Bible, God has spoken to people. First, he gave Adam and Eve instructions as to how they were to live and enjoy life on this earth. Then after they had sinned and were hiding in fear, "they heard the sound of the Lord God walking in the garden" (Genesis. 3:8) and heard the voice of God calling to them. But the fruit of human sin was banishment from that close fellowship with God, and people had to learn to listen to God's Word through men like Moses, Elijah, and other prophets.

It was a sad day in Israel when there was no one to hear from God. In 1 Samuel 3:1, we read, "And the word of the LORD was rare in those days; there was no frequent vision."

We know that God "is there and he is not silent." The challenge is to become sensitive to his voice. It will not always come clothed as we expect it. It will often surprise us and may even cause us pain and dismay. But his voice, his Word is life and hope.

> He speaks, and list'ning to his voice
> New life the dead receive,
> The mournful broken hearts rejoice,
> The humble poor believe.
>
> Hear him, ye deaf; his praise, ye dumb,
> Your loosened tongues employ;
> Ye blind, behold your Savior come,
> And leap, ye lame, for joy!
> (Charles Wesley, 1740)

A Prayer: Make my ears attentive, O Lord, to your voice. May I yearn to hear your word and be quick to perform it. For Jesus' sake. Amen.

1. How can you become more sensitive to God's voice?

2. During these past four weeks, have you discovered God speaking to you in new ways? List them.

Listening to God's Prophet
Daily Reading: Exodus 20

"You speak to us and we will hear; but let not God speak to us, lest we die." (v. 19)

In the previous chapter, Israel said to Moses, "All that the LORD has spoken we will do." God, in order to confirm to the people that he indeed was speaking by Moses, allowed them to hear the thunder of his mighty voice. The experience was so frightening that they wanted an easier way to hear from him. From that time on, God raised up prophets to speak to the people and to their rulers.

It was an awesome responsibility to be a prophet. The prophet was accountable to God for what he said, no matter how difficult his message. Naturally, some prophets found such a task too difficult, so they would change the message or make up one of their own which was more agreeable to the hearers. One of the marks of the true prophet was that he often warned the people about where they were wrong and what would happen if they did not change. The false prophet was frequently more pleasant!

The gift of prophecy did not stop with the coming of Jesus. Indeed, the Book of Acts says that the latter day will see "your sons and daughters" prophesying. That means that there will be many who speak the divine message to God's people by the power of the Holy Spirit.

When we hear someone with a word from the Lord, whether in sermon, teaching, or otherwise, are we attentive to it? Do we, like Israel, say, "All that the Lord has spoken we will do"? Or do we think to ourselves, "Who is this person to be speaking for God?" There are still false prophets, of course, and we are told "Do not despise prophesying, but test everything and hold fast what is good" (1 Thessalonians 5:20-21). They must exalt Jesus Christ and be faithful to the written Word of God; otherwise they are not true prophets at all. But we should be humble enough to hear God through his servants whom he has called and anointed for that purpose. They have been given to the Church to build us up in the faith and to bring us to maturity in Christ.

A Prayer: Father, give me the humility to hear your voice through your servants whom you have sent and ordained for this holy purpose. As they preach, teach, and speak the Word of God to me, give me ears to hear and a heart to understand. Amen.

1. Do you find it difficult to believe that God speaks to you through other people? Why?

The Still Small Voice
Daily Reading: 1 Kings 19:1–18

And after the fire, a still small voice (v. 12)

Elijah had had a tremendous spiritual victory over all the prophets of Baal at Mount Carmel. The false prophets had tried in vain to prove the power of their god, and Elijah had waited, taunting them in their failure. Then, at the time of the evening sacrifice, he "repaired the altar of the Lord," which had fallen into disuse. The sacrifice was then prepared, and God answered his prayer by fire from heaven, consuming the entire sacrifice, and the altar as well! The people were impressed, to say the least! "The Lord, he is God!" they cried over and over again. And in that moment, Elijah acted—having the 450 false prophets seized and slain on the spot, seeking to rid the country and the people of the false religion which was destroying them.

Then Jezebel, the wicked queen, sent Elijah word, promising to do to him just what he had done to her Baal prophets, and Elijah was frightened. He felt alone because he knew her power over her husband the king. So he fled from the capital city and finally came to a cave many miles away, broken, full of self-pity and anger. God displayed his might in wind, earthquake, and fire—reminding Elijah that his hand is not shortened that it cannot save! But the real message came after the display, in "a still small voice."

We tend to look for God in the big things, the great and impressive displays of his miracles and his might. How easy it is to ignore the still, small voice within. He often speaks in our conscience, a little warning, a little, quiet reminder of what he wants us to do. But unless we are attentive, we will hasten on, looking for the big event. In the small things of everyday, he is still speaking.

A Prayer: Lord, you have made us for fellowship with you. Give me ears to hear the still, small voice within. May I treasure that inward communion above all earthly delights, and grieve not your Holy Spirit. Amen.

1. When in your life recently have you, like Elijah, forgotten all God has done and instead you have fled into self-pity and anger?

2. How do you believe you can become more keenly aware of the "still small voice" of God speaking to you daily?

Listening to Jesus
Daily Reading: Mark 9:1–29

"This is my beloved Son; listen to him." (v. 7)

How they were to listen to Jesus was very clear. They were with him physically, and he spent much time talking to them and training them for what was to come. Even so, they did not understand much of what he was saying until after he was crucified. We may envy them and suppose it was easier. But they did not have the advantages we have. We have not only their later witnesses of his glorious resurrection and ascension to God's right hand, but we have the testimonies of twenty centuries of followers who have found him a Friend indeed. So we need not envy the fact that listening to him was a clear and direct thing.

Instead, we need to listen to him today. "He speaks to me everywhere," says the songwriter. Look about you today and listen for his voice. He is the Creator of all, and not only the birds, the stars, the sun and moon "proclaim his praise," but to the listening ear come intimations, thoughts, a sense of knowing—which we can learn to identify as his voice to us, not in some vague, romantic way, not in some super-spiritual way, but as the living communication of our Living Christ.

His Words in Scripture, especially Jesus' words in the Gospels, are powerful words to us. Inwardly digest them, savor them as you read. They burned their way into the hearts of their hearers and later were "written down for our instruction" (1 Corinthians 10:11). Let them burn their way into your mind as a strong word of help and guidance. He speaks through them as well as through his living Spirit today. "He that has ears to hear, let him hear."

A Prayer. Lord Jesus, sanctify me in the truth. Thy Word is truth. Amen.

1. Where have you had a "sense of knowing" that God is speaking to you this week?

2. When and where is it easiest for you to hear God? Why?

Listening to Scripture
Daily Reading: 2 Timothy 3

All scripture is inspired by God, and profitable for teaching, for reproof, for correction, and for training in righteousness, that the man of God may be complete, equipped for every good work. (vv. 16-17).

How important it is to hear God in the Holy Scriptures. It is our safeguard against untold errors, and in them is contained all things necessary for our salvation. Paul here is giving some very basic advice to his son in the faith, young Timothy. Timothy is called on to lead people who have not had the advantage he, Timothy, had in associating closely with Paul. They need someone who has learned faith and learned it well. Paul reminds Timothy that he had been acquainted with the Scriptures since his childhood, and in another place, speaks of Timothy's mother and grandmother as having been believers before him. Now that Timothy is "on his own," so to speak, the Scriptures are a safeguard against the deceptions and deceivers he is meeting in the world.

The same is true for us today. Many erroneous and strange teachings are for sale today in the Christian marketplace. Some of them sound very attractive, and offer us quick gratification, telling us that we are wonderful and that we have nothing to worry about. Others play on guilt, fear, uncertainty about the future, and enslave their hearers in new bondages. What is the remedy against such error? The Holy Scriptures.

It is not by accident that the Church has referred to the Bible as the word of God. It is a treasure and storehouse of divine wisdom and truth. We have been given the Holy Spirit as our enlightener and guide, and the Church itself as a check against any possible private interpretations that might lead us astray. With those two safeguards, we can open the Scriptures expectantly. They are profitable for teaching, reproof, correction, and training in righteousness. God speaks through them to our conditions. Those whom he has anointed often interpret them to our good. "Thy word is a lamp to my feet, and a light to my path. I have laid up thy word in my heart, that I might not sin against thee" (Psalm 119:105 and 11).

A Prayer. O that we, discerning its most holy learning, Lord, may love and fear thee, and evermore be near thee!
(Henry W. Baker, 1861)

1. Where have you allowed the Holy Spirit to speak to you specifically this week through the Scriptures themselves?

2. Do you need help to hear God speak to you through the Bible? (If your answer is yes, who can you talk with about this ?)

God Speaks Through Our Circumstances
Daily Reading: Isaiah 30:8–33

And though the Lord give you the bread of adversity and the water of affliction, yet your Teacher will not hide himself anymore, but your eyes shall see your Teacher, and your ears shall hear a word behind you, saying, This is the way, walk in it, when you turn to the right or when you turn to the left (vv. 20-21).

God was speaking to his people through the circumstances of their life. "Woe to the rebellious children who carry out a plan but not mine" is the first word of warning. If we insist on doing things our own way, working out our own wills, God warns us lovingly that we will come to regret it!

Israel would go through times of great affliction. She would be battered and tossed about as the great nations around her played with her like a pawn on a chessboard. But God was keeping watch. His business with Israel was to bring her, chastened and fashioned into a new time. "The LORD waits to be gracious to you" (v. 18).

It is so with us. Our ways end up in affliction, confusion, and distress. Most of us know from firsthand experience what that means. And God through those circumstances is calling us to give up our ways to take on his. He is speaking through the everyday conditions of your life and mine, if we but have ears to hear and hearts to understand.

If our way is hard and we cannot see how it is going to work out for good, it is time to trust. "In returning and rest you shall be saved; in quietness and trust shall be your strength" (v. 15). If our way is smooth and pleasant, let it be a reminder of how greatly we are loved, and let it spur us on to more faithful obedience to the Lord.

Halts by me that footfall:

Is my gloom, after all,

Shade of his hand, outstretched caressingly!

(Hound of Heaven, F. Thompson, 1859–1907)

A Prayer: Lord give me eyes to see you and ears to hear what you are saying through the circumstances of my life. I thank you that you are with me in them and that the darkness in them is "the shade of your hand, outstretched caressingly." In Jesus' Name. Amen.

1. Where in the circumstances of your life has God been speaking to you?

2. What have you done about it?

Listening to Others

Daily Reading: Ephesians 4:15–32

Rather speaking the truth in love, we are to grow up in every way into him who is the head, into Christ. (v. 15)

This week we have been thinking about hearing God in various ways. One of the hardest ways for most of us is to hear him is through other people. Yet we are told very clearly here to "speak the truth in love" to one another. Further on, Paul tells us, "Let everyone speak the truth with his neighbor" (v. 25).

Robert Burns, the Scottish poet, has a little verse which says, "O would some Power the giftie gie us, to see oursel's as others see us." As a matter of fact, Christians have been given that "giftie." If we are truthful with one another, we cannot only see ourselves as others see us, we can begin to get a better view of ourselves as God sees us.

We know, or we should know, what the prophet Jeremiah said about the human heart—about our own hearts: "The heart is deceitful above all things, and desperately corrupt; who can understand it!" (Jeremiah 17:9). Our hearts tell us all that we are good, that we mean well, that we are right. But others often tell us a different story. If we will but listen to those who speak to us—even if we think they are speaking out of their own sin—God will honor that, and we will begin to get a different and healing view of ourselves. That is the word of testimony of many people who have subjected themselves to the discipline of listening to others.

Pride and ego can build a wonderful but false image of ourselves to ourselves. The truth begins to tear down and destroy that image. It is painful, but it is worth it, because in its place God offers us freedom from having to keep up that false image, freedom from having to feed the monster ego which is never satisfied, and replaces it with the joy of simply being in him.

"A man who flatters his neighbor spreads a net for his feet" (Proverbs 29:5). Do we seek flattery or truth? Do we speak the truth in love, or do we spread nets for the feet of friends?

A Prayer: Spirit of truth, give me a love for thee.
Let me not despise nor reject thee in any guise.
Let me welcome and receive thee and be wise.
In Jesus' Name, Amen.

1. What areas are there in your life in which you need to grow up?

2. What steps can you take?

Chapter Review

Listening is often harder than speaking. It is especially true if God is speaking what we do not want to hear.

1. Where is God speaking to you and how is he speaking?

2. Do you hear God when he is telling you when you are disobedient?

3. Think about one situation where you believe you heard God and you took action as a result.

THE BLESSING OF OBEDIENCE

"He who has my
commandments
and keeps them, he
it is who loves me;
and he who loves
me will be loved by
my Father, and
I will love him and
manifest myself to him."
John 14:21

FIVE

A Blessing and a Curse
Daily Reading: Deuteronomy 11:8–32

"Behold, I set before you this day a blessing and a curse: the blessing if you obey the commandments of the LORD your God, which I command you this day, and the curse, if you do not obey the commandments of the LORD your God, but turn aside from the way which I command you this day, to go after other gods which you have not known." (vv. 26–28)

Obedience brings blessing—obedience to God, that is, instead of obedience to "other gods." Our scripture makes very plain that two ways are set before us—God's way and the way of "other gods." The one path is the path to blessing. The other is the path to ruin. Israel is being challenged to "choose life."

We all know that children are not naturally obedient. Their nature is to do what they like, and it is with careful (sometimes painful) training that they learn that obeying mother and father brings more satisfaction than getting away with whatever they want to do. As parents, we know, too, how difficult it is to be consistent in requiring obedience for the sake of the children.

God is not an unreasonable tyrant. He has not so constructed his world that he requires obedience for capricious reasons. He requires obedience because of his love. Everything that he asks of us is grounded in his love for us. We should always look at the requirement of obedience in that light, even though obedience may seem less rewarding in the short run than disobedience! The *truth* is here: blessing, if we obey the commandments of the Lord. It is built into the very nature of things.

The sad story of Israel throughout the Old Testament is the story of people who did not learn to be obedient and suffered the consequences. God did not abandon them, and still sent words of hope and promise, but what a lot of grief and suffering they could have been spared had they learned to be obedient.

All of us are still learning. We are not yet perfected in obedience. Only One was perfectly obedient—Jesus our Lord. But the same blessing promised of old still holds—if we will set our wills to be obedient. Start where you can! Keep at it! Don't give up! The blessing is worth it.

A Prayer. Great and many are the blessings I have already received from you, O Lord. I pray for the grace of an obedient spirit, in Jesus' Name, Amen.

1. Where are you discovering the blessing of obedience in your life?

If You Love Me
Daily Reading: John 14:15–31

"If you love Me, you will keep My commandments." (v. 15)

This is a strong and disturbing verse. It clearly says that obedience is the proof of love and the expression of love. In another place, Jesus says, "Why do you call me 'Lord, Lord', and do not do the things that I say?" (Luke 6:46)

"Yes, Lord, you know that I love you!" That is what Peter said to Jesus when they met after the Resurrection. It was not spoken hastily or lightly for Peter remembered with shame and sorrow how he had deserted the Lord after vowing that he would give his life and die for him if necessary. But Peter could only say in spite of all he had done, in spite of all he had not done, "Lord, you know all things. You know that I love you."

Jesus gives us this strong and disturbing word because we need it. Self-love is so strong that unless we are pulled up short, it can easily take over and crowd out our love for him. Like the weeds in the parable of the sower, "the cares of the world, and the delight in riches, and the desire for other things, enter in, and choke the word and it proves unfruitful" (Mark 4:19).

We cannot, in and of ourselves, love him. That is his gift to us. With St. Paul, we must admit that without Jesus Christ and the work of the Holy Spirit within, we are locked in a nature that is totally self-oriented and self-concerned, often confounding us with our own contradictions! But, if he has given us grace to love him, then he will give more grace. Obedience brings added grace, and we can move from strength to strength.

Jesus, what didst thou find in me
That thou hast dealt so lovingly!
How great the joy that thou hast brought!
So far exceeding hope or thought!
Jesus my Lord, I thee adore:
O make me love thee more and more!
    (Henry Collins, 1854)

A Prayer: Make us of quick and tender conscience, O Lord; that understanding we may obey every word of thine this day, and discerning, may follow every suggestion of thine indwelling Spirit. Speak, Lord, for thy servant heareth; through Jesus Christ our Lord. Amen.

1. How does your self-love express itself?

2. How can you break out of self-centeredness?

If You Keep My Commandments
Daily Reading: John 15:1–11

"If you keep My commandments, you will abide in My love, just as I have kept My Father's commandments and abide in his love." (v. 10)

Yesterday we thought about obedience as the proof and acid test of our love for Jesus. Today's scripture turns the subject around, and reminds us of the promise of what obedience will bring.

"You will abide in my love." What does it mean to abide in his love? It means to be one in spirit with all that he is and all he is doing. It means to live in the daily, moment-by-moment blessing of his grace and favor in our lives.

Perhaps you have experienced a small taste of this with another human being. You loved that person, and as long as you and the other person were in unity of spirit, there was an atmosphere of freedom and trust between you. You wanted to please the other because you loved, and you were pleased by the other because you were loved by him or her.

This is an inadequate but helpful picture of what he is saying. Breaking the commandments brings about disjuncture, a fracturing of the relationship. We are injured by our own disobedience, and our Lord suffers, too. Otherwise, we had no part in his crucifixion and death, if our sins do not really hurt. And so, when we willfully disobey, we are not "abiding in his love." That does not mean that he ceases to love us; it does not even mean that we have ceased to love him. But it does mean that the fellowship and oneness are broken, and all the blessing that flowed to us from that oneness is cut off, waiting to be restored and renewed.

Jesus felt that abiding in his Father's love was worth everything that obedience cost. He even endured the cross, despising the shame. He promises no less for us; if we obey, the blessing of abiding in his love will be worth everything it costs!

A Prayer:
I rest upon thy word, the promise is for me;
My succor and salvation, Lord, shall surely come from thee.
But let me still abide nor from my hope remove,
Till thou my patient spirit guide into thy perfect love. Amen.
(Charles Wesley, 1742)

1. Have you seen any place in your life recently when you have been willfully disobedient? Where?

2. What were the results?

Slaves of the One You Obey
Daily Reading: Romans 6:12–23

Do you not know that if you yield yourselves to any one as obedient slaves, you are slaves of the one whom you obey, either of sin, which leads to death or of obedience, which leads to righteousness? (v. 16)

Paul here in this sixth chapter of Romans develops further the intimate, almost organic, relationship between obedience and abiding in Christ.

The figure of speech he uses is that of slave. We cannot be absolutely free even though we may fool ourselves that we are free when we do as we please. The truth is, that we are in that very moment (if what we please is disobedience!), yielding ourselves as slaves of sin! We can choose our master, but it will be one or the other—sin or Christ.

That puts the matter quite plainly: We choose who is going to have dominion over us. Once we had no choice—our nature took care of that, as members of Adam's fallen race. But Jesus Christ entered our race, took our human nature upon himself, lived a life of perfect obedience and died in our place, in order that sin need not have dominion over us any more. He is the Key of David who unlocks the prisonhouse of our old self-bondage. With him, we can become "slaves of obedience," which Paul says leads to righteousness.

Someone may ask, "What kind of a choice is that—just a choice of masters?" Yet to answer it, we have only to look back at where the other kind of slavery—slavery to sin—took us; or where it takes others whom we know and love. Becoming obedient does not mean that we lose the temptation to choose sin, nor does it mean that we have entered a new kind of bondage. For with obedience comes life, grace, peace, and joy. Against these, who can complain?

A Prayer: O God, who art the author of peace and lover of concord, in knowledge of whom standeth our eternal life, whose service is perfect freedom, defend us thy humble servants in all assaults of our enemies; that we, surely trusting in thy

defense, may not fear the power of any adversaries, through the might of Jesus Christ our Lord. Amen.
(Service of Daily Morning Prayer, Book of Common Prayer)

1. How do you feel about not having your own way?

2. What do you do with how you feel?

I Was Not Disobedient to the Heavenly Vision
Daily Reading: Acts 26:1–32

"Wherefore, O King Agrippa, I was not disobedient to the heavenly vision." (v. 19)

This week we are thinking about the blessing of obedience and the importance of obedience. Small things are important. Jesus said, "He who is faithful in a very little is faithful also in much" (Luke 16:10). Let us try to see our disobedience in God's perspective!

But today's scripture speaks of another dimension of obedience. Paul's obedience "to the heavenly vision" was an indispensable element in his faithfulness to Jesus Christ. It was not simply a matter of doing right things, avoiding wrong things as it had been in the days when he was a practicing Pharisee. Now his obedience included faithfulness to the vision the Lord had given him. When we think back to the fruit of that obedience (He was the first great Christian missionary!), it is impossible to overestimate its blessing. His letters to churches and individuals make up some of the most valuable and helpful portions of the Holy Scriptures, so that even today, our debt to him is immeasurable.

Are we obedient to our "heavenly vision"? Have you been given some inspiration, some goal, some worthy thing to do, which you believed came from God? Treasure it, and be faithful to it. "Where there is no vision, the people perish" (Proverbs 29:18). Without this long-range goal toward which we can strive and move, life can mire in the concerns of the moment, and our spiritual muscles can become flaccid.

A Prayer: O Lord God, when thou givest to thy servants to endeavor any great matter, grant us also to know that it is not the beginning but the continuing of the same until it be thoroughly finished which yieldeth the true glory. Amen.

(Sir Francis Drake, 1540–1596)

1. List ways you have sought to be obedient this week.

2. What were the results?

Be Subject to One Another
Daily Reading: Ephesians 5:1–33

Be subject to one another out of reverence for Christ. (v. 21)

Perhaps the hardest part of obedience is learning to subject our wills to the will of another. None of us likes to be told what to do! We fear that to subject ourselves to another will mean the loss of freedom and possible annihilation of our own personalities.

Yet we are clearly instructed: "Be subject to one another out of reverence for Christ." Strength—physical or psychological—

should not be the determining factor as to whose way prevails. The strong should serve the weak, and those who seem weak are often psychologically stronger than the physically strong! And so Paul instructs wives to be subject to their husbands "as to the Lord," and husbands to lay down their lives (including their own "rights") as Christ laid down his life for the Church. No one, then, would be lording it over anyone else, for there would be a mutual subjection to one another. In the Gospels we read Jesus' words: "The kings of the Gentiles exercise lordship over them, and those in authority over them are called benefactors. But not so with you; rather let the greatest among you become as the youngest, and the leader as one who serves" (Luke 22:25-26).

If we are subjecting ourselves to one another out of reverence for Christ, this means that we are hearing what Jesus has to say to us through another person. If we become suspicious enough of our own willful tendencies, we will not be so afraid to put down our own will to do what someone else suggests, when we know that they are not leading us into anything sinful or wrong. It is not an easy assignment. But this attitude is essential if we are to "walk in love, as Christ loved us." (v. 2) Remember that he said he came, not to do his own will, but the will of him who sent him. This, too, should be our goal in being subject to one another out of reverence for Christ.

A Prayer Thought: If there be any good in thee, believe that this is much more in others—that so though mayest preserve humility within thee.

(Thomas à Kempis)

1. Note any other things the Lord has shown you about obedience.

2. What fear do you have about being obedient to others?

Faith Without Works
Daily Reading: James 2:8–26

So faith by itself, if it has no works, is dead. (v. 17)

We have thought about obedience as the path to blessing, as a proof of our love for God, as underwritten by God's promises of his abiding presence. We have considered the option of being slaves to sin and death or to obedience and life, and noted that the long-range vision as well as the duty of the moment demands our faithful obedience. We have thought about the problem of subjecting ourselves to do what another person tells us or wants us to do.

Today's scripture was written with people in mind who insisted that faith alone was all they needed, and who disregarded the necessity of obedience to the truth. James is greatly concerned that we see the deception of such thinking and that where faith is alive, works (read "obedience") follow. Doing good things is not the way to God, but neither is "head belief" without works that demonstrate the sincerity of one's faith.

This brings us back to the basic struggle we all face as Christians. It is the struggle between self, in all its devious ways of deception, and the call to obedience, with its disarming simplicity. All of us face this struggle every day, and as we seek to be faithful in simple obediences, we find that we understand better the nature of the struggle going on within us.

Thank God for a living faith that can produce obedience as its fruit! Let us pray daily for an increase of that faith!

A Prayer Thought: Pray him to give you what Scripture calls "an honest and good heart," or "a perfect heart," and, without waiting, begin at once to obey him with the best heart you have. Any obedience is better than none.

You have to seek his face; obedience is the only way of seeing him. All your duties are obediences. To do what he bids is to obey him, and to obey him is to approach him.

(John Henry Cardinal Newman, 1801–1890)

1. Describe any struggle that might have gone on within you this week between self and the call of obedience.

Chapter Review

You have been learning about obedience. It is not always easy.

1. Are you discouraged about your faith journey? If so, have you been honest about your feelings to allow God to change your heart? Sometimes we are blessed in a different way than we had in mind.

2. What other areas in your life do you find difficulty in being obedient?

NOBODY TELLS ME WHAT TO DO! (REBELLION)

"Behold, to obey is better than sacrifice, and to hearken than the fat of rams. For rebellion is as the sin of witchcraft, and stubbornness is as iniquity and idolatry."

1 Samuel 15:22b-23 (KJV)

SIX

Rebellion Is As the Sin of Witchcraft
Daily Reading: 1 Samuel 15

"For rebellion is as the sin of divination,
and stubbornness is as iniquity and idolatry."
(v. 23a)

Saul put his own judgment ahead of God's clear command. He reasoned that since Agag was king, he should not be destroyed along with other Ammonites. He reasoned that it would be a shame to kill the good sheep, oxen, fatlings, and lambs (as he had been instructed to do). So when Samuel arrived at Gilgal, Saul confidently exclaimed, "I have performed the commandment of the LORD." "What then is this bleating of the sheep in my ears, and the lowing of the oxen which I hear!" asked Samuel. Saul's explanation was to no avail. His reasoning did not matter. What mattered was obedience to the clear command of the LORD. "Why did you not obey the voice of the LORD?" Samuel persisted. And Saul then did a very interesting thing (not at all unlike the things we do when we are confronted with our wrong). He said, "I have obeyed. . . . I have gone on the mission. . . . I have brought Agag. . . . I have destroyed. . . . But the people . . ." In order to excuse his own disobedience, he put the blame "on the people."

There is an important lesson for us all in this passage. The inner rebellion against whatever God is requiring of us leads to all kinds of reasoning, rationalization, and excuse-making. It may fool us for awhile. But it does not fool God. There has to be a reckoning time, and the spirit of rebellion within must be dealt with. Better that it be dealt with early, before it has time to do its destructive work in us and in others around us. Equating it with witchcraft or divination (a kind of fortune-telling) is intended to show us the depth of its wickedness, so that we may turn from it with abhorrence.

A Prayer: O our God, bestow upon us such confidence, such peace, such happiness in thee, that thy will may always be dearer to us than our own will, and thy pleasure than our own pleasure. All that thou givest is thy free gift to us, and all that thou takest away is thy grace to us. Be thou thanked for all, praised for all, loved for all; through Jesus Christ our Lord. Amen.

(Christina G. Rossetti, 1830–1894)

1. This very clear picture of Saul's disobedience can speak to us. Where have you seen that you blame others to excuse yourself?

2. Where have you rationalized your decisions or your behavior?

A Stubborn and Rebellious Generation

Daily Reading: Psalm 78:1–20

And that they should not be like their fathers, a stubborn and rebellious generation whose heart was not steadfast whose spirit was not faithful to God. (v. 8)

The psalmist relates here a parable, "a dark saying from of old, that he had heard from 'our fathers'." It was a sad but glorious story of God's faithfulness and Israel's rebellion. This long psalm becomes a kind of "Reader's Digest" history of

Israel, citing the wonderful deliverances of God and the sad tendency of the people to turn away from him.

As we read it, however, we are aware that it is more than the story of an ancient people and their God. It is also the story of our rebellion and of God's judgments and mercies. For we know that he is the same, yesterday, today, and for ever.

What did God do to meet this rebellion? "He established a testimony in Jacob and appointed a law in Israel" (v. 5). That was his first move, to set up the evidence of his merciful deliverance (the testimony) and what he required of those who would be his people.

Paul discusses the Israelites failure to keep the law, and concludes that the law declares us all guilty before God—Jew and Gentile alike—so that we are all in need of his mercy and forgiveness.

But see here the compassion of God, and his infinite patience with his chosen people. His manna in the wilderness and the water from the rock should have been ample testimony of his care.

What about the testimony, the witness of God's mercy in your life and mine? Do we ignore it, or do we let it work life in us? That is the question. For he has established a testimony, a record of loving deeds for us as surely as he did for Israel of old!

A Prayer: Grant to us, Lord, we beseech thee, the spirit to think and do always such things as are right; that we, who cannot do anything that is good without thee, may by thee be enabled to live according to thy will; through Jesus Christ our Lord. Amen.

1. Against what specific things do you find yourself rebelling?

2. How can you cooperate with God in your daily life in order that you can choose God's will?

Yet They Rebelled
Daily Reading: Psalm 78:32–72

Yet they tested and rebelled against the Most High God, and did not observe his testimonies, but turned away and acted treacherously like their fathers. (vv. 56-57a)

The latter part of this psalm catalogues the folly of continued rebellion in the face of all God's dealings. His "destroying visitations" seemed to produce a temporary return to God. "When he slew them, they sought for him; they repented and sought God earnestly." (v. 34) But these returns were short-lived, and soon the pull of the old ways was stronger than their fear of God's judgments.

Does that sound familiar? Do we not do the same—return under affliction, and find the mercy free flowing, and then find that our self-will and old habits pull strongly against what we know to be the will of God?

Our rebellious nature is something we have to recognize. Otherwise we will be like Saul at Gilgal, affirming that we have done everything the Lord wants us to do, when in reality we are doing what we want to do. That is one of the reasons why it is important to let others have some authority in our lives, permission to tell us what to do in one or more areas.

Israel was finally carried away, never to be seen again as a result of her rebellion. Only little Judah remained to carry on the testimony of God. Israel stands as a permanent warning to us of the effect of persistent rebellion against a Holy God.

Perverse and foolish oft I strayed
And yet in love he sought me,
And on his shoulder gently laid
And home rejoicing brought me.

Henry Baker, 1868 (based on Psalm 23)

A Prayer. I know, O Lord, and do with all humility acknowledge myself as an object altogether unworthy of thy love; but sure I am, thou art an object altogether worthy of mine. Do thou then impart to me some of that excellence, and that shall supply my own lack of worth. Help me to cease from sin according to thy will, that I may be capable of doing thee service according to my duty.

(St. Augustine, 354–430, abridged)

1. Self-will and old habits often rob us of spiritual gains. How can we stand against these?

2. How can you begin to establish new habits?

Do Not Harden Your Hearts

Daily Reading: Hebrews 3

But exhort one another every day, as long as it is called "today," that none of you may be hardened by the deceitfulness of sin. (v. 13)

One commentator on these verses says, "Tomorrow is the day when idle men and fools repent. Tomorrow is Satan's today; he cares not what resolutions you form, if only you fix them for tomorrow."

Whenever we are called on to make any forward progress in our life of personal discipline and obedience, the tempter whispers, "This one time won't matter that much." Whenever we are tempted to disobey or ignore one of the disciplines, the same thing comes into our minds. In this way, we are hardened by "the deceitfulness of sin." The old pattern is continued, becoming fixed in a kind of "conditioned response" to a given situation. Something happens that makes us feel sorry for ourselves, or we get angry or resentful, we are disappointed, or actually hurt or put down by someone else. In such a case, look out! The tempter will come and whisper, "You can resume your discipline tomorrow!"

It is very important that we see this part of human nature, and guard ourselves against it. "Exhort one another every day," says the writer of Hebrews. Exhort yourself, and help anyone else whom you have responsibility for—and be willing to ask for help from family or friends when the temptation comes to ignore or give up discipline!

The hardened heart through the deceitfulness of sin only sets us up for more painful situations later on. Since God is working with us to bring us more fully into conformity with his will, we must expect that he will keep on working, in many and various ways, to soften our hearts and to clarify our vision, so that we be not blinded with the deceitfulness of sin.

A Prayer Thought: "Blake has told us that Satan is the god of things that are not, 'the traveller's dream under the hill.' He is the god of the rainbow in the next field but one, in seeking whom men miss the true God in the meadow where they stand."

(Arthur Clutton-Brock)

A Prayer: Make and keep my heart soft, O Lord, and sensitive to the moving of your Holy Spirit. In Jesus' Name. Amen

1. What are you tempted to do when you feel sorry for yourself, angry, or resentful?

2. Where have you been willing to ask for help when you are finding a disciplined life difficult or you are feeling "stuck" somewhere?

I Have Rebelled
Daily Reading: Lamentations 1

"The LORD is in the right, for I have rebelled against his word." (v. 18a)

Lamentations is a book of tragic songs, sung by the prophet Jeremiah as he saw Judah and Jerusalem being destroyed and carried away captive. In it we see the grief and anguish of the prophet's heart as Jerusalem reaps the reward of her rebellion. Here in the first chapter, Jeremiah speaks for Jerusalem, confessing her sin and waiting for the mercy of God.

All this week we are thinking about the reality of rebellion in the human race, and of our own specific part in it. Rebellion demands punishment on God's part if he is to remain Lord of his own universe. "The LORD is in the right."

The rebel is in the wrong. Man cannot excuse his uprising against God's government, and we cannot excuse our own rebellion against what we know God requires of us. What is sown is reaped, and the effects can be heartbreaking.

D. L. Moody is reported to have said once to a group of students, "Don't forget that 'whatsoever a man soweth, that shall he also reap.' You have got to reap what you sow. Do you ask, 'if I repent and God forgives me, will I still have to reap?' Yes, you will; nothing can change that law. But if you repent, God will help you in the hard work of reaping."

It should neither surprise us nor dismay us when we see the results of our rebellion displayed in our life situations, our relationships, our children, and so on. That is no time for despair, the throwing up of hands and giving up. Instead, we can say, "The Lord is in the right, for I have rebelled against his word." We can begin to cooperate with him, so that he can bring good out of evil, and can help us "in the hard work of reaping." He is using it all for good and for his glory, and that should be a tremendous word of hope and encouragement to any of us!

A Prayer: Lord, open my eyes to see the true nature of rebellion before too many seeds are sown for a sad harvest. And anything that I must walk through because of past rebellion, do be with me, and give me grace to see your loving hand. In Jesus' Name. Amen.

1. Where have you come to see yourself excusing your rebellion?

2. Rather than despair, where do you see you can cooperate with God to bring blessing out of your disobedience?

The Rebellion of Korah
Daily Reading: Numbers 16

"Therefore it is against the LORD *that you and all your company have gathered together; what is Aaron that you murmur against him?" (v. 11)*

The rebellion of Korah and his followers stands as an extreme and graphic example and warning to Israel and to all of us against the sin of rebellion. A conspiracy had been formed and two hundred and fifty men were involved in it, challenging the leadership of Moses and Aaron. Here are some thoughts for our meditation:

First, their rebellion was rooted in jealousy. When we find ourselves inwardly resisting or resenting those in places of leadership, we should be suspicious of our own motivation. Jealousy is an insidious sin, and it quickly spreads, feeding on small dissatisfactions and resulting at times in major crises. More harm is done to Christian fellowship by this sin than any other.

Second, the rebellion was aided by backbiting. The dictionary defines backbiting as "saying mean and spiteful things about a person who is absent." Jealousy uses backbiting in order to do its destructive work. Rebellion could not become conspiracy without it.

Third, those who engaged in rebellion were the ones who were ultimately harmed. God has pledged himself to protect and defend his work. "Lo, I am with you always," said Jesus, "even to the close of the age." But if we place ourselves, even unwittingly, against what God is doing then we endanger our own interests. In every group, church, congregation, or fellowship, it is important to guard ourselves against, the spirit of rebellion; every discipline carries with it the temptation to resist and rebel. So let us behave wisely in the light of what we are seeing.

A Prayer: O merciful God, bless thy people throughout all the world, and all who love thee in sincerity, although they follow not with us in all things. Heal all strife, division, and discord, and make us all thine in willing devotion as we are all thine by redemption and grace; for the sake of Jesus Christ our Lord. Amen

1. Prayerfully go over your life and make a list of people in leadership or authority of whom you have been jealous.

2. Go over the list and confess this jealousy to the Lord, accept the forgiveness of God and go on rejoicing and change!

The Fruit of Rebellion
Daily Reading: Romans 1:18–32

Therefore God gave them up in the lusts of their hearts to impurity, to the dishonoring of their bodies among themselves, because they exchanged the truth about God for a lie, and worshiped and served the creature rather than the creator, who is blessed forever! Amen. (vv. 24-25)

This section has been aptly referred to as the darkest description of human nature in the Bible. Paul is concerned here to shock us with the ultimate direction in which rebellion takes us. He wants us to be sickened by the description of men and women abandoned to what is in them apart from the grace of God.

We are confronted here with the terrible wrath of God which has been revealed from heaven against all sin—small and great. Everywhere men's consciences register his wrath, until by continually rebelling against him, the conscience becomes so seared and deadened that it can no longer register God's wrath, and so are given up by God to whatever is in the heart. "Willful resistance of light," says David Brown, "has a retributive tendency to blind the moral perceptions and weaken the capacity to apprehend and approve of truth and goodness; and thus is the soul prepared to surrender itself, to an indefinite extent, to error and sin." The key term is "willful resistance to light." We are not responsible for what we have not been taught. "The times of this ignorance God winked at," says Acts 17:30, "but now commands men everywhere to repent." In other words, we are morally and spiritually responsible for the light we are given. This is especially important when we are hearing it from someone else, and do not like what we are hearing. Instead of "willful resistance to light," we should struggle against ourselves to receive the light within, that knowing where we are wrong, where we need to change, where we need to repent, we can step further in the light, and manifest more of Jesus' likeness.

The fruit of rebellion, when God gives a person up to the lusts of the heart, is frightening indeed. Let it warn us away from its earlier motions.

A Prayer: Make us of quick and tender conscience, O Lord; that understanding, we may obey every word of thine this day, and discerning, may follow every suggestion of thine indwelling Spirit. Speak, Lord, for thy servant heareth; through Jesus Christ our Lord. (Christina G. Rosetti, 1830–94)

1. Note anything else the Lord has shown you about rebellion.

Week Review

When we hear the word "rebellion," we think of extremely "bad" behavior—something easily recognized. In reality, rebellion is simply not being willing to be obedient. Rebellion can also be very subtle, especially when you think you have an excuse to be disobedient.

1. Think about those specific places in your life where you are rebellious. Do you need any help?

2. Have you discovered any habit patterns that encourage your rebellion?

3. What are you putting off "until tomorrow"?

4. How do you overcome rebellion?

"THOSE WHOM I LOVE I REPROVE" (CORRECTION)

For the Lord
disciplines him
whom he loves,
and chastises
every son whom
he receives.

Hebrews 12:6

SEVEN

Bearing the Burden of Correction
Daily Reading: Galatians 6:1–10

Brethren, if a man is overtaken in any trespass, you who are
spiritual should restore him in a spirit of gentleness. . . .
Bear one another's burdens, and so fulfill the law of Christ.
(vv. 1-2)

It comes as a distinct surprise to many Christians that they may have some obligation to correct other Christians! This is so foreign to the experience most of us have had in the church that it may seem to be a new or strange teaching. Actually, the "new and strange teaching" is the idea that has crept into Christianity that we do not have responsibility for dealing with one another's faults.

If a person is in a fault or "trespass," how can he or she be "restored" unless the trespass is talked about? And if it is talked about, it must be done lovingly but in the spirit of truth and frankness. Such a thing is almost unthinkable in today's church, except where small groups of people covenant together to give and receive correction one of another. It may seem very risky, and certainly no one is going to enjoy (for the moment) receiving correction by others. But what it can do, when it is carefully and lovingly done, is to open up a depth of caring Christian fellowship which can be the greatest blessing imaginable.

The "burden" of speaking correction to a brother or sister in Christ means that we feel the risk of being rejected by that person if we tell them the truth. That burden, however, can open the way to forgiveness, freedom, and a new joy when the other person has "been restored."

Each person has to bear his or her own load, too. That means (at least in part) that when we receive correction from others—wife, husband, employer, friend, parent, etc.—we can and must "bear" it, in order to become free of false estimates of ourselves. The way is very clear, and the blessings are abundant, if we are willing to walk in it.

1. Some people are easier for you to be honest with than others. Who is the hardest for you, and why?

But When I Saw They Were Not Straightforward...
Daily Reading: Galatians 2

But when Cephas came to Antioch I opposed him to his face, because he stood condemned. (v. 11)

Cephas is Peter. Apparently Peter had difficulty at this point in his life in living out what he really believed in the face of opposition. He cared what other people thought about him! When he came to Antioch, at first he mingled with the non-Jewish Christians and ate with them as equals. Then came "certain men from James," representing a group who felt that all Christians should be circumcised and follow the Jewish rites. It had become quite a point of controversy in the Jerusalem church, and they were concerned when they heard that Paul and Barnabas were not requiring Gentiles to become Jewish proselytes when they became Christians.

Paul himself had been the strictest kind of Jew, and he knew from personal experience what observing the law meant. He also knew that God had thrown open the door of the kingdom to all—to the Jew first and also to the Gentile! And when Peter, fearing criticism from the delegation from

Jerusalem and the "folks back home," jumped up from the Gentile table and went over to a table made up of Jews only, Paul "opposed him to his face."

This is a good example of how correction worked in the early church. The concern for truth was greater than the concern for personal feelings. That, of course, can be an excuse for erupting one's feelings out of jealousy, anger, hurt feelings, and other motives, if we are not concerned with the other aspects of our fellowship: receiving as well as giving correction, and maintaining the "unity of the spirit in the bond of peace."

But the point is important. Christians must be willing to speak when another Christian is in the wrong. Usually it is wise to have a third person (see Matthew 18:16) when speaking to someone about a fault or trespass.

A Prayer: Lord, make me quick to hear a word of reproof, and willing to speak the truth to my brothers and sisters as led by your Holy Spirit. Above all, help me to see myself, first, as "the chief of sinners," so that my self-righteousness will not be a stumbling-block. In Jesus' Name. Amen.

1. What do you really care more about—the concern to be honest, or what other people think? Why?

Let Everyone Speak the Truth
Daily Reading: Ephesians 4

Therefore putting away falsehood, let every one speak the truth with his neighbor, for we are members one of another. (v. 25)

As we are considering the subject of correction or reproof it is well to ask the Lord wherein we are dishonest in our relationships with fellow Christians. Do we flatter insincerely? Do we change the facts to make them a little more acceptable when repeating something to another? Do we pretend to approve of some attitude which we know to be wrong and hurtful? Do we indulge in repeating hearsay and gossip which does no good, and serves to divide the fellowship? Do we listen to gossip, even if we do not repeat it? And if so, do we realize that listening makes us as guilty as if we spoke it ourselves?

The young church at Ephesus was a church in a hostile environment. At this time Christians were often ostracized and shunned for their faith. Paul himself writes the letter from prison. "I therefore, a prisoner for the Lord, beg you to lead a life worthy of the calling to which you have been called," (v. 1). If that young fellowship did not learn to be *truthful* within itself, it would have no inner strength to stand against the forces outside.

Today, we are yet again in great need of the spiritual buttressing received when Christians speak the truth to one another in love. It is a freeing experience. We truly cannot know ourselves without the help of others who will speak the truth to us.

"Truth is the secret of eloquence and of virtue, the basis of moral authority; it is the highest summit of art and of life."
(Henri-Frederic Amiel, Journal, 1883)

A Prayer: Almighty God, Who hast sent the Spirit of truth unto us to guide us into all truth, so rule our lives by thy power, that we may be truthful in word, deed, and thought. O keep us, most merciful Savior, with thy gracious protection, so that no fear or hope may ever make us false in act or speech;

and bring us all to the perfect freedom of thy truth; through Jesus Christ our Lord. Amen.

(Bishop Westcott, 1825, abridged)

1. Have you seen any places that you flatter insincerely or change the facts to make them more acceptable? Where?

2. Where recently have you been willing to speak the truth with your neighbor (or family)?

Have I Become Your Enemy?
Daily Reading: Galatians 4:8–31

Have I then become your enemy by telling you the truth?
(v. 16)

The truth is, that in our feelings this is exactly what happens when someone speaks unpleasant truth to us. We often do not even recognize it as truth. It seems like criticism, condemnation, even rejection. Our reaction, then, is hurt, anger, self-defense! We are attacked and the person speaking is the enemy.

Paul knew that this was probably the way the Galatian Christians were reacting to his rebuke. The whole letter is a stern and loving rebuke of a man who had poured out his life to give these people the Good News of Jesus Christ! Now he saw them in danger of selling their spiritual birthright for a mess of legal pottage, and he was angry! He was angry at those who had come into the flock of new Christians and upset their faith, and he was appalled at the Galatians for being so gullible. But there is power in truth. There is light and healing in it. When it is spoken, the hearer has the opportunity of choosing to believe it, even though feelings may go in exactly the opposite direction. After all, if we are ruled by our feelings, none of us is very stable! So we can choose to give up considering the person who speaks to us as "the enemy." We can choose to put down our defenses, and pray for even a small corner of agreement, where we can "agree with our adversary quickly." In this way, we treat the person as a friend and helper instead of an enemy, and once we have given up the self-righteous defense mechanism all of us have, we can begin to come into greater light and understanding, repentance and freedom. It is a secret too few of us know and fully appreciate, but one which saints and heroes of faith have long treasured. It allows the Cross to work on our old nature, as the truth convicts and sets us free.

Truth being truth,
Tell it and shame the devil.
    (Robert Browning)

A Prayer: Help me the slow of heart to move, by some clear, winning word of love. Teach me the wayward feet to stay, and guide them in the homeward way. Amen
    (Washington Gladden, 1879)

1. Is there someone specific you resist when they speak to you? Who? Why?

2. Where have you allowed the truth spoken to you to set you free and help you change?

Respect Those...Who Admonish You
Daily Reading: 1 Thessalonians 5

But we beseech you, brethren, to respect those who labor among you and are over you in the Lord and admonish you, and to esteem them very highly in love because of their work. (vv. 12-13a)

Admonish. 1a. To indicate duties or obligations to. b. to express warning or disapproval to, especially gently, earnestly, and solicitously. 2. to give friendly, earnest advice or encouragement.

The word comes from the word meaning "to warn." Those who admonish us are those who warn us of possible or real dangers in our lives if we follow certain courses of action.

What place has admonishment in our lives as Christians? Do you ever feel a warning for someone else who is going through a difficult time and asks for help? Do you expose your own struggle and temptation, so that others may give you "friendly, earnest advice or encouragement"?

Leaders, pastors, and others, have a responsibility for those entrusted to their care, to give such help as they can. *All* of us without exception, need to be admonished from time to time. We have seen Paul admonishing Peter. We read many examples of admonishing in the New Testament. To avoid being admonished is to run the danger of leaning on our own understanding and placing ourselves above all others. Such an attitude breaks fellowship and separates us from our families and other members of the body of Christ.

A Prayer. Lord Jesus, yours is the most humble of hearts; I confess that by nature I am inclined to haughtiness and that

*my heart's evil spirit is poisoned by pride, the root of all sin.
Grant me true lowliness so that I may imitate your holy
humility, becoming like a child. Amen.*

(Johann Arndt, c. 1600)

1. What are some of the ways God has admonished you?

2. Where have you cared enough for people to lovingly and
mercifully admonish them?

The Rebuke of the Wise
Daily Reading: Ecclesiastes 7:1–20

*It is better for a man to hear the rebuke of the wise than to
hear the song of fools. (v. 5)*

By nature we all love to hear good things about us. There is
a term current today called "positive stroking." It means saying
good things to people about themselves to make them feel better.

We all need to hear encouraging, heartening words at times.
But if we know our strong bent to be praised, to be "loved,
honored, worshiped, and adored," we should be leery of that
within us that swells with pleasure when we are praised.
"Well done!" is one thing, but being told we are wonderful
is a different "kettle of fish."

How then do we receive rebuke from *anyone if* we believe
we are wonderful? How could we? It would not seem fitting
or proper or even truthful. Yet, as our scripture tells us,
"Surely there is not a righteous man on earth who does good
and never sins" (v. 20). Somerset Maugham once observed,
"People ask you for criticism, but they only want praise."

That may be well and good for the world apart from God. It is not well and good for Christians who know "a more excellent way," the way of receiving correction and letting it work for us. "The rebuke of the wise" refers to something spoken out of greater light than we have at the moment, greater discernment and understanding. Most of us at times have such a word for others, and most of us have need of such a word from others. If we begin to see the love of God and the spirit of Jesus behind such words, then we can appreciate them for what they are.

> And blest is he who can divine
> Where the true right doth lie,
> And dares to take the side that seems
> Wrong to man's blindfold eye!
>
> Oh, learn to scorn the praise of men!
> Oh, learn to lose with God!
> For Jesus won the world through shame,
> And beckons thee his road.
>
> And right is right, since God is God;
> And right the day must win;
> To doubt would be disloyalty,
> To falter would be sin!
> *(F. W. Faber, 1814–1863)*

1. What value do you think merciful honesty has in your experience?

Do Not Be Weary of His Reproof
Daily Reading: Proverbs 3:1–12

My son, do not despise the LORD'S *discipline or be weary of his reproof, for the* LORD *reproves him whom he loves, as a father the son in whom he delights. (v. 11-12)*

Reproof and correction are expressions of love. It is vitally important that we learn the truth of this as we go on in our walk with Jesus Christ. The writer of the Proverbs encourages us to choose to see God's discipline and God's rebukes as expressions of his fatherly love and care for us.

Most of us are neophytes or newcomers to this concept. We may have accepted (even unwillingly) the fact that our parents did correct us in love, even though we know as parents ourselves, that parental correction does not always come without sin. Nevertheless, it is better for the child to be corrected than not to be corrected, and there are no sinless parents around, so we have to accept the fact that our parents did the best they knew, and be grateful for it. At the same time, we can commit ourselves as parents to do the best we know, and trust God with the results. It goes without saying that at the time, no discipline is welcomed by any child—but remembering back, we can testify that discipline did us good.

Even when we recognize the Lord's hand in a certain discipline, however, self-pity can still rise up and we can grow "weary of his reproof." Self-pity says, "it is too much. Even though I need to change or am wrong in such and such an area, this is unjust and too much!" This is when we need to gird up ourselves, call someone for help, get busy doing something to distract our self demands, and pray mightily for a new measure of grace and the presence of the Lord. Small victories lead to larger ones. Small indulgences lead to larger ones. The choice, in the midst of temptation, is ours.

A Prayer: O God, Who hast folded back the mantle of the night to clothe us in the golden glory of the day. chase from our hearts all gloomy thoughts, and make us glad with the brightness of hope, that we may effectively aspire to unwon virtues, through Jesus Christ our Lord. Amen.

(Bp. Charles H Brent)

1. Where, in your life, have you seen that reproof and correction are expressions of loving concern?

Chapter Review

Correction is something which is difficult to get across— and yet something that has changed many lives. Correction is a stepping stone into eternal life.

1. Did this topic sound a little stern at the start of the readings? Why?

2. Did you feel more comfortable by the end of the reading? Why?

3. Are you able to speak the truth in love to anyone around you?

4. Is anyone really honest with you?

"IF WE CONFESS OUR SINS"

*If we confess our
sins, he is faithful
and just, and will
forgive our sins and
cleanse us from all
unrighteousness.*

1 John 1:9

EIGHT

I Know My Transgression
Daily Reading: Psalm 51

The fifty-first Psalm is perhaps the greatest prayer of confession ever composed. It came from the heart of one who was truly convicted of his sin, truly sorry for it, and who was willing to throw himself on the mercy of God in the belief that God is merciful to sinners. So it makes a good point at which to start this week's meditations on the combined subjects of "Repentance, Confession, and Forgiveness."

The Holy Spirit is the Spirit of truth. He searches out the inward parts, and reveals to us our condition. Thank God we have such an inward light. Jesus said, "if the light in you is darkness, how great is that darkness!" But we have the light of the Holy Spirit to shine like a floodlight on the sin areas, exposing all the hidden creepy-crawlies within.

We cannot repent when we do not know our transgression. It would be a terrible thing to be left in the darkness of delusion, because then we would be unable to repent. Like those people described in the first chapter of Romans, we would be "given up" by God to all that was within us. If you have ever had a good look at what is inside, you know that it is not very pretty to see. But when we have been convicted by the Holy Spirit of our transgression, we know our transgression, our wrongness, and we can then begin to repent. We can ask for mercy, for washing and cleansing, and like the psalmist we can say to God, "thou art justified in thy sentence, and blameless in thy judgment." In other words, we agree with God's judgment about where we are wrong.

When a surgeon begins to operate on a person, he has to know where the trouble is—and have a pretty good idea what it is. And there is a lot about it that the patient would prefer to avoid, but knowing that what lies ahead is joy and health, goes through with the pain of it. That is a fairly accurate picture of the process of conviction and repentance. There is pain, and we might rather avoid it. But for the joy set before us, we endure it knowing that in Jesus Christ there is mercy, forgiveness, restoration, and joy!

A Prayer:
Come as the light to us reveal
Our emptiness and woe,
And lead us in those paths of life
Whereon the righteous go.
                    Andrew Reed, 1829)

1. How did David react when confronted with his sin?

2. How do you respond when faced with your sin?

So Turn and Live
Daily Reading: Ezekiel 18:21–32

"For I have no pleasure in the death of anyone," says the Lord GOD; *"so turn and live." (v. 32)*

God is so loving, so giving, so generous that he desires to give life. He is the Source of life, and he created us for life. Throughout the Bible, we glean this picture of him in his infinite patience with his people. He desires life for them all!

It is a reassuring and encouraging thought amid the struggles of our lives, to know that God desires life for us. Jesus said it in another way: "I have come that they may have life and have it abundantly" (John 10:10). It is not just existence that he gives us and desires for us. It is life in fullness and abundance, life as it was created to be in the heart of the Creator and that he longs to give his children.

What holds us back from that life? It can be nothing but ourselves. It cannot be that God is unable to give what he wills to give. No force in heaven or earth can stay his hand. But because of the unique place he has given us, he will not over-rule or destroy our wills. He will not make robots out of us, even though he could. Instead, he allows us to stumble, to fall, to taste the fruit of our sin, to feel the pain of the separation we have made from him—to the end that we will turn and live.

In this chapter from Ezekiel, the wicked man is encouraged to turn from his way and live. The righteous man is encouraged not to turn from his way to die. God's will is life for us all. The way to life has been opened for us by our Lord Jesus Christ. He has fought the battle, and invites us to share in the benefits of his victory.

But in order to do that, we must turn, over and over again, when we have gone out of the way, when we have lapsed back into our old nature; then the way back is to turn from our way, to his way, and find that abundant life again. If you do not have a deep sense of repentance, pray for it. It is a precious gift which leads to life.

A Prayer Thought: How true it is that if you fight with your conscience and lose, then you win.

(J. Moulton Thomas)

1. How is God's faithfulness demonstrated as we confess our sin?

No Longer Worthy
Daily Reading: Luke 15:11–32

This story of the prodigal son can be read with several different objects in mind—the merciful, waiting father, the wayward but finally repentant son, or the jealous elder brother. Certainly one of its most endearing qualities, however, is its picture of a young man who decided to go his own way, found that all he thought would bring him happiness led him finally to being willing to eat pigs' food, and coming to his senses, returned to his father's house. What had happened inside that young man is the thing we need to see, as we think about repentance, confession, and forgiveness.

First, his repentance came about when he realized where he was and what he had done. "He came to himself" (v. 17). We have talked about that in earlier devotional readings—this process of realizing who we are and what we have done. He no longer lived with blinders over his eyes, expecting that things would get better. He took responsibility for where he was, and decided to do something about it! "I will arise and go to my father!"

Second, his confession is expressed in these words: "Father, I have sinned against heaven and before you; I am no longer worthy to be called your son." Even though his father had come out to meet him "while he was yet at a distance," and had embraced and kissed him, the son knew what he had to say. He had to acknowledge with his words the reality of what he had seen about himself.

Third, his repentance and confession brought the assurance of forgiveness. They did not earn forgiveness, for you cannot earn forgiveness—it is a free gift. But they did enable him to receive and enjoy the father's forgiveness.

This is our pattern. It is God's pattern for us, and as we follow it, we enter over and over again into his fellowship as his beloved children.

> My God is reconciled;
> His pard'ning voice I hear;
> He owns me as his child;
> I can no longer fear.
> With confidence I now draw nigh,
> And, "Father, Abba, Father," cry!
>   *(Charles Wesley)*

1. How did the young man "come to himself'?

2. How do you take responsibility for "where you are" and decide to do something about it?

Confess Your Sins to One Another
Daily Reading: James 5

Therefore confess your sins to one another, and pray for one another that you may be healed. (v. 16)

When should we confess our sins to another person? That seems a legitimate question. Certainly it is unwise to confess sexual misconduct to anyone other than a trustworthy pastor, priest, or mature counselor. Otherwise, it can become a stumbling block and a snare. A timely warning against such an unwise course is in order!

There are, however, many sins which can and should be confessed to other Christians—to members of a prayer group, or wherever God has provided people willing to "bear one another's burdens, and so fulfill the law of Christ."

Sometimes confessing our sins in secret to God does not seem to bring relief from the burden or guilt of them, and we need additional help from others. Here again, Bonhoeffer's words seem appropriate:

God has willed that we should seek and find his living word in the witness of a brother, in the mouth of a man. Therefore, the Christian needs another Christian who speaks God's word to him. He needs him again and again when he becomes uncertain and discouraged, for by himself, he cannot help himself without belying the truth. He needs his brother man as a bearer and proclaimer of the divine word of salvation

That "word of salvation" is often the assurance of forgiveness after we have exposed our sin of jealousy, rebellion, hatred, or whatever. That we are loved and accepted, forgiven and cleansed is a cause of rejoicing and fellowship in the entire body of Christ, represented by the person to whom we have made our confession.

That "word of salvation" may also be additional light thrown on the problem we are talking about, as we come to see more clearly that we are behaving out of subconscious, buried feelings and motivations. Once we see them, and they are brought into the light, we can have the peace of God which passes understanding. "And pray for one another, that you may be healed." The healing is first inward, and then, oftentimes physical as well.

O Savior Christ, thou too art man;
Thou has been troubled, tempted, tried;
Thy kind but searching glance can scan
The very wounds that shame would hide.
    (Henry Twells, 1868)

1. When should we confess our sins to another person?

2. When recently have you received the assurance of forgiveness and experienced restored relationships after you've exposed and confessed your sin?

The Repentance of Nineveh
Daily Reading: Jonah 3

When God saw what they did, how they turned from their evil way, God repented of the evil which he had said he would do to them, and he did not do it. (v. 10)

Nineveh was renowned for its wickedness. In Chapter 1, God's word came to Jonah saying "Arise, go to Nineveh, that great city, and cry against it; for their wickedness is come up before me." There was no doubt about Nineveh's need for repentance. But there is an unusual feature to this story. Apparently Jonah's message was only to "cry out" against Nineveh's sin and to declare its impending doom. There was no call for repentance as such. This should give us a clue as to how God sometimes deals with us. Something may come into our lives that seems clear-cut, definite, and unchangeable. It may be clear to us that it is the judgment of God on us, or someone may be angry with us for something we have done and cannot undo. What is our response? Anger? Self-defense? Hurt? Withdrawal and passivity?

A good example of what not to do in such a case is seen in 1 Samuel 3, where young Samuel was given a message to deliver to Eli, the priest, promising judgment on Eli's house because of his sons' wickedness. Eli's answer, "It is the Lord; let him do what seems good to him" (1 Samuel 3:18). He made no effort to change!

But Nineveh was wiser in this case. Though the prophet did not hold out any hope, the king said, "Let us repent, and perhaps God will be gracious." And they did.

The implication here is that if the wicked people of Nineveh could repent, there is no reason that God's people cannot repent when confronted by the Holy Spirit with their wrongness. It is true today as it was then!

> Search out our hearts and make us true,
> Wishful to give to all their due;
> From love of pleasure, lure of gold
> From sins which make the heart grow cold
> Wean us and train us with thy rod;
> Teach us to know our faults, O God.
> (William Boyd Carpenter, 1841–1918)

1. If you are truly sorry for your sin, you will want to change. What specific steps are you taking to allow God to change you?

2. What is the difference between remorse and repentance?

Purified with Blood
Daily Reading: Hebrews 9

And without the shedding of blood there is no forgiveness of sins. (v. 22b)

The entire Old Testament sacrificial system begins to make sense when we see it as a foreshadowing of the "one, true, pure immortal sacrifice" of Jesus Christ. The blood of bulls and lambs and goats was shed in anticipation of the Lamb of God who would take away the sin of the world.

What does that mean to us as Christians? First, it means that the shedding of Jesus' blood is a sacrifice for our sin, and that forgiveness and remission are applied when that sin is brought "under the blood." We need the soul-cleansing blood to free us from the stain and pollution of sin. That comes about when we recognize the sin, take responsibility for it, confess it, and seek the blood-washing. 1 John 1 says, "if we walk in the light, as he is in the light, we have fellowship with one another, and the blood of Jesus his Son cleanses us from all sin" (v. 7). Notice that it is when it is "in the light," and not hidden in the dark that we have the blood-cleansing. 1 John 1 goes on to say, "if we say we have no sin, we deceive ourselves, and the truth is not in us." This clearly refers to our acknowledgment and confession of sin as a part of the cleansing and healing process.

Secondly, it says that our good works cannot make up for our wrongs. Too many of us fall back into the old pattern, even after becoming Christians, of trying to compensate for our wrongness by doing good or right things. The way out of sin is confession and forgiveness—not working harder at being right. Out of the blessedness of forgiveness, and the gratitude of our Lord for his sacrifice for us, we bring forth "works that befit repentance," the fruit of obedience in our lives.

But if we ever fall back into thinking that we do not need the shed blood of Jesus, that our own goodness and righteousness is enough, then we have fallen from grace into dead works. No life comes forth from dead works, and we will be hardened Pharisees, while claiming with our lips our loyalty to Jesus. May God save us from such a fate!

1. Where recently have you tried to make up for your wrongs by good works?

2. What does "the one true pure immortal sacrifice" of Jesus Christ mean to you personally?

He Will Forgive ... and Cleanse
Daily Reading: 1 John 1

He is faithful and just, and will forgive us our sins, and cleanse us from all unrighteousness. (v. 9)

George Adam Smith wrote, "The forgiveness of God is the foundation of every bridge from a hopeless past to a courageous present."

That's what we need: a courageous present. A present that is as free from fears and hang-ups, from bondage to old habits and ways of reacting as is possible at this moment. We are not yet there, we are not yet perfect, we have not yet arrived—but we are on the way! Praise be to God!

"Why, then," you may ask, "all this talk about repentance and forgiveness? I'm a Christian, and Jesus forgave me my sins when I accepted him, and he has cleansed me from the past!"

Indeed, as we came to Jesus in our need, he did forgive and cleanse. But we find that there are new expressions of the old self cropping up (or leaking out) all along the way. And we may get so discouraged that we might even wonder if we are Christians at all! That sad state has plagued many sincere people. They thought they had accepted Jesus with all their heart, but they did not find the ongoing victory they had heard about, and they felt that they either had to pretend to be better than they were, or find out why it was the way it was.

Here, in this little verse is the answer. What is born of God, the life of the Holy Spirit within us, does not sin. That is there, and it is given, the Presence of God within every true child of his.

But the old, Adamic nature is also there, seeking to express itself in the old patterns of hurt, desire to be loved, desire to be number one, to win, lusting after the things of this world. And there is the adversary, the Devil, using the old nature, appealing to it, and tempting us to wander far from the Lord. We all know the tug and pull of it.

But there is a way out of this mess. It begins here—"If we confess our sins, he is faithful and just, and will forgive us our sins and cleanse us from all unrighteousness." The more we learn it, believe it, and practice it, the more we can advance in our life in Christ.

1. What does it mean to you to be forgiven?

Chapter Review

Have you caught a glimpse that it is safe to recognize and admit that we are sinners. We simply confess it, repent of it, receive forgiveness and go on in the joy of a soul set free, praying for the grace to change.

1. Do you believe that God sent his Son to die for wrong people, needy people, sinners and not those who consider themselves right? Why is that important to you?

2. Is it safe yet for you to be wrong?

3. Do you still think and feel that your acceptance by God, and by other people is based on your goodness?

EMOTIONS:
WHAT TO DO WITH THEM

Rejoice with
those who rejoice,
weep with those
who weep.

Romans 12:15

NINE

The Anger and Sorrow of God

Daily Reading: Genesis 6:1–8, Deuteronomy 9:13–29

And the LORD *was sorry that he had made man on earth,*
and it grieved him in his heart. (Genesis 6:6) And the LORD
was so angry with Aaron that he was ready to destroy him.
(Deuteronomy 9:20)

These and many other passages show us what we could
term the "emotions of God." The Bible does not reveal a God
who is placid, without feeling, dwelling in eternal calm. It
reveals to us a God who acts, speaks, and yes, feels.

What are some of the things that bring sorrow to God?
"Woe to those," says the prophet Amos, "who lie on beds of
ivory, and stretch themselves on their couches, eat lambs from
the flock . . . sing idle songs . . . drink wine in bowls, and
anoint themselves with the finest oils, but are not grieved over
the ruin of Joseph!" (Amos 6:4-6). The ruin of his people, the
sin that blemishes and deforms his creation—these bring grief
and sorrow to the Father's heart.

What produces anger? In the scripture for today, it is clear
that the readiness of the people to trample underfoot all that
God had done for them, the miracles of the Passover, the Red
Sea, and all the other deliverances—and to turn away to their
own inventions—this kindled the holy anger, the righteous
wrath of a Holy God.

This week we are looking at emotions, and asking what we
can and should do about them. It is good in the beginning to
see that some of the emotions we least want to recognize in
ourselves are attributed to God himself in the Bible. His, of
course, are without sin. Ours are not. But knowing that God,
too, feels anger, grief, sorrow, and the like, should make it

easier to see that it is all right to recognize these in ourselves. Pray this week that the Lord will give you grace to get in touch with your real feelings and begin to learn how to deal with them more constructively.

A Prayer: There is no place where earth's sorrows are more felt than up in heaven; there is no place where earth's failings have such kindly judgment given.

(F. W. Faber, 1814–1863)

1. What does it mean to you to know that God feels all your sorrows and griefs?

2. Is it a relief to you to consider that it is safe to recognize feelings that you have such as anger, jealousy, and fear? Why?

The Rejoicing of God
Daily Reading: Isaiah 62

As the bridegroom rejoices over the bride, so shall your God rejoice over you. (v. 5)

As we think about our emotions, it is good to see how the Bible also ascribes emotions or feelings to God. Here is a good example of God being pictured as rejoicing over his people. In Luke 15, Jesus reminds us that there is great rejoicing in heaven over one sinner who repents.

All of this should help us to see that our feelings are an integral and essential part of being made in the image of God. Because we *can* feel joy, love, sorrow, grief, anger, and so on, we are *persons*.

If we do not deal with our negative emotions, it is a sad truth that we lose the ability to rejoice. The entire feeling level becomes so depressed or repressed that it becomes impossible for us to experience the excitement and joy we may have known as children. No wonder Jesus said, "Except you are converted and become as little children, you cannot enter the kingdom of God" (Matthew 18:3). We need to treasure and, if necessary, recapture our ability to truly rejoice. Only then can we be in harmony with heaven which rejoices over one sinner who repents, and with God, who rejoices as a bridegroom rejoices over his bride.

Couple this with such commands to us as these: "Rejoice always" (1 Thessalonians 5:16), "Rejoice in the Lord always; again I will say, Rejoice" (Philippians 4:4).

The ability to rejoice is commensurate with our wholeness in the Lord. Never take it for granted, or think that it is all right if you grow dull in your willingness to rejoice!

Let all the world in every corner sing,
My God and King!
The heavens are not too high,
His praise may thither fly;
The earth is not too low,
His praises there may grow.
Let all the world in every corner sing,
My God and King!
(George Herbert, 1633)

1. Where have you seen that when you refuse to deal with your negative emotions you lose the ability to rejoice?

A Man of Sorrows
Daily Reading: John 11:1–44

When Jesus saw her weeping, and the Jews who came with her also weeping, he was deeply moved in spirit and troubled; and he said, "Where have you laid him?" They said to him, "Lord, come and see." Jesus wept. (vv. 33–35)

The prophet Isaiah called him "a man of sorrows and acquainted with grief." "Is it for nothing," asks one, "that the Evangelist, some sixty years after it occurred, holds up to all ages with such touching brevity the sublime spectacle of *the Son of God in tears*? What a seal of his perfect oneness with us in the most redeeming feature of our stricken humanity. . . . The tears of Mary and her friends acted sympathetically upon him, and drew forth his emotions. What a vivid outcoming of real humanity!"

Knowing that we have a great High Priest who is able "to sympathize with our weaknesses" (Hebrews 4:15), we should not be ashamed to face our own feelings of weakness, sorrow, grief, fear, and need. These things we often try to deny, but it is very encouraging to know that Jesus did not try to hide them. He was indeed an example to us, the example of perfect manhood. But we have thought that such feelings were unacceptable, and many of us have made a practice of denying them—so that we become deadened inside and may not know how we feel on any given subject, because we do not feel anything very much. Such a state is unnecessary for a Christian to remain in, and we can begin to get in touch with feelings—good, bad, and in between. The more we allow our feelings to surface, the freer we become to grow into the kind of whole people we were meant to be.

A Prayer: Lord Jesus, we read that in the days of your flesh, you offered up prayers and supplications with loud cries and tears (Hebrews 5:7). May I not be ashamed to cry when I need to, and finish when it is fitting, and become the whole person you want me to be. In your Name. Amen.

1. What unacceptable feelings have you sought to deny?

2. How do you express positive emotions? Negative emotions?

Be Angry and Sin Not

Daily Reading: Ephesians 4:17–32

Be angry but do not sin; do not let the sun go down on your anger (v. 26)

Charles Haddon Spurgeon, the great English nineteenth-century preacher, has an interesting word to say about anger:

"Anger is not always or necessarily sinful, but it has such a tendency to run wild that whenever it displays itself we should be quick to question its character with this enquiry: 'Doest thou well to be angry?' It may be that we can answer, 'Yes.' Very frequently anger is the madman's firebrand, but sometimes it is Elijah's fire from heaven. We do well when we are angry with sin because of the wrong it commits against our good and gracious God, or with ourselves because we remain so foolish after so much divine instruction, or with others when the sole cause of anger is the evil they do. He who is not angry at transgression becomes a partaker in it. Sin is a loathsome and hateful thing, and no renewed heart can patiently endure it. God himself is angry with the wicked every day, and it is written in his Word, 'Ye that love the Lord, hate evil.' "

The apostle here seems to differentiate between being angry and sinning. Yet many of us have been so conditioned to think of anger as always being wrong and ugly, and we have so wanted not to be wrong and ugly, that we have repressed the anger that came up in us, and tried to deny its very existence! It may even have been "righteous anger," a justifiable reaction to sin and the harm that it was causing in someone else's life. But if we think that anger is not becoming to a Christian, that we are always supposed to be calm and unflappable, then our tendency will be to push it down and deny its existence.

Here the Bible is saying "Be angry, but do not sin." Phillips translates it like this: "If you are angry—be sure that it is not a sinful anger. Never go to bed angry—don't give the devil that sort of foothold!" When we check out our anger and find that it is sinful and wrong, we should be quick to do something about it. On the other hand, we must allow room for the fact that being who we are, we do get angry, and that it is a part of our essential emotional make-up that we can get angry. Many of us need much freeing of bottled-up anger which we have not admitted to ourselves.

1. List the things that make you angry.

2. What do you do with your anger?—confess it, push it down inside you, or refuse to recognize it?

When I Am Afraid
Daily Reading: Psalm 55, 56

When I am afraid, I put my trust in thee. (Psalm 56:3)

Fear is one of the "basic emotions" with which we are made. It has a very important function in our lives, warning us of danger, enabling us to put forth greater effort when needed, and so on. A healthy fear is essential to our well-being.

Moreover, we are told, "The fear of the Lord is the beginning of wisdom." We need to have a holy fear of God—knowing that he is our Maker and we are accountable to him. Without it, it is doubtful that we will be moved toward obedience. Few if any of us could claim to obey solely on the basis of our love for God.

Yet, "perfect love casts out fear." There is in fear the potential of going beyond its useful function, and becoming a devastating and controlling emotion. Fear then becomes the enemy. ("We have nothing to fear but fear itself," said a famous president once.) Satan uses fear to paralyze, to make us hesitant when we should be bold, and to sap our energy and distract our attention from the Lord.

The psalmist knew what it was to be afraid. In Psalm 55: 4-5 he says, "The terrors of death have fallen upon me. Fear and trembling come upon me, and sorrow overwhelms me." Fear, when it reaches such proportions can cause tragic results.

So what is the solution? First, do not deny its reality. One of the most dangerous and foolish things is to "pretend to be brave" when we are not! Fear cannot be controlled in that way. Rather, we need to face its presence and confess it to the Lord. "When I am afraid." Not if, but *when*. We all are at times, when our lives seem out of control: at news of an accident, or illness or when we are informed that we ourselves may be in danger of some unknown illness. Confess to the Lord that you are afraid, and that it is because you do not trust him as you should! He is trustworthy! That's what the psalmist is saying. God "whose word I praise, in God I trust without a fear." We can move from fear to faith—over and over again, because we can choose to trust in our heavenly Father!

A Prayer: I call upon you, Lord, and you will save me. I utter my complaints and my moans, and you hear my voice. What then can flesh do to me? By grace, I choose to give up my fear and trust you more and more. In Jesus' Name. Amen.

1. List the fears in your life.

2. How can you move from fear to faith over and over again?

Learning to be Genuine
Daily Reading: Romans 12

Let love be genuine; hate what is evil; hold fast to what is good; love one another with brotherly affection; outdo one another in showing honor. (vv. 9-10)

This week we are considering what to do with our emotions, with a lot of emphasis on facing them as a real part of our lives. Hiding them, denying them, disowning them, if you will, are the most harmful ways of dealing with them.

The goal of the Christian life is to become integrated, whole persons, God-directed instead of self-directed. The wholeness comes as we are inwardly healed by the presence of the Holy Spirit, enlightened by the truth. In another way of describing it, we might say that it means having all our parts connected correctly to one another and functioning as God created them to function.

This twelfth chapter of Romans deals with our relationships with one another in the Christian fellowship. The apostle recognizes that there are forces outside and inside that keep us from being what Jesus Christ means us to be. "Do not be conformed to this world" (v. 2). The world is constantly trying to "press us into its mold," as someone has put it. And we must resist by allowing the transforming power of God to work in us. But there are inner forces, too, which distort us." I bid every one among you not to think of himself more highly than he ought to think" (v. 3). Can we plead innocent on that one? Thinking too highly of ourselves opens us up to get hurt, feel rejected, to become jealous, and, in general, to infuse a dark, negative element into the Christian fellowship. What can we do about it? Unfortunately, what some people do, is to try to cover it up with a surface politeness and friendliness, which belies what is underneath. So Paul says, "Let love be genuine." Let it be sincere. But we cannot be sincere unless we honestly deal with the negative feelings we have about one another. *Then*, by God's grace, love does flow through us to others, and we can receive God's love through them to us. Love becomes genuine as we become real, because of Jesus Christ.

We cannot be sincere and have genuine love unless we deal with the negative feelings we have toward one another.

A Prayer: Lord let me learn to be real that my love may become genuine. In Jesus' Name. Amen.

1. What negative feelings do you have toward people you live with, your friends, and in the church fellowship?

2. What can you do with these negative feelings?

First the Inside
Daily Reading: Matthew 23:1–28

"Woe to you, scribes and Pharisees, hypocrites! for you cleanse the outside of the cup and of the plate, but inside they are full of extortion and rapacity. You blind Pharisees! First cleanse the inside of the cup and of the plate, that the outside also may be clean." (vv. 25-26)

The scribes and Pharisees were caught up in outward performance and appearance. They did not set out to be hypocrites; they just were hypocrites because they had been blinded by their own rightness.

Jesus did not encourage "bad behavior." But neither was he put off by "good behavior." He looked beyond the outward pattern to see what was in the heart. And in the hearts of the Pharisees, he saw self-deception and hypocrisy.

We need to take this to ourselves. When we have made a life-pattern of denying feelings we had—ugly, wrong feelings that needed to be dealt with—we can be nothing but hypocrites. It is not that we mean to be hypocrites; we just are, because we are not connected up right. Our feelings and our ideas are not "tracking together," as the phrase goes.

Even when our words and our faces express joy or love, or some other positive emotion, if our heart is not right, then what comes out of us is cloudy, confusing, and hurtful. There is no way around it: either we have to learn to be honest with ourselves and others, or we will continue to live in the same darkness that the Pharisees lived in. They could not hear what Jesus was saying, because their hearts kept telling them he was wrong and they were right.

Facing our ugly emotions, admitting them before the Lord and one another, and seeking his power in overcoming them, is the healthy wholesome way into fuller, freer life. The Pharisees, for the most part, stayed in their sin of delusion. We do not have to, for we know Jesus Christ has the answer to our needs.

A Prayer: Thank you, Lord that I do not have to deny my negative feelings nor live in them. There is a way out, through you. Thank you that you love me so much that you are leading me day by day, in finding that way. Amen.

1. During this week what ugly emotions have you faced? Have you admitted them before the Lord and others?

2. How are you seeking his power to overcome them?

Chapter Review

Emotions help us express what is going on inside of us, and we do not need to be afraid of them. As you begin to recognize these emotions, positive or negative, and ask the Lord to help you to not be controlled by them, your whole life can come into balance.

1. What emotions are you most aware of in your life?

2. Have you seen any relationship between your emotions and your daily habits/lifestyle?

3. Are there any feelings that you try to hide from yourself or others?

4. What does God want us to do with our emotions?

WHEN LIGHT IS DARKNESS

*"You will know
the truth, and the
truth will make
you free."*

John 8:32

TEN

The Truth Will Make You Free
Daily Reading: John 8:31–59

"If you continue in my word, you are truly my disciples, and you will know the truth, and the truth will make you free." (vv. 31-32)

This week we are thinking about the "lies we believe." By that we mean that many things we have been taught, or have picked up ourselves, which we have believed to be true, are in reality *false*.

Perhaps you have never thought much about it. But think a moment. If you think something is true, and act upon it, it makes a great deal of difference whether it is true or not.

There was a story told years ago about a worker in a factory whose clothing caught fire. A fellow worker grabbed a bucket labeled "water," (as factories had in those days) and threw it on his co-worker. But the bucket contained gasoline. It was labeled wrong!

Think about that in connection with things we believe to be true, some of which are mentioned in your Bible studies this week. How vital it is for your own welfare and that of others, to begin to be able to discern truth from falsehood.

Jesus said, "if you continue in my word . . ." That is a clue. He not only has the truth, he is the Truth, and we can expect his active help and assistance as we seek to come more and more into the truth that sets free.

This week should be an exciting one, as you begin to discover lies which you have thought to be truth, and start on the adventure of renouncing the lies (for Satan is the father of lies) and affirming the truth (for Jesus is the Truth).

Expect miracles!

1. Can you think of one "truth" in your life that turned out later to be a lie?

2. How has believing that lie affected your life?

If the Light in You Is Darkness
Daily Reading: Matthew 6

"But if your eye is not sound, your whole body will be full of darkness. If then the light in you is darkness, how great is the darkness!" (v. 23)

Throughout history, further light has proved old light to be darkness. For many centuries theories about the universe, about the human body, about the shape and structure of the earth prevailed. Then discoveries proved old theories wrong and made new advances possible. Perhaps nowhere has this been more dramatic than in the advance of medical science.

A poet said it like this:
New occasions teach new duties,
Time makes ancient good uncouth.
They must upward still and onward
Who would keep abreast of truth.
(*James Russell Lowell*)

Because we live by faith rather than facts provable in a laboratory, it is possible to think that "one opinion is as good as another." But Jesus issues a stern warning against such a relativity. He plainly says that unless what comes in is real light then what we think is light is really darkness. The Old

Testament is the history of the struggle of truth, the truth about God and his Nature and his purposes, against the false gods of the nations. If we Christians are to be the light of the world, as Jesus said we are, then we must be careful to reject false ideas, especially our own false ideas about ourselves and what makes life enjoyable, and "buy the truth and sell it not!" (Proverbs 23:23).

Keep at it, and seek the Spirit of truth to show up the many wrong things you believe about what makes life worth living. You may be surprised how many they are!

A Prayer: Spirit of truth, prevail! In Jesus' Name. Amen.

1. Do you believe that correction is rejection? Why?

2. How would your life be different if you knew that correction is not rejection but really love?

Recognizing and Destroying Delusion
Daily Reading: Acts 19:1–20

And a number of those who practiced magic arts brought their books together and burned them in the sight of all; and they counted the value of them and found it came to fifty thousand pieces of silver. So the word of the Lord grew and prevailed mightily. (vv. 19-20)

The whole area around Ephesus was shaken and affected by the gospel. God's power was evidenced in the changed lives and the healings, both physical and emotional, which accompanied the preaching of Paul.

Satan sought to frustrate and hinder the work, but God's word prevailed over all opposition. The influence which the truth had is clearly seen in this passage, as we read the summary of the two years' work of Paul in Ephesus. Those who had become believers "came, confessing and divulging their practices" (v. 18). The Lord was putting the power of the truth alongside the power of the evil lies by which these people had lived, and they came to see that, whereas lies bind and delude, the truth frees. So they brought out this horde of books on magical arts and occult practices, knowing that they had been in bondage to the prince of lies, Satan himself!

The delusions by which Satan seeks to bind us are based on our human sinful desire to be God. Since this is the same nature he, Satan, has, he recognizes its likeness in our fallen nature, and appeals to it. His lies offer us instant gratification, pleasure without pain, without responsibility, and without price. But one does not go very far down that path without seeing that something is wrong. Still, we may go on in delusions of various kinds for many years, because they appeal to our vanity and ego and desire for an easy way.

How wonderful it is that when we taste the truth, and get a foretaste of what it means to be a child of God, that we begin to get willing to pay the price of going further into the truth. These people brought their books, which represented an investment that is staggering to the imagination even by today's standards. It was a price to pay—but they paid it gladly, for they were beginning to taste what it really means to be free. So the word of the Lord grew and prevailed mightily. May it grow and prevail mightily in us, too. Amen!

1. A few lies you may believe and live by:
   —Peace at any price is good.

—Being hurt is the worst thing in the world.

—If you love me you'll accept me as I am.

Are you willing to see these as lies and choose truth?

2. What would be the truth in each of the above instances?

How Long will You Seek After Lies

Daily Reading: Psalms 4-5

O men, how long shall my honor suffer shame? How long will you love vain words and seek after lies? (Psalm 4:2)

We are told that the Hebrew word in this verse of "O men" is a word denoting distinction and honor. "God ironically gives them this title of honor in reference to their own high opinion of themselves."

These psalms seem originally to refer to those who had joined David's son Absalom in rebellion against their anointed king. "How long will you seek after lies?" he asks, because they deluded themselves as to what was really going on. Absalom had used religion to cloak his real purpose (2 Samuel 15:7-8) and had relied on falsehood and flattery to draw the people to himself and away from his father. Thus the entire project would collapse because it was based on lies and treason.

Why do we "seek after lies"? Is it not because, like these "distinguished men of honor," we prefer them to the hard truth? Do we not rather seek those who tell us good things about us, and tend to avoid those who tell us "bad things"?

We can see a parallel between them and ourselves—as long as we avoid the truth.

A Prayer: May your Spirit, O Lord, who proceeds from you, illuminate our minds, and as your Son promised, lead us into all truth, through the same, your Son Jesus Christ our Lord Amen.

1. Ask God to reveal specific lies you have believed that have controlled and influenced your life. Make a list of them.

Misplaced Trust
Daily Reading: Jeremiah 7:1–20

"Behold, you trust in deceptive words to no avail." (v. 8)

Judah thought that since they had the temple of the Lord in their midst, and since they were God's chosen people, all would surely be well. The prophet is warning them that it makes no difference how much they trust "deceptive words"it will do them no good. God holds them accountable for their faithfulness or lack of it to himself, and all their wishful thinking will not stay his judgment. He reminds them that they can go to Shiloh, once the mighty capital of Israel after the kingdoms had divided in two following the death of Solomon. Shiloh was a great city, full of wealth and military power, proud and lifted up. But when Jeremiah spoke, the people were reminded that Shiloh was only a memory. "Go and see for yourself," they were told.

It was a stern lesson, but coupled with the positive side of our weekly theme, it is vitally important. Our trust will betray us if it is misplaced. If we build our lives and hopes on lies and delusions, they will not, cannot save us.

Instead, the truth is offered to each one of us as we are open to it. We know the folly of some of the delusions we have entertained. There are more for all of us. And God will lead you step by step in discovering and discarding them.

When you find that you have been believing a lie, pray something like this: "Lord, I confess that I have believed a lie. (State what it is.) I take responsibility for believing this, and I am sorry for it. I accept your forgiveness. I renounce this lie and all its effects in my life. I state the truth. (State the truth which you have seen in the place where you believed the lie.) I ask you to fill me with this truth, and let it bear fruit in my life. In Jesus' Name." Do this with each false idea and each delusion you discover you have believed. The effect is truly remarkable.

1. Why is truth so important for us from God's point of view?

Obeying the Truth
Daily Reading: Galatians 5:1–25

You were running well; who hindered you from obeying the truth? (v. 7)

The Galatian Christians were young in the faith. They had heard Paul's preaching about Jesus, and they had believed what he said, and they had accepted Jesus Christ as their Lord and Savior. The Holy Spirit was a reality in their lives, and they found their lives totally different from the old days.

But they were not stable, mature people. They quickly turned to listen to others who came telling about Jesus, who convinced them that in addition to believing, they also had to be circumcised and keep the Jewish law. They were persuaded that they would be superior Christians if they followed this new plan.

Paul was furious with those who had come and unsettled his converts. He had risked his life over and over again to carry the Good News to those who had not heard it. And now the Judaizers had slipped in behind him and were sowing confusion and controversy in the church. The Letter to the Galatians could be called a "correction" letter, because Paul in his love and concern for them fears that they are going to turn to "another gospel," and turn away from the truth.

"You were running well," he says; "who hindered you from obeying the truth?" Probably the biggest thing that had hindered them was their desire to be right. This is in many ways the deadliest foe for Christians, because it is a counterfeit for being obedient. On the one hand, we are called to be obedient, but on the other, being right has subtle pride built in it that robs God of his glory and feeds our self-righteous, high opinion of ourselves. This is one of the hardest but most important lessons Christians have to learn. The truth makes us free to "walk in the Spirit," not gratifying the demands of the flesh, which includes "self-conceit" and "envy," as well as the gross sins of the flesh. One could well spend some time in prayer asking that the Spirit of truth reveal where we are striving to be right instead of striving to be obedient.

Unless we obey the truth, we will fall prey to the subtle lies of the enemy. Truth is not only to be believed, it is to be obeyed.

A Prayer: Lord Jesus, I see your obedience to the truth, to your father's will. As you show me the truth, help me to treasure it and to obey it, so that I neither fall into sin nor run into any kind of danger. Amen.

1. Truth is not only to be believed. It is to be obeyed. In your life, where do you see the truth that you should obey?

I Would Have Been Untrue

Daily Reading: Psalm 73

If I had said, "I will speak thus," I would have been untrue to the generation of thy children. (v. 15)

The psalmist believed alot of things that were untrue. He looked about him, and saw arrogant, wicked men prospering. They seemed to have healthier bodies, less trouble, more success than people who were striving to do right. He looked at their pride and their violence. "Their eyes swell out with fatness, their hearts overflow with follies." They were contemptuous of others, and even snickered their blasphemies against God.

Then he noticed something else. In spite of all this (or because of it!) they were praised as though they had no faults!

Bitterness entered his heart. "It's no use trying to serve God and keep one's hands innocent of wrong" he thought.

But wait—"If I had said, 'I will speak thus,' I would have been untrue to the generation of thy children." Something stopped him when he went into the house of God. There he saw a deeper truth, and he knew that if he had allowed the jealous, envious feelings and thoughts about the wicked to stay in his heart, he would have betrayed others as well as himself.

When we harbor lies and delusions in our hearts, we are a menace to others as well as ourselves. For what comes out of our mouths will be accusing words against God, words which can mislead and cause others to stumble. And we all have been guilty of this.

"When my soul was embittered . . . I was stupid and ignorant!" says the psalmist. And when we allow ourselves to become full of bitterness, we are just the same!

"Truly God is good to the upright!" (v. 1). "But for me, it is good to be near God" (v. 28). That is a place reserved for those who seek him. The Father's presence is for those who love him. Let the wicked and arrogant go. God is our strength and portion forever!

A Prayer: When I am tempted to envy the godless, turn my eyes away to thee, Lord Jesus. Thou art my joy, my hope, and my life. May that truth steady me to the end. Amen.

1. What else has God shown you this week about living in truth versus living in falsehood?

Chapter Review

We have considered this week that many things we believe and have based our lives on, which we have believed to be true, are in reality, false.

1. What difference do you think believing and living by the truth should make in your life?

2. Does the word "lie" seem so ugly and "sinful" to you that you find it hard to consider there might be lies in your own life? Why?

3. What about "little white lies"? Do you ever tell them? Give some examples.

YOUR MIND:
A BATTLEGROUND

*We destroy
arguments and
every proud
obstacle to the
knowledge of God,
and take every
thought captive to
obey Christ*

2 Corinthians 10:5

ELEVEN

We Destroy Arguments
Daily Reading: 2 Corinthians 10

We destroy arguments and every proud obstacle to the
knowledge of God, and take every thought captive to obey
Christ (v. 5)

This week we are thinking together about the battle which
goes on in our minds—the battle between light and darkness,
between the Lord and the devil, between the Spirit and the
flesh. It is the battleground on which the Christian's primary
warfare is to be fought.

Paul is writing to the Corinthians, a particularly arrogant
and haughty group of Christians. He knows that they listen to
"arguments," because they allow their minds to become
captivated with the wrong kind of thinking. How often do we
indulge in imaginary conversations in our minds, thinking of
the clever things we might have said, if only we had thought
of them in time? We may be thinking of things we hope to say
when we have the opportunity. Perhaps our thoughts may
grow out of anxiety and fear, as we try to figure out a way to
prevent some fearful thing from happening. At any rate, these
vain imaginations are a part of the weaponry of our adversary,
the devil, and if we do not recognize him, then we fall head-
long into his trap.

"We destroy arguments," says Paul. How? By the truth.
Martin Luther's great hymn says it thus:

And though this world, with devils filled
Should threaten to undo us,
We will not fear, for God has willed
His truth to triumph through us.

The prince of darkness grim,
We tremble not for him;
His rage we can endure,
For lo! his doom is sure:
One little word shall fell him.

Satan's deceptive arguments are destroyed when we begin to recognize them for what they are, and apply the light of truth against them. In the name and power of Jesus Christ, we can win the battle!

A Prayer: O Lord of Hosts! Enable us to fight the good fight of faith, to recognize the wiles of the enemy, and to bring every thought captive to obey Christ. We ask it in his Name, Amen.

1. Be perfectly honest and write down some of the thoughts that run through your mind in a single day.

2. Make a list of the thoughts that are good constructive thoughts.

3. Make another list of bad thoughts—thoughts of jealousy, anger, lust, fantasy, or day dreaming.

The Case of Judas
Daily Reading: Luke 22:1–33

Then Satan entered into Judas called Iscariot, who was of the number of the twelve; he went away and conferred with the chief priest and captains, how he might betray him to them. (vv. 3-4)

Judas has been the subject of many studies. What made him do as he did! Surely he did not join the disciples with the idea of becoming the betrayer. Nothing in the Gospels indicates that he did. In John's Gospel we do read "he was a thief, and as he had the money box he used to take what was in it" (John 12:6b). In other words, he pilfered from the funds of the group for his own purposes, and thought it was hidden from the others. What does this suggest to you? That it is dangerous to try to get away with little things— little dishonesties, little "harmless" lies. This may be especially tempting when we have taken on some kind of special discipline.

The danger with these little dishonesties is that they open up our minds to Satan's further plans. Do you remember the "Cat in the Hat" stories of Dr. Seuss? When the children opened the door to the "Cat in the Hat," the cat took over from there on, and they watched in amazement and consternation at his antics. That, it seems, is a humorous picture of what happens when we inadvertently let Satan in through some "harmless" dishonesty. His plans are for your destruction, gradually or quickly. The battle becomes joined when you or I give him ground through our sin, for he has a right to any area where we have given him permission to come in. We give this permission by entering into sin. His reasonings may sound perfectly harmless and logical. But they are leading us into harmful paths. That is why the Lord taught us to pre-pray against temptation, and for divine protection. We do not always recognize it when it comes! This is the subtlety of the battle for the mind, for we can be in the thick of it and not even know it is going on.

Judas stands as an extreme and tragic example of one whose "little sins" led him progressively into greater darkness.

Instead of thinking of Judas as different from ourselves, we should recognize the same potentiality in ourselves of being deluded and becoming betrayers of the very One we seek to follow.

A Prayer: Stab me awake, Lord, to the danger of letting my thoughts run into paths of jealousy, resentment, lust, and vindictiveness. Help me not to give the enemy ground to destroy your work in me. In Jesus' Name. Amen.

1. Are you able to control your thoughts, or do your thoughts control you?

2. What are your most difficult thoughts to deal with?

Out of the Abundance of the Heart
Daily Reading: Luke 6:17–49

"The good man out of the good treasure of his heart produces good, and the evil man out of his evil treasure produces evil; for out of the abundance of the heart his mouth speaks." (v. 45)

God knows and Satan knows that it is in the "heart," (read "mind") that our actions flow. Some of them come out of our subconscious, and we do not even understand what we are doing. Paul talks about this dilemma in Romans 7. But there is the need to do battle against the "evil" thoughts which seek to invade our minds at a conscious level. Then the Holy Spirit will bring to light those things that are buried in the unconscious which we need to be aware of, so that we do not have to fear them or be controlled by them.

What happens when a dark, evil thought enters your mind? Do you greet it, welcome it, entertain it, and hold friendly discourse with it? Do you assume that it is correct in all its suspicions, in its judgments against your fellow men, in its dark and jealous feelings of resentments that others have what you would like to have? If so, you are storing up a horde of "evil treasure," and out of that abundance your mouth will speak.

Do you ever surprise yourself by making some cutting remark (perhaps humorously disguised) that really puts another person "in his place"? If so, it may be because you have stored up a treasure of evil thoughts and feelings against him.

What can be done to rid ourselves of the horde of evil treasure (we all have some of them, of course), and to build up for ourselves a store of "good treasure" so that our words and actions can be consistent with our Christian commitment!

First, you can do battle with these thoughts when they come. Confess your jealousy, your resentment, your greed—or whatever—to the Lord as soon as the thoughts begin to appear. Then tell Satan to go with his thoughts in the Name of Jesus, and begin to pray positively for the person against whom you have harbored hurt, etc. It does work! And you can begin to see and tell the difference. Try it today!

A Prayer: Arm me for battle, Lord, against all the wiles of the devil. Help me to be watchful and alert and ready to guard that which is good, which comes from you. I reject everything from Satan, and I choose everything from Jesus Christ. Amen.

1. Is there anyone about whom you particularly think bad thoughts? Who? Why?

2. When is the best time to attack and do battle with a thought?

Blinded Minds
Daily Reading: 2 Corinthians 4

In their case the god of this world has blinded the minds of the unbelievers, to keep them from seeing the light of the gospel of the glory of Christ, who is the likeness of God. (v. 4)

All this week we are thinking about light and darkness in our minds, and the struggle between the two that is going on. Paul here clearly describes the unbelieving world as being "blinded" by the god of this world, Satan. In Chapter 3, he speaks of Israel's mind being "hardened" (v. 14), so that when they read the Old Testament, their eyes are veiled and they do not perceive the truth they are reading. There is a relationship between the "hardening" and the "blindness" being spoken of here.

When we harden our minds to the truth of God, our minds become progressively darkened. Eventually we cannot discern truth from falsehood, and we are then in total deception about reality. You can see this in people who have become increasingly unreachable by others until they finally are hospitalized "out of reality." It is not mysterious; it is a process by which the mind hardened against seeing its wrongness becomes more and more right and unreachable, until it is completely "blind."

"This happened in the case of Tom, a splendid young man in his early twenties. Tom had tried for days to argue with me on the hate-filled issues of neo-Nazism, anti-Semitism, and white racism. Finally I turned to Tom and asked, 'Which do you want—to be right on these issues or to get well so you can leave this hospital!'

"Without a moment's hesitation he answered, 'Be right! I don't care if I never get out of this hospital!' " (*Kingdom of Self,* Earl Jabay, p. 27)

Let us pray for a new awareness of those things which harden our hearts and blind our minds, so that our minds may be filled with God's light and truth, and so that his wholeness may be manifest in us.

A Prayer: Lord, let it be so, In Jesus' Name. Amen.

1. What is the best way of dealing with evil thoughts?

2. What part do work and/or disciplines play in this battle?

The Wiles of the Devil
Daily Reading: Ephesians 6

Put on the whole armor of God, that you may be able to stand against the wiles of the devil. (v. 11)

According to the dictionary, a *wile* is "a trick or stratagem intended to ensnare or deceive." It is certainly possible to become too "devil-conscious," and to have an unhealthy attention to what we think are evidences of his presence or power. But it is equally possible to be so unaware of his wiles that we become easily ensnared by them, without ever knowing what is happening. Paul here is cautioning us to recognize that there are spiritual enemies arrayed against us. "We are not contending against flesh and blood, but against the principalities, against the powers, against the world rulers of this present darkness, against the spiritual hosts of wickedness in the heavenly places" (v. 12). These are all unseen forces or powers at work against us, and if we are not aware of them, how can we fight against them?

What are some of the "wiles of the devil," the tricks by which we are readily ensnared or deceived? Some of them may be; . . . we are tempted to think too highly of ourselves or something we have done, making us overly sensitive to criticism or lack of praise.

. . . we may suddenly find ourselves very suspicious of others, and looking for ways to be hurt by them.

. . . we are tempted to think that we are hopeless, or our situation is hopeless.

. . . we are tempted to think that no one understands us, and that whatever it is we want to do will not make any difference to anyone else.

Perhaps you may know how the tricks work in your own case. The mind is the battleground in which these tricks or wiles must be fought. If we accept lies as the truth, then we are on slippery ground indeed! The whole armor of God is needed and is available to us, when we recognize our need of his help.

1. How do you think we should try to fight against mind wandering and encourage spiritually healthy thoughts?

The Renewal of Your Minds
Daily Reading: Romans 12

Do not be conformed to this world, but be transformed by the renewal of your mind, that you may prove what is the will of God, what is good and acceptable and perfect (v. 2)

Dear Lord and Father of mankind
Forgive our foolish ways.
Reclothe us in our rightful minds,
In purer lives thy service find,
In deeper reverence, praise.
      (John Greenleaf Whittier)

Our minds need to be "renewed." They were darkened by the fall of our first parents, Adam and Eve, and throughout history men's minds have dwelt in the natural darkness which resulted from the fall. "The people who walked in darkness have seen a great light; those who dwelt in a land of deep darkness, on them has light shined" (Isaiah 9:2). That light is Jesus Christ, who has shined in our hearts by the power of the Holy Spirit to bring us out of everlasting night!

But our minds are not renewed overnight. This is plain as Paul addresses the Christians at Rome about their need to resist the pressure of the world and to be "transformed by the renewal of your mind."

"The children of light, being risen with Christ, have a life of their own—the life of pardoned and reconciled believers: renewed in the spirit of their mind, they breathe a new air, they have new interests and affections, and their sympathies are all heavenly and spiritual" (David Brown: *Critical, Experimental and Practical Commentary, Vol. VI, p. 264).*

As inheritors of the kingdom of light, we can choose to live in a continual renewing of our minds, learning more and more to separate light from darkness, good from evil. We *have*, as children of God, the transforming energy of the Holy Spirit to help us in our struggle against our old darkened ways of thinking and to bring us to a new place in him. No matter where we are in our Christian walk—how new or old, how successful or what failures we have been, we *can* lay hold of that transforming energy by faith through obedience and repentance today. God is with us! Who can be against us!

1. What part does obedience play in the battle for your mind?

2. What part does repentance play in the battle for your mind?

The Mind of Christ
Daily Reading: 1 Corinthians 2

For who has known the mind of the Lord so as to instruct him? But we have the mind of Christ. (v. 16)

What a startling thing to say! That we actually have available to us the mind of Christ. C. T. Craig reminds us that Paul is not talking "of the mental faculties with which Jesus was endowed. He means the Spirit which dwelt in Christ, who was himself the Spirit (2 Corinthians 3:17) and the giver of the Spirit" (*Interpreter's Bible, Vol. 10, p. 41*).

This is where the battle for our minds can be won, because Jesus himself has won the victory over all the powers of hell and darkness, and has given us his Spirit to dwell within every believer. Because of this, we have the light we need, and the help we need, and the thoughts we need, if we will but lay hold on them!

When Paul talks about the spiritual man here in this second chapter of 1 Corinthians, he is not talking about some few, specially endowed people who are head and shoulders above the rest of us. He is talking about you and me—all who have received Jesus Christ in our hearts by faith. When we receive him, we receive the Holy Spirit, for God cannot be divided. As he dwells in us, we have access to his light and influence to guide us in our thoughts. It is an exciting, almost unbelievable thing that God has made his guiding Spirit available to us.

Holy Spirit, faithful Guide,
Ever near the Christian's side;
Gently lead us by the hand,
Pilgrims in a desert land.
Weary souls fore'er rejoice
When they hear that sweetest voice
Whisper softly, "Wanderer come!
Follow me, I'll guide thee home."
            (Marcus M. Wells, 1858)

We do not struggle alone! God is with us, Christ is for us! Let us never give up!

1. What does it mean to you that you actually have available to you "the mind of Christ"?

2. After this week's emphasis on "Your Mind: A Battleground," what changes have you felt in your daily thought life?

Chapter Review

All sorts of thoughts invade our minds. We need to do battle against the evil thoughts that invade our minds at the conscious level. As we seek to do battle with our conscious thoughts, the Holy Spirit will do battle for us against any evil thoughts buried at the unconscious level.

1. After the week of study on the mind, are you more aware of your thought life? How?

2. Why does this battle seem overwhelming to you?

3. What is your biggest battle in your mind?

WHAT IS DISCIPLESHIP?

*"If any man
will come after
me, let him deny
himself and take
up his cross daily
and follow me."*

Luke 9:23

TWELVE

What Must I Do?

Daily Reading: Mark 10:1–31

And Jesus looking upon him loved him, and said to him, "You lack one thing. Go, sell what you have and give to the poor, and you will have treasure in heaven; and come, follow me," (v. 21)

One of the most interesting things about this word of Jesus to the rich young man is that he tells him *first* to go and sell what he has and give to the poor, *then* come, follow me. The first was the means by which he would become a disciple. Discipleship was the goal.

Disciplines are not ends in themselves, but are to be followed as the means toward a long-range goal, one harder to reach, yet near at hand: the goal of becoming more genuine followers or disciples of Jesus.

For the rich young man, his money was really not his problem, although it is plain he didn't want to part with it. His real problem was that he did not want to be told what to do! He had rigorously kept "the commandments," meaning that he had built up a tremendous treasure of "rightness," and yet he kept thinking that God required something more. That "something more" was the spontaneous obedience which he would have to display if he was to be a disciple of Jesus Christ. Getting rid of the money was only a first step to free him for such obedience. Getting rid of whatever store of "treasure" we have—self-righteousness, opinions, prejudices, tastes, hurts, resentments,—is only a way of getting us free to become true disciples, followers, "obedient ones" of Jesus Christ.

How little, then, the price we have paid in these simple disciplines if they lead us toward *this* goal.

A Prayer: Lord Jesus, I long to be fully and completely yours. I thank you for the means by which you are setting me free to follow you in whole-hearted obedience. By your grace, I will follow on. Amen.

1. How have you learned the blessings of obedience? Describe.

Counting the Cost
Daily Reading: Luke 14:15–35

"Whoever does not bear his own cross and come after me, cannot be my disciple. For which of you, desiring to build a tower, does not first sit down and count the cost, whether he has enough to complete it?" (vv. 27-28)

How many projects have you started with good intentions, only to find that after a few days or weeks, the work and struggle grew wearisome, and you gave up? Or how many resolutions have you made, only to break them before the New Year had scarcely begun?

Counting the cost. What can that mean? Too many people start out their spiritual life with a "gung-ho" attitude, only to find themselves lagging after a few months. It is little wonder that people regard the enthusiasm of a new Christian with some skepticism!

Thomas à Kempis says in his classic devotional book, *The Imitation of Christ:*

Each day we should renew our resolution and bestir ourselves to fervor, as though it were the first day of our conversion, and say, "Help me, O Lord, God, in my good resolve and in your holy service; grant me this day to begin perfectly, for hitherto I have accomplished nothing."

(Book I, Chapter 19)

Jesus did not quibble about what it was going to cost to be a follower of his. There was no easy, cheap price. He himself leads the way, by going to the cross and laying down his own life for our sakes. He warns all who are drawn to him that there will be a cost involved in finishing our course. Of course it is all grace! We have nothing of ourselves to bring but our need! And what a joy it is that we can begin again, day after day—knowing that his grace is greater than our sins and failures. But we must be prepared to carry through—go all the way. No turning back! That's the key.

A Prayer: I thank you, Lord Jesus, that you know who I am and all that I have done, and that you still call me to follow you. No matter what, with your help I choose to follow you Grant me grace to fulfill this good purpose. Amen.

1. Counting the cost. What does that mean to you?

Let Us Hold True
Daily Reading: Philippians 3

Only let us hold true to what we have attained. (v. 16)

In this chapter, Paul is confessing that he has not yet arrived. "Not that I have already attained this or am already perfect," he says in verse twelve. But having confessed this, and his determination to "press on," he admonishes us to hold true to what we have attained.

What have you attained by grace, through discipline and obedience?

Paul knows that not only he, but his readers as well, need to "hold on" to what they have attained in Christ.

The same is true for us. Wherever we are, whatever plateau we may have reached in our upward climb, we need to remember how easy it is to relax, let go, and allow old habit patterns of thought and feeling to dominate us again.

The same temptations which have lured us in wrong paths in the past are all still with us. Our human nature is still vulnerable at certain points to be carried away in hurtful patterns of self-love or self-hate. We still have to fight the feelings of jealousy, the desire to control others, judgmental thoughts, and nursed resentments.

How do we hold true to what we have attained? By remembering who we are, keeping our eyes steadfastly on Jesus and who he is, and allowing him free reign to shepherd us through every situation of our lives. By being obedient to the light we have, and being open to more light. By not giving up when the going is tough, and not despairing if we fail!

I would be true, for there are those who trust me,
I would be pure, for there are those who care.
I would be strong for there is much to suffer,
I would be brave, for there is much to dare.
     (Howard A. Walter, 1918)

1. How can you see the benefits of daily discipline in your life?

2. How can you keep from letting old habit patterns of thoughts and feelings dominate you again?

Take My Yoke Upon You
Daily Reading: Matthew 11

"Come to me, all who labor and are heavy-laden, and I will give you rest Take my yoke upon you, and learn from me; for I am gentle and lowly in heart, and you will find rest for your souls. For my yoke is easy and my burden is light." (*vv. 28–30*)

As we think about the cost of discipleship, we need also to remember the promise of discipleship. Jesus says that his is an "easy yoke." "Discipleship," says Dietrich Bonhoeffer, "means joy." And he adds, "The command of Jesus is hard, unutterably hard, to those who try to resist it. But for those who willingly submit, the yoke is easy, and the burden is light. "His commandments are not grievous" (1 John 5:3). The commandment of Jesus is not a sort of spiritual shock treatment. Jesus asks nothing of us without giving us the strength to perform it. His commandment never seeks to destroy life, but to foster, strengthen, and heal it." (*Cost of Discipleship, pp. 40-41*)

To go on with Jesus from where you are at this moment means coming under his yoke. The oxen is yoked for labor, and is guided by his master. Our yoke is our submission to Jesus, to be guided in all things by him. He himself was subject to his Father in all things. The more we subject ourselves to him, the more complete will be the rest we find for our souls.

"Our hearts are restless till they find their rest in thee," said St. Augustine. He knew that after years of rebellion and looking elsewhere for true satisfaction, that the only rest, true rest, was to be found in subjection to the Lord Jesus Christ.

Discipleship is the continuing path on which we walk as we seek to let our wills become conformed to his will, so that one day, by his grace, we may have the simplicity of heart to have our wills and his be one.

God doth not need
Either man's work or his own gifts.
Who best bear his mild yoke, they serve him best.
(John Milton, 1608–1675)

1. What are you discovering as you submit yourself to Jesus more and more?

His Daily Cross
Daily Reading: Luke 9:7–27

And he said to all, "if any man would come after me, let him deny himself, and take up his cross daily and follow me." (v. 23)

What is discipleship? Learning to will what he wills. Learning through pain and failure, through victory and joy that his way is best. Dying daily to the demands of the old nature, allowing oneself to be crossed out without demanding that things go the way one wishes. All this is discipleship.

What is discipleship? To set one's hand to the plow and not turn back. To be one of those who goes on into deeper understanding of God's truth, further repentance for who we are, more absolute dependence on Jesus Christ. All this is discipleship.

What is discipleship? Renewing daily one's love and loyalty to him who died that we might live. A relationship of leader and follower. A relationship of growing trust. More of him and less of me. All this is discipleship.

The Gospel of Luke says it succinctly, that we are to "take up our cross daily" and follow him. Many are the days when we do not want to take up any cross. We feel we have had enough, and we are tired of fighting against our old Adamic nature. We would rather give in and express the old selves we thought we had left behind!

Beware, disciple! Pray for added grace, and look again at all you have to lose and all you have to gain. Death and sickness, guilt and sin left behind, if we go on with him. Can we make any other choice!

Man am I grown, a man's work I must do,
Follow the dear! follow the Christ, the King,
Live pure, speak true, right wrong, follow the King
Else, wherefore born!
(Alfred Tennyson, 1809–1892)

A Prayer: Almighty God, whose most dear Son went not up to joy but first he suffered pain, and entered not into glory before he was crucified: mercifully grant that we, walking in the way of the cross may find it none other than the life and peace, through the same thy Son Jesus Christ our Lord Amen.
(Book of Common Prayer, 1979)

1. What does discipleship mean to you?

I Have Given You an Example

Daily Reading: John 13:1–35

"For I have given you an example, that you should do as I have done to you." (v. 15)

In washing the disciples' feet, Jesus, the Lord, took the place of the servant. The act of kneeling down and washing the feet of guests was one of the lowliest of servant-tasks. But this is not just any Rabbi. This is the Lord of Heaven and Earth, stooping to serve fallen mankind.

From the beginning of the Gospels to the very end we have this strange paradox pictured before us—the lowliness of God, the servanthood of Jesus. In his birth, in his life, and in his death there is this strange mixture of lowliness and glory.

What does it mean for us, as far as our discipleship is concerned? He says, "I have given you an example." In the First Letter of Peter, chapter 2, we are told, "For to this you have been called, because Christ also suffered for you, leaving you an example that you should follow in his steps" (v. 21). We are to look to his life as our pattern, not just as a means of our salvation from sin. He has lived as we are called to live.

In another place he says, "I came not to do my own will, but the will of him who sent me." That is an example for us.

And again he says, "My food is to do the will of him who sent me and to finish his work." That is an example.

In the Garden of Gethsemane, he said, "Father, if it is possible, let this cup pass from me. Nevertheless, not what I will, but thy will be done." That is an example for us.

As we look and learn from him, let us pray that his image will be formed in us, his life grow in us, so that what we shall be, will be like him.

O to be like thee! Blessed Redeemer,
This is my constant longing and prayer.
Gladly I'll forfeit all of earth's treasures, Jesus,
Thy perfect likeness to wear.
O to be like thee, Blessed Redeemer,
Pure as thou art;
Come in thy sweetness, come in thy fullness;
Stamp thine own image deep on my heart.
 (Thomas O. Chisholm)

1. The "lowliness of God"—What does that mean to you in your daily life?

If Anyone Serves Me
Daily Reading: John 12:20–50

"If any one serve me, he must follow me; and where I am, there shall my servant be also; if any one serves me, the Father will honor him." (v. 26)

Here in today's verse is both a warning and a promise. First, the warning. If we are to serve Jesus, we must follow him. It is not a matter of "being good," "doing the right thing," obeying the Law, or doing good works. It is a matter of following the living Christ. He is alive, he has a will for us, and he is present with us. Let that reality become more and more a part of your daily consciousness. Brother Lawrence was a cook in a French monastery in the seventeenth century. He learned a wonderful secret, since retold many times in a little book called *The Practice of the Presence of God*. He says,

I make it my only business to persevere in his holy Presence, wherein I keep myself by a simple attention and an absorbing passionate regard to God, which I may call *an actual presence of God*; or, to speak better, a silent and secret conversation of the soul with God. . . .

Second, the promise. Jesus says, "If any one serves me, the Father will honor him." That is his promise, and you can depend on it. No one truly serves and loves the Son who is not honored by the Father himself. What greater reward could we ask, what great enticement to the way of discipleship?

If I find him, if I follow
Is he sure to bless?
Saints, apostles, prophets, martyrs
Answer, "Yes!"
        (John M. Neale, trans.)

A Prayer: Thank you, Father, for the disciplines and the joys of these past weeks. Thank you for beginning a new work of grace and love in my life. Bless all who traveled with me, and grant us grace to go on, knowing that the way leads home. In Jesus' Name. Amen.

1. What have you gleaned from these weeks of devotions?

Chapter Review

Following these readings, you are now aware that there are definite areas in your life where you need God's help.

1. What are these areas of need?

2. What weekly theme(s) and/or daily reading was most helpful to you? Why?

3. What is the ultimate goal of your life?

THE JOY OF BEING OPEN
COME OUT OF YOUR SHELL

*Now the
company of those
who believed
were of one heart
and soul.*

Acts 4:32a

Hide and Seek
Daily Reading: Genesis 3:1–13

"Adam and Eve had Someone bigger than themselves to reckon with. They had to meet God; and they did meet him, *walking in the garden in the cool of the day*. Childlike as the form of the story is, note how dramatic and spiritually deep is its suggestion. The Eternal Righteousness moves in a great peace and calm; but Adam and Eve, with their guilty consciences, are hot and embarrassed when they meet him. . . .

Thus always the confusion of conscious wrongdoing is confronted by the steady truth that is inescapable. Eat forbidden fruit against our better knowledge, and it turns out to be not the tree of life but the tree that is deadly to self-respect and peace of mind. Try to know better than God to break the laws of life, to imagine that our cleverness and our clutching after power can say the final word, and we stand at the end of the day dumb before the quietness of God. . . ." (Walter Russell Bowie, *The Interpreter's Bible*, Vol. 1, p. 507.)

And that is where the game of hide and seek begins, and that is the root of it. For all of us, since earliest infancy, we have learned to hide certain feelings, thoughts, and deeds from others—so that we would be able to keep them, felt we had a right to them, and so on. Hiding for many becomes a way of life. Unspoken thoughts are supposed not to have any negative or bad effect!

Adam and Eve finally had to come out of hiding to receive both their clothing and their reward for their disobedience. Sooner or later, we too must give up our old protective techniques if we are to enjoy the freedom and joy which God has for his children. At times it will be painful, and we will have to face the wrongness of our thoughts and feelings. So what? If they are wrong, is it not better to recognize it earlier rather than later? If we have misjudged someone, if we have been fearful when there was no reason to be, if we have been hurt when no hurt was intended—how much better to get it into the light and resolved, so that we can be free from its nagging effects!

A Prayer: Father, I thank you, as we begin this new adventure, that we do not have to play "hide and seek" with you. You have sought us and found us; you have loved us and redeemed us. And now you call us to come to you, where it is safe to be ourselves, and where there is healing for every wound, and an answer to every need. All praise and thanks to you, through Jesus Christ our Lord. Amen.

1. What are you afraid may happen if you are willing to expose certain feelings, thoughts, or deeds to others?

2. What thoughts or emotions have you begun to recognize that you would rather keep hidden than talk about, or "bring into the light"?

Open Your Hearts
Daily Reading: 2 Corinthians 6:1–13, 7:14

There is alienation and estrangement between Paul and the Christians at Corinth as he writes this epistle. What an example of wise diplomacy the entire letter is! There are illusions to the trouble, but always they are couched in the framework of positive, loving concern which Paul had toward these, his spiritual children. He knows that his name has been sullied by others, and that some necessary rebuke he has given has caused some of them to grow cold and resentful toward him. But he moves in the confidence that they are related in Christ, and that the Holy Spirit of truth will be present to bring understanding out of misunderstanding, reconciliation out of alienation.

"Our mouth is open to you, Corinthians; our heart is wide. You are not restricted by us, but you are restricted in your own affections. In return—I speak as to children—widen your hearts also. . . . Open your hearts to us."

It is a great example and encouragement to us who seek to be related to others on something other than a superficially pleasant, polite basis. There may be moments of confrontation; moments of tension, even of hostility. But they are only steps toward a deeper, lasting, trusting, open relationship in Christ. Once we have tasted that kind of fellowship, few want to go back to the shallow, surface kind.

In order to reach that kind of fellowship, however, we really have to open our hearts to one another. We have to express the real needs (as we become aware of them) and give other people permission to react honestly to us, so that we can see ourselves "as others see us." There is a hymn which says it beautifully: "transient pain may be but a path to thee."

A Prayer: Lord Jesus, thou didst give thyself freely to us and for us, holding nothing back. Enable us so to open our hearts toward others that we may learn and experience the joy of deep fellowship in and through thee, who with the Father livest in the unity of the Holy Spirit, God for ever and ever. Amen.

1. In what relationships have you chosen a superficial and a pleasant, polite basis rather than risk moments of confrontation, tension or even hostility?

2. Why do you think you have chosen this shallow way rather than to come to a trusting open relationship in Christ?

One Heart and Soul
Daily Reading: Acts 4:32–37

Today's scripture reading is a very short one. It is intended to give us a taste and whet our appetite for the kind of Christianity experienced by those first believers. Through the centuries, the Church has referred to this as a model of Christian community, and it has formed the inspiration for Christian communities in every century.

These words were not written to entice us to form "communities," but rather to inspire us to want the kind of oneness of heart and soul which these Christians felt. The quality of their life was such that we should envy it and desire to experience it ourselves.

Today's Christian is apt to find himself or herself feeling like an isolated individual. Individualism has so permeated the thinking of our time that no Christian tradition is exempt from it. We do not like (and often do not accept) authority of any kind over us, especially in spiritual matters. For all intents and purposes, we make ourselves the final court of appeal in any question of dispute! How different from these early Christians. "They were of one heart and soul," and you do not get that way by staying in independent, individualistic separatism. You *submit*, first one thing and then another, to the group, testing and tasting, to see if it seems good. And little by little, you learn to trust God, working through others, and to *distrust* your own understanding. Maybe it is only a little at first, but every step counts. For as long as our understanding has the last word, we have made it a god and the final arbiter of right and wrong. But when we give others permission to talk to us, and when we take the risk of talking freely with others, we allow the Holy Spirit permission to do a miraculous work within us and among us. We are actually *changed*, and our hearts and souls are knit together in a new and wonderful way.

Does it sound attractive? Do it prayerfully, tenderly, and above all, gratefully. For it is a gift from God and should not be treated lightly! Search and seek until you find it. It is there, and God will not fail you!

A Prayer: How wonderful it is, Father, that you choose to use my need and failings to open to me, a new and wonderful adventure in fellowship. I am still afraid at times, overly cautious in sharing what I feel or think, fearing that I will be rejected or hurt. But that is self feeling that way, and I choose instead to venture out—taking the risk, trusting Jesus. Great grace was on the early disciples, and I know that your promise is still valid. And so, with that grace, I will learn to be more open and learn to receive as well as to give. In Jesus' Name. Amen.

1. In what areas have you been discovering that you have made your own understanding a god, and a final arbitration of right and wrong?

2. Where have you been learning little by little to trust God working through others?

A Simple Yes and No
Daily Reading: Matthew 5:33–38, 6:1

Jesus said, "Let what you say be simply 'Yes' or 'No'—anything more than this comes from evil." (Matthew 5:37)

As we think about the joy of being open with one another, here is a text we should ponder again and again. Jesus is drawing a picture of a new kind of righteousness, one that "exceeds that of the scribes and Pharisees." This new righteousness is not the legalistic, hard kind of rightness that religious people sometimes display. It is an inner attitude which is without guile, without the desire to conceal or deceive. That, it seems, is the point being made here.

Our communication with each other should be so unreserved, so uncalculated, that all we need is a simple yes or no to show the truth of what we are saying. If that is what we desire in our hearts, we have to be willing to pray, "Cleanse thou me from secret faults," and "Search me, O God, and know my heart, try me and know my thoughts, and see if there be any wicked way in me" (Psalm 139:23-24). For we do not always know if our simple yes or no reflects all that is in our hearts, and we must desire the light of the Holy Spirit to acquaint us with the hidden depths.

God uses and blesses our imperfect efforts and adds the light and guidance of the Holy Spirit to our human words and thoughts. The result is something of a miracle: increased self-understanding and deepened fellowship in Christ.

As these happen, we are more intensely and effectively aware of what Jesus Christ means to us in a practical, everyday way, and we rejoice in the newness of life which is ours.

Do not be afraid to seek this simplicity and openness of heart!

A Prayer: Father, you know that I am often closed, self-protective, hidden, and isolated from others. Yet I long to know more fully the fellowship of those who are committed to you and to one another. Without this, I will remain stunted spiritually and prey to many hidden dangers. I thank you for the opportunity to learn greater openness with fellow Christians. By your grace I will be faithful to this opportunity with a grateful heart. In Jesus' Name. Amen.

1. What are some of your hidden places that the Holy Spirit is showing you?

2. When and where have you experienced "the joy of being open"?

Healing in Confession
Daily Reading: James 5:13–20

Confession is a serious thing. Some things can be confessed in a group, and we can experience the forgiveness of God mediated through the attitude of the group in a very helpful and healing way. Many reactions of jealousy, pride, self-righteousness, etc., can and should be dealt with in this way. Confessing them to God alone does not do the crucifying work to the ego that happens when we obey this injunction in James, "Confess your faults one to another, and pray for one another that you may be healed." That is the Church in action when it is the Church as it was meant to be.

There are confessions that cannot be made this way. Sins of a sexual nature cannot and should not be spoken of in a group. The very act of talking about them can lead to further temptation, and should always be avoided. Rather, if one has problems of this kind which cause guilt, or continuing harassment, he or she should seek out a priest or pastor who is trained and experienced at hearing such confessions and prepared to offer counsel and the assurance of God's forgiveness. Sometimes a retreat is a useful place and time for such "housecleaning" of the soul, and many people use them for such needed purposes.

But a great many people unnecessarily carry burdens they do not need to carry because pride keeps them from humbling themselves to confess before another human being the sin which is crippling them.

Healing comes in many ways, not the least of which is the relaxation and inner peace which grow out of a clear conscience. When we have sought a repentant spirit, confessed as best we can, and "intend to live a new life, walking henceforth in his holy ways," we are already on our way to spiritual healing and often to physical healing as well. After all, *salvation* and *health* in some languages come from the same root word—showing that our ancestors understood this truth very well indeed.

A Prayer: Lord of all power and might, whose wisdom is over all thy works, and who lovest all thy children: hear us, we pray, and stretch forth thy hand to heal all those who call upon thee. Thy power to heal has been known from of old. Thy presence in thy Church has never ceased. Thy healing gifts everywhere abound and surpass all we can ask or think. Before we call, thou art listening. All our ways are in thy hands.

Heal first our souls; forgive our sins, of which we heartily repent and resolve to sin no more; so that thy healing power may flow freely into us and through us, filling our whole being, body, soul, and spirit, renewing our minds and strengthening our wills. Then let us, renewed and refreshed, rise up to do thy will, O gracious Father, and walk in the paths thou hast set before us, well and strong ourselves and able to share thy gifts with others; in Jesus' Name. Amen.

(Adapted from a prayer by Frederick C. Grant)

1. Where are you finding freedom to confess some of your hidden reactions to others, as well as to God?

2. Pride and ego want to protect the image. In what areas of your life do you know you are trying to protect yourself from humbly exposing your sin and need?

3. Are you willing to ask God to give you the grace for this kind of honest confession, in order that you may experience healing and peace?

Joy in Forgiveness
Daily Reading: Psalm 32

Our hymnals are full of references to the joy of being forgiven. Here are a few of them, taken at random:
Amazing grace! how sweet the sound
That saved a wretch like me;
I once was lost, but now am found,
as blind, but now I see!
(John Newton)

O hope of every contrite heart,
O joy of all the meek:
To those who fall, how kind thou art,
How good to those who seek.
   (Bernard of Clairvaux)

Come we that love the Lord
And let our joys be known;
Join in a song with sweet accord
And thus surround the throne.
   (Isaac Watts)

Here would I feed upon the bread of God,
Here would I drink the royal wine of heaven;
Here would I lay aside each earthly load
And taste afresh the calm of sin forgiven.
   (Horatius Bonar)

But there can be no joy of forgiveness as long as we hold onto our sin (especially our wrong attitudes) and refuse to give it up. The psalmist knew the burden of carrying around self-justifying thoughts, accusations against others, hurt, guilt, and so on. It was so dreadful that he says, "my body wasted away through my groaning all day long" (v. 3). It is a great load to carry—our petty grievances, our old resentments, our wounded pride. We may think we have a *right* to carry them, but in the long run, we pay dearly for it.

There is a better way! There is a path of freedom and joy which the psalmist discovered as soon as he acknowledged his sin to God. There is a world of meaning in that one little phrase. For we could look at it as *finally* recognizing that he had something to acknowledge before God. Before that he may have pictured himself as innocent, a victim, etc. But the moment he was willing to acknowledge that *he* was wrong, the situation dramatically changed. And so it can with us.

And the large part of the reason why we don't like to be as open with others as we should is that we are afraid we will be *convinced* of some wrongness in attitude or action which we don't want to give up! It's that simple.

But, oh! the joy of sin forgiven!

1. Where recently have you experienced the freedom of acknowledgment of your sin and the joy of sin forgiven?

2. What are the areas in your life where you are still trying to see yourself as the innocent victim?

Bearing One Another's Burdens
Daily Reading: Galatians 6:1–10

We come today to the crux of this week's theme: the joy of being open. What greater joy is there than entering into another's life, sharing the pain and the joy, being accepted and accepting the other as a brother or sister in the Lord. Surely it is one of the great gifts God has given us in the Christian family.

Paul elevates this aspect of our life in Christ to the highest possible value, saying "Bear one another's burdens, and so *fulfill the law of Christ.*" We hear an echo of the words of Jesus, reminding us that we are to love God with all our heart, mind, soul, and strength, saying that it was "the first and great commandment." Then our Lord added, "The second is like unto it: Thou shalt love thy neighbor as thyself." "Bearing one another's burdens" is a way of fulfilling that, treating our neighbor as though his or her interests were our own.

In spite of all kinds of improved communications, the modern world is said to be increasingly impersonal. In our work, our mass-produced clothes and goods, our supermarket style of shopping and in many other ways, the personal touch is removed, and the human heart longs for fellowship—real and deep fellowship. Even an e-mail or a telephone call lacks something of the personal touch, though that is better than no touch at all! Meeting with friends in a weekly group may seem artificial and contrived—but only if we fail to see beneath it the possibility of reaching out and touching someone else's life in a meaningful and life-changing way. *That* takes the artificiality out of it, and allows it to become a vehicle of the Holy Spirit to bless everyone concerned.

When one is facing a problem that seems unsolvable, just having people to share it with helps. Millions have found it so, and when we bring it to the Lord together, miracles still happen.

A Prayer: Father, by thy grace I would be faithful in sharing others' burdens and allowing them to help bear mine. So fill all of us with a love of thee and shed thy love abroad in our hearts that we may grow in likeness to Jesus Christ our Lord. Amen.

1. Are you sensitive and responsive to the needs in the lives of others? If not, why not?

2. In what ways do you believe you could reach out and touch other lives?

Chapter Review

Openness with other Christians and with those people who are close to us is a way of living in truthfulness. It is a way of living that invites honesty from others and that pays the price of being honest with them, even when that honesty brings us into conflict. The desire to live without conflict leads many Christians to choose a closed, protective relationship with others, and they miss the tremendous joy that comes when feelings are expressed and worked through with forbearance and forgiveness. "Our mouth is open to you . . . our heart is wide," says Paul. A large part of our faith journey is learning to trust a few others enough to speak our feelings honestly— to tell of our hurts, fears, angers, jealousies, failures, and foibles. Most of us do not need help in speaking of the good feelings we have, though even they are closed and hidden for some of us. Coming out of the shell of protectiveness and hiddenness can be a great joy indeed!

1. How do you handle your feelings about situations where it is impossible or unwise to express them to the other person or persons involved?

2. What is the difference between "airing" your feelings and confessing them before another person? (Hint: It has something to do with seeing your own wrongness no matter how wrong the other person may be.)

3. How can we be helpful to other Christians who are close to us when they are going through a struggle with their own feelings?

4. Give the best example you can remember of being freed inside by getting out negative feelings and dealing with them honestly. Was it as bad as you feared it would be?

LEARNING TO FORGIVE YOURSELF
WHITER THAN SNOW!

*"Blessed are the
merciful, for
they shall obtain
mercy."*

Matthew 5:7

FOURTEEN

Accepting Yourself as Imperfect
Daily Reading: Philippians 3:12–21

This week's theme, *Learning to Forgive Yourself*, will cover several aspects of the problem many of us face. Not only are we critical and hyper-sensitive to the faults of others, we have a deep underlying, unforgiving attitude toward ourselves. In fact, we are reminded that our super-critical attitude toward others may be a symptom of our deep refusal to accept ourselves as imperfect.

Paul demonstrates the problem and the cure in a graphic way. He was of a religious bent, we would say. He had been well-trained as a boy in the Jewish Law, and had taken it with great seriousness. He had studied for the ministry (as a Rabbi) under some of the finest teachers of his day. But his heart was not satisfied, for he could not be sure that he was perfect in God's sight. Religious rightness did not satisfy his deep soul's needs. In an effort to assuage his deep anxiety about his own rightness, he became zealous, over-zealous for the defense of the faith. When he heard of Christians who seemed to be teaching some dangerous perversion of the Scriptures, he hastened to help those who were trying to stamp out the movement in its infancy. Why? Because Paul was not at ease within himself. On the Damascus Road he met the living Christ, and his life turned around. He found the answer that had always eluded him. "Since we are justified (made righteous) by faith, we have peace with God through our Lord Jesus Christ" (Romans 5:1). What a wealth of meaning in that verse. It tells of heart-rest. It tells of a peace which passes understanding. It tells of a ceasing to be right, because Paul has faced his wrongness and has found God's answer to it in Jesus Christ.

When he wrote the Christians at Philippi, thanking them for their concern and the gifts they had sent him in prison, he was an old warrior for Jesus. He had travelled far and wide, and had seen many people come into that wonderful assurance that God had forgiven and cleansed them of their sinful past, and had given them a new life to live. He was willing to die for that truth, because it was the most precious thing he had ever found. He was a hero in the eyes of many of those who had come to know Jesus through his ministry.

Yet writing to the Philippians, he says that he "counts everything as nothing for the sake of knowing Christ and the power of his resurrection . . . that, if possible, I may attain the resurrection from the dead." And then he says a very significant thing. This saint, this old warrior for Christ says, "Not that I have already attained it, or am already perfect . . ." (v. 12). He recognizes that he still has far to go. He accepts the fact that he is still an imperfect, unfinished child of God.

If you are hung up on being perfect—the perfect husband, the perfect wife, the perfect mother, etc.—you cannot know what Paul was talking about! In your striving for perfection you miss the joy of grace, the acceptance of yourself as one who needs to be saved and is being saved. Think about it! Forgiving yourself involves giving up the demand that you be perfect! God will teach you the deep inner meaning of this, if you seek it with a whole heart.

A Prayer: Forgive me, Father, for thinking too highly of myself, and help me to remember and to accept the freeing truth that I am not yet perfect, and that you love me and came to free me from the demand to achieve perfection on my own. In Jesus' Name. Amen.

1. Where in your life are you demanding to be perfect?

2. What are the imperfections in other people that you criticize because you won't face the same imperfections in you?

3. How can you give up the inner demand to make yourself perfect?

If Any One Does Sin
Daily Reading: 1 John 2:1–6

Christians find sin embarrassing! We know that we should not sin, and therefore often fight off any suggestion that sin might be in the picture. F. B. Meyer has a helpful word for us. "Men are apt to say that they have no sin. It is a profound mistake on their part, arising from defective ideas of what sin is, or from self-ignorance. If they realized what God's standard of holiness and sinlessness is; if they understood that sin consists in coming short of his glory as much as in distinct violation of his will; if they knew that there may be sin in motive as much as in act, and even in lack of love—they would not speak thus." (F. B. Meyer, *Great Verses Through the Bible.*)

We may not even welcome such clarification, since it unmasks some of the thinly veiled excuses we make for ourselves. But let's look at it positively. Self-deceit is going to fail us sooner or later. Better to unmask it now, and come clean with ourselves and with God, and find his answer to the problem.

We are commanded to be merciful to others, and to forgive. That is a spiritual necessity laid upon us all. Holding grudges, keeping accounts against other people is specifically forbidden to us all. What then do we do when we are faced with our own sin—the wrongness of our attitude toward another, our jealousy, our bitterness, or our unhealthy desire to be loved? Are we willing to be forgiven and then to *accept* that forgiveness? Accepting forgiveness can be very painful to pride, but it is tantamount to forgiving yourself.

Every one of us has carried wrong attitudes. We have all violated our own consciences, and "done those things which we ought not to have done." Even more, "we have left undone those things which we ought to have done." But once we confess, accept the forgiveness which Jesus Christ our Lord has made available by shedding his precious blood, we can go on our way in peace and joy. The key to accepting his peace is our earnest desire not to continue in the old sin, and our willingness to humbly forgive our own failure to measure up. This is not to make light of sin, but to accept the way which Jesus offers into a newness of life.

A Prayer: Cleanse me, O Lord, from pride and self-righteousness, and let me know the freedom and joy of one whose sins are forgiven and washed away. Then in that freedom, may I offer you all that I am and can be, to live according to your blessed and holy will. In Jesus' Name. Amen.

1. What do you do when you face wrong attitudes in yourself, such as jealousy, bitterness, or anger?

2. Why is it difficult for you to forgive yourself?

Who is to Condemn?
Daily Reading: Romans 8:31–39

Many of us use up a lot of energy worrying about those who might condemn us. Is it not one of the roots of self-consciousness—fear of being condemned by others?

Paul seems to be saying "Relax!" Remember what and who you are, where you have come from, and how much God has done for you. Remember the testimonies of others who have found God "a very present help" in their time of need, and keep your face toward him.

Every life, no matter how easy, how "put together" it may look on the outside, has its rough times, its trials, and testings. These trials and testings may come suddenly, or we may fall into a kind of slough of hopelessness from time to time. The important thing is this: You have been claimed by God for his purposes, he loves you, has redeemed you, and is at work, *even in the most discouraging moments*, working everything *together* for your good (Romans 8:28).

The real "condemner" is none other than our old adversary, the devil, who goes about seeking those whom he may devour. Temptation is offered, aimed at whatever weak point we may have exposed at the moment. Especially we have to watch (1) times when we have been really disappointed that we could not have what we wanted; (2) times when someone has hurt our feelings and we are feeling sorry for ourselves; and (3) when something has gone especially well, and we feel exhilarated and want to celebrate. They are all danger points, when we may need special help. But the real purpose of the temptation is not just to get us to be disobedient. It is to plunge us into condemnation and hopelessness. For *that* is the condition our adversary finds really most effective in making us of no effect for Jesus Christ. What is sadder than to see a Christian who has started out the walk of faith, become so discouraged and down that he or she just wants to give up, quit trying. Such a person can become a negative witness, a false witness, saying, in effect, "It doesn't work. Jesus failed me." And that is what the adversary wants.

Who is to condemn? So, you're not perfect? So what? You have a Savior! You have the Holy Spirit within you. Up and be doing! He is the strength you need this very day!

A Prayer:
Arise, my soul, arise! Shake off thy guilty fears!
The bleeding Sacrifice In my behalf appears;
Before the Throne my Surety stands,
My name is written on his hands.
(Charles Wesley)

Father I thank thee for Jesus, my strength and my Hope!
Amen.

1. How can you overcome self-consciousness and the fear of being condemned by others?

2. How can you "shake off guilty fears" and discouragement?

Having Mercy
Daily Reading: Matthew 5:1–11

As we think about forgiving ourselves, we need to make clear again and again that we are not making light of sin. That is what the world does. In fact, a recent survey in one

European country revealed that ninty or ninty-five percent of the people no longer believe in sin! But we are thinking within a context where we all recognize sin as a reality in human life, and as a serious problem. Christianity can never survive among those who have no sense of sin, because it is God's answer to the sin problem. The Holy Spirit is the Convicter of sin and the One who remits our sins.

Having said that, let us think about these familiar words of Jesus which we call "The Sermon on the Mount." Among the many strange and incredible things he says in this sermon (such as "Blessed are the poor, those who mourn," and so on), he says, "Blessed are the merciful, for they shall obtain mercy."

(1) First of all, we must need mercy, or this would hold no appeal for us at all. I would not be interested in obtaining mercy if I did not need it. But realizing my need is a first step toward attaining it. Having known that, I am ready to listen to what he says. And the word here is "Blessed are the merciful."

(2) Second, if I am to have the experience of being "mercied," I must learn to be merciful to myself. This is not the same as loving myself, or approving myself, or excusing myself. It is learning to follow the leading of God in dealing with unworthy sinners. God does not wait until we are pure, perfect, holy, and obedient to love us. He accepts and loves us because of who he is, not because of any merit on our part. That is grace. Mercy is seen in his dealing with our wrongness. He allows us to continue on our way until our way becomes so intolerable that we decide to go his way. But he does not force or coerce. He is patient, waiting for the right moment to move us forward in our spiritual growth.

In dealing with ourselves, can we not see the wisdom of such an approach? How many good resolutions, new starts have you begun and abandoned?

Having mercy on one's self is recognizing that force and coercion are not God's ways. When we find ourselves straying in thought, instead of berating, gently lead the mind back in the right areas. And when temptation presents itself, remember that you are weak, that years of undiscipline have made you prey to such thoughts, and gently distract yourself with other interests. It is a way that has worked for many in problem areas of life. Being merciful is not being soft on yourself. (We've all done enough of that!) It is showing the wisdom and patience of God in keeping our long-range goal in mind and remembering who we are.

A Prayer: Thou are merciful and gracious, O Lord, slow to anger and abounding in steadfast love. Thou art good to all, and thy mercies are over all that thou hast made. Blessed art thou, O Lord, for ever and ever. Amen.

(Adapted from the Psalms)

1. Where have you recognized your need of mercy in your life?

2. What is the difference between excusing yourself and having mercy on yourself?

I Have Calmed My Soul
Daily Reading: Psalm 130 and 131

We are thinking about the miracle of forgiveness—God's forgiveness of us, our forgiveness of others, and our forgiveness of ourselves. Today's scripture consists of two psalms. In the first, the psalmist begins by describing where he has come from. "Out of the depths I cry to thee, O LORD!" That is a good place to start—in the *depth* of our need, in the *depth* of our despair of our self-condemnations! It takes some effort, though, even to cry out to the Lord in those depths, because it is the very nature of those depths to cause us to feel that God is far away, does not hear, does not care. That is the effect that such depths have on us spiritually. So, the psalmist cries, "Lord, hear my voice! Let thy ears be attentive to the voice of my supplication!" It is urgent pleading of the needy child.

The psalmist then goes on to ask a freeing kind of question. "If thou, O LORD, shouldst mark iniquities, Lord, who could stand?" (v. 3). This comes close to what someone has called "the good news of sin." It is comforting, somehow, to know that we are not the only one who gets into this kind of shape. It does not excuse our disobedience, it does not deliver us from the depths, but it is helpful to contemplate that "God has consigned all men to disobedience, that he may have mercy on all" (Romans 11:32). It is somehow an expression of haughtiness (a kind of inverted haughtiness) to believe that we are in such a bad situation, in such terrible condition that even God cannot help us! Yet many people have come to believe they are beyond help, "gone too far." What foolishness!

"But there is forgiveness with thee, so that thou mayest be feared" (v. 4). There is the key to hope! There is the ray of light in our darkness! Whatever seems to be holding us back, separating us from God and from the life we know we should be living—it can be dealt with, because "there is forgiveness with thee!" Nothing is hopeless and no one is hopeless!

And since God chooses to deal with us in such unqualified, undeserved mercy "so that he may be feared," why, then, should we not take a step of faith, and shake off our guilty fears? Why should we remain in the dim shadows of self-condemnation, when we can move into the clear light of God's love and hope?

"Steadfast love" and "plenteous redemption" await every one of us as we turn from our darkness and despair to his light.

And then, what a beautiful thought in that brief Psalm 131. "I have calmed and quieted my soul like a child quieted at its mother's breast; like a child that is quieted is my soul." That is the peace that passeth understanding, which is ours by faith and trust in our Lord Jesus Christ. "O Israel, (fill your own name in here) O _____ , hope in the Lord from this time forth and forevermore."

A Prayer: Out of my bondage, sorrow and night Jesus, I come, into thy freedom, gladness, and light Jesus, I come to thee. Out of my sickness into thy health; Out of my want and into thy wealth; Out of my sin and into thyself, Jesus, I come to thee, Amen.

(W. T. Sleeper, 1886)

1. How are you coming to really know that nothing is hopeless, no one is hopeless and you are not hopeless?

I Will Remember Their Sin No More
Daily Reading: Jeremiah 31:27–34

There is such a thing as a blessed forgetfulness. Some Christians, striving for rightness and perfection, fail to deal constructively and healthfully with their failures. It is no good, of course, to "sweep them under the rug," so to speak, and pretend that they are not there. Our subconscious will play nasty tricks on us and remind us at very vulnerable moments of our past failures. It may not even be conscious, but may be in the form of certain binding feelings, over-reactions, fear, or anxieties that refuse to go away. The way to deal with all past failures, sins, transgressions, disobediences is to confess them humbly before God, accept his forgiveness through the sacrificial blood of Jesus Christ, and ask him to change our hearts. Then we can go thankfully forward, cleansed, renewed, and strengthened. If some troublesome area persists, we should seek a minister or priest who can listen to our confession and give us needed counsel and the assurance that God has indeed forgiven us. (Pride can be a strong barrier to making such an open confession, but it should only be done with one who is trained and spiritually able to hear it rightly. It is very foolish to make intimate confessions to the wrong people.) Having done with sin should mean letting go of the accusation, guilt, and despair with which some people flail themselves. A clue to the freedom in Christ to change and grow is not to think too highly of ourselves. Oddly enough, this "thinking too highly" is often associated with a harsh unforgiveness toward oneself. Thus, instead of leaving the past behind and going on in Christ to new obedience and joy, a person can stay locked into remorse and self-hate.

"I will forgive their iniquity, and I will remember their sin no more." This is God's attitude toward our sin, once it is repented of and confessed. It is gone. A well-known Christian teacher used to say, "God says he will cast our sins into the depth of the sea. And," she would add, "I think that he puts a sign up reading, 'No Fishing!'" There is indeed a world of difference between remembering the pit out of which we were dug (where we have come from and how God has delivered us) and rehearsing our failures, reiterating our weaknesses, fretting about our imperfections. If this is a problem with you, and if you are one of those Christians who misses the joy and freedom that comes when you accept yourself as "a wrong one," pray that the Lord will free you and enable you to live in his life. Our own life, including our own high standards for ourselves, is bondage. His life frees us to appropriate the strength we need for each moment. Live it!

A Prayer: I am thine, O Lord. I have heard thy voice, and it told thy love to me. But I long to rise in the arms of faith, and be closer drawn to thee. In the freedom, Lord, that thou dost give, in the life thou dost impart; Let me even now look up and live, with a glad and grateful heart. Amen.

(Fanny Crosby and H.M.H.)

To deal with past failures, sins, transgressions, and disobediences is to confess them before God, accept his forgiveness through Jesus Christ's blood, and ask him to change our hearts.

1. Where have you put this into practice this week?

2. Where else do you need to do this?

Repentance, the Key
Daily Reading: Luke 18:9–14

Today's reading is the familiar parable Jesus told of the Pharisee and the publican (or tax collector). It is one of the most basic lessons in the Christian life, and yet it is one we seem to have difficulty really accepting and absorbing. The Pharisee was a great deal like many of us. He was religious, upright, moral, circumspect, well-behaved. (Perhaps you could name a few other characteristics you think would fit such a person.) The truth is that the Church has always been the favorite place for Pharisees. The biggest problem the Pharisee had was his spiritual pride. He thought he was better than others. In truth, objectively speaking, he was better-behaved than that tax collector! But he failed to take into account what was really inside himself, and how far short he fell of God's perfection. In one place, the Bible reminds us that even the heavens are not pure before God. In other words, as Jesus said, "Why do you call me good? There is only one good, and that is God." Lacking that healthy perspective on himself, the Pharisee foolishly prided himself in his comparative righteousness, because he could plainly see how much worse the old publican was than himself.

The tax gatherer couldn't make a case for himself. When he went to the temple, he was suddenly aware of God's holiness. He was convicted that his own life fell far short, and he was thoroughly ashamed of himself and sorry. So, looking at no one else, he simply beat his breast, saying, "God be merciful to me, a sinner!" It was the only thing he could think of.

Jesus then drives home his point. "I tell you, this man went down to his home justified rather than the other."

One meaning of the word "justify" is "to be pronounced free of guilt." The difference between the state in which these two men left the temple is this: One went away forgiven and free, while the other went away bound in self-righteousness and unforgiveness. He could not accept God's forgiveness because he would not forgive himself, nor even face where he was wrong.

The key to getting rid of this hidden bondage is facing where we are wrong (not just in acts or outward behavior, but inward attitudes, motives, and feelings), accepting God's mercy and forgiveness, and forgiving ourselves. Then we can go on into newness of life, freed from the necessity of trying to convince ourselves and others of our rightness.

A Prayer: God be merciful to me, a sinner, for Jesus' name sake. Amen.

1. In what way do you see yourself as the Pharisee?

2. How can you cooperate with the Lord in your life so that you might be freed from the necessity of trying to convince yourself and others of your rightness?

Chapter Review

It is surprising how many Christians have accepted God's forgiveness, but have not deeply forgiven themselves for being who they are. Inwardly they still carry on the battle to prove that they are really almost all right. Yet Jesus said, "I did not come to call the righteous but sinners to repentance." (You can read "sinners" as "wrong ones" or "un-right ones.")

1. Write a description of the things you like most about yourself.

2. Write a description of the things you dislike most about yourself.

THE HIDDEN BITTER ROOT
JEALOUSY: THE GREAT DESTROYER!

Wrath is cruel,
anger is
overwhelming;
but who can
stand before
jealousy?

Proverbs 27:4

FIFTEEN

Who Can Stand Before Jealousy?
Daily Reading: Proverbs 27:1–6; 6:34–35; Galatians 5:19–24

If we are going to be disciples of Jesus, we are going to have to face our personal jealousies. Of course, none of us wants to have to look at it, or even to admit that it is there. But the human soul is, by reason of its fall from original purity, tainted with jealousy. Some people have a greater struggle with it than others. But we all experience it from time to time. So the first thing to do is to recognize "the good news of sin," which is, that we all share in like natures!

There is no reason to be discouraged about the fact that we sometimes "become jealous" or "experience jealousy" or "fall into jealousy." It may come at an unexpected moment, just when we think that we are going along in great fashion with our life in Christ. All of a sudden, we may find ourselves bowled over, as it were, with strange, dark, unhappy feelings. The green-eyed monster has reared its head again!

There is a story about an old saint, an ascetic, who lived in the desert, and denied himself every form of carnal pleasure. The devil tried to tempt him with all sorts of pictures and allurements, but the man of God was too firmly fixed in his devotion to be swayed by them. Then the devil whispered in his ear, "Did you hear that old friend, brother Ambrose, has been made bishop?" And across the saintly face, a scowl of envy and jealousy signaled that the devil had hit his mark!

What can be done if we find ourselves in this situation? Expose it to the light—to yourself, to another if you can, and to the Lord. Ask for and accept the forgiveness of Jesus Christ, and do active battle in your mind to put away judgmental, critical, or unloving thoughts toward the person or persons of whom you are jealous. Pray for their greater success, and thank God for blessing them! It works! Jealousy does not have to keep the upper hand in the life of a child of God!

A Prayer: O Lord by thy grace so work the truth of this lesson in my heart that I may no more hide my jealous thoughts and feelings from myself or from thee. May the truth work deeply in my heart that I may turn over for thy cleansing and forgiveness any jealousy that I may still harbor, that I may live in new freedom and joy, in the name of Jesus. Amen.

1. How do you recognize jealousy in your life?

2. What specific steps can you take so that jealousy doesn't keep the upper hand in your life?

The Sin of Lucifer
Daily Reading: Isaiah 14:12–20

Christian tradition tells us that this passage in Isaiah refers to none other than the devil himself, Lucifer, the Angel of Light, son of the Dawn. It pictures the angel who stood at the right hand of God, but who was not content with his creaturely status. "I will ascend above the stars of God, I will set my throne on high. . . . I will make myself like the Most High."

It is interesting that when Satan first tempted Eve, it was with the suggestion that if she disobeyed God and tasted the forbidden fruit, she would "be like God, knowing good and evil" (Genesis 3:5). So it was with the same deadly desire, to rise above the limitations which God had placed on us, that our first parents sinned and fell from light and fellowship with God. Human nature has ever been subject to this subtle and powerful temptation, to play God; and to forget that we are not in charge, either of our lives or our world.

What does this say about you and me? That we are subject to being tempted along the lines of wanting to control our lives, wanting to be the center, wanting to be in charge of the circumstances, of the people around us, and that, failing to accomplish our desire to "play God," we often use food, rest, idleness, and entertainment as ways of compensating a consolation prize.

But unlike Lucifer, we have a Redeemer, One who is available to us in our great need.

Satan's cunning is that he attacks us in the point of our weakness and our most vulnerable place. If we have for years indulged in these little consolation prizes it is the likely place where he will strike us unawares. Beware! Be on guard! When the thought comes, *flee* to Jesus, for he is our help and defense. We are not able on our own to fight Satan and win. But with Jesus, we can experience victory.

Our hope and our *way out of temptation* is Jesus.

A Prayer: Lord, I know that I cannot stand alone against temptations when they come. Yet this does not excuse me nor does it make me a victim. I choose to flee to you, and to keep on fleeing to you, rejecting the pull of the flesh and the devil, and choosing rather the better part—obedience to your holy will. For grace and strength, Lord, I pray. In Jesus' Name. Amen.

1. Where are the places in your life that you are tempted to:

    (a) control your own life?

    (b) want to be the center?

    (c) want to be in charge of the circumstances of the people around you—play God?

2. How are you using food, money, relatonships, work, TV, or a computer as a compensation—or comfort—in your life?

The Root of Bitterness
Daily Reading: Hebrews 12:7–17

The writer of today's scripture reminds us of the high price Esau paid for a single meal: He sold his birthright! That may seem fantastically foolish, but wait! Do we sell our birthright as children of God for less?

This week's subject is jealousy, and we are reminded that our natures are, from the days of Adam and Eve, prone to jealousy. That means that we are subject to feelings of envy, jealousy, and bitterness toward those who seem to have what we are denied, or who seem to be preferred, or who seem to be getting along beautifully when we are having to struggle! Who has not felt the dark bitter feeling in such cases! Especially if, in our judgment, the person is less worthy than we!

Our birthright, however, has nothing to do with anyone else. Jesus loved us so much that he would have died for one of us alone! Such is the story we have in the parable of the lost sheep, where the Shepherd "left the ninety and nine in the wilderness" to go in search of the *one* sheep that was lost. I love the verses by Sarah Pratt Green, which go like this:

Po' lil' brack sheep dat strayed away,
Done los'in de win'an' de rain
And de Sheherd he say, "O hirelin',
Go fin' my sheep again."
An' de hirelin' say, "O Shepherd,
Dat sheep am brack an' bad,"

But de Sheherd he smile, like dat lil' brack sheep
Wuz de onliest lamb he had.

And de Sheherd go out in de darkness
Where de night wuz col' an' bleak,
An' dat lil' brack sheep, he fin' it,
An' lay it agains' his cheek.
An' de hirelin' frown; "O Shepherd,
Don' bring dat sheep to me!"
But de Sheherd he smile, and' he hol' it close.
An'—dat lil' brack sheep—was—me!

If we will but keep our eyes on Jesus, and his great love for
us, we can root out the bitter root of jealousy before it
destroys our fellowship and poisons our relationships.
Because our relationship with *him* and our place *in* him is the
thing that really counts!

*A Prayer: Lord Jesus, I thank you that you so loved even me,
that you were willing to take the lowest place, the place of
shame and dishonor—that I might be raised to communion
and fellowship with you. I thank you that you have given me
many blessings and comforts, and friends with whom I can
share the way. Fill me, Lord, with such thanksgiving and
wonder that there will be no room to harbor any thought or
concern that is not from you. Amen.*

1. Where do you have feelings of jealousy or bitterness toward
anyone who seems to be preferred or to be more successful
than you?

2. How can you overcome these feelings and be set free?

Sibling Rivalry
Daily Reading: Luke 15:11–32

We usually read this parable of Jesus with our eyes focused on the prodigal son and the Father's welcome when he finally woke up, came to himself, and decided to return home. Of course that dimension of the story will always be dear to us, and we treasure rightly the picture of God as the waiting and forgiving Father who accepts us in all our unacceptability.

But the real point of the parable seems to lie in another direction. That little bit about the older brother and his feelings toward his rebellious brother has not gotten the attention it deserves. Yet it is important, or our Lord would not have put it into his story.

Someone years ago asked a group to read this story and then write down with whom each one identified. I assumed that everyone always identified with the prodigal and his shame at being far from his Father's house, and his repentance in returning home. To my surprise, a good number of people said they identified with the elder brother, and felt he got a raw deal! It turned out that they had in their experience some situation which was similar enough to this story that they felt someone else was "getting away with" something, while they remained "good, true, loyal, and faithful."

Most of us have experienced conscious or unconscious rivalry with brothers or sisters, or with someone else important in our childhood. We have competed with the other person for attention, approval, and favor. When they seem to have gotten it without effort, we may have gone into vindictive patterns, tried other ways to gain approval, or made up to ourselves for what we felt was lacking. The wonderful thing is this: whether we are the prodigal who ran away to "live it up," or the good son or daughter who stayed behind, we can have freedom in Christ to forgive and be forgiven, to get free from patterns which may long have bound us in fruitless competition.

We do not have to win our place in Christ. It is grace, pure grace. We are accepted and loved, not because of worth or work on our part, but because of who Jesus is. It is his love which is the foundation of our faith, and we can completely and absolutely trust in that at all times.

That faithful love which offers to receive back the prodigal, and offers to welcome the "stay-at-home" to the party, is a picture of God's tender mercy. That same mercy, then, leads to reconciliation, healing, growth, and change in our relationships.

What an exciting and fulfilling life this way of discipleship is!

A Prayer: Jesus, too late I thee have sought;
   How can I love thee as I ought?
   And how extol thy matchless fame
   The glorious beauty of thy Name!
   Jesus, my Lord I thee adore,
   O make me love thee more and more!
      (Henry Collins, 1854)

1. In what way have you seen yourself as:
    (a) the prodigal—the younger brother?
    (b) the older brother?

2. If you are a sibling, list the places you have sought (or still seek) to win a place over your brother(s) or sister(s).

The First Shall Be Last
Daily Reading: Matthew 20:1–16

"It isn't fair!" How often have you said or felt that? And what may seem like perfectly good, righteous indignation may be nothing more than jealousy in disguise! Truth to tell, most of us do not burn with holy indignation at unfairness unless it affects us personally! There is, of course, a righteous anger against injustice and exploitation. The prophets make it perfectly clear that God sees and that his wrath is set against all injustice and unrighteousness.

But having said that, look at this parable again and your own reaction to "unfair" situations. How often is it jealousy in disguise? That was certainly the case with these men in the story Jesus told. Those who were hired early in the morning were promised a certain wage. Then about 9 AM (the third hour) the householder went out, found others idle and open for employment, so he hired them with the promise to give them "whatever is right." Again at noon and at three in the afternoon, he did the same. And at the end of the day, he paid them all the same amount. "Unfair!" shouted those who were the first to be hired. "We have borne the burden of the day and scorching heat, yet you give those who have worked only one hour the same as you paid us." "Ah," replied the other, "I am giving you what we agreed on in the morning. In giving them the same, I am doing you no wrong. Do you begrudge my generosity?"

The truth is, that when jealousy rears its head within our hearts, we do begrudge God's generosity to others. It makes a very bad companion for anyone who wants to be a follower of Jesus. For our resentment cannot keep God from being generous and from blessing those who love him. If such thoughts and feelings come, we need to treat them as dangerous symptoms, go for help to God, and to others if we have people (or a person) who can help us get rid of the danger. Jealousy does hurt others, but it hurts the one who harbors it much, much more.

Never begrudge God's blessing and generosity toward others! Rejoice in it, and pray that they may have it more abundantly! Your blessing will come back to you—in a closer walk with God and in a healthier state of soul. And for the rest, why not leave that to the generosity of God, too!

A Prayer: Jesus, what didst thou find in me,
That thou hast dealt so lovingly!
How great the joy that thou hast brought,
So far exceeding hope or thought.
Jesus, my Lord, I thee adore:
O make me love thee more and more,
        (Henry Collins, 1854)

1. When have you begrudged God's blessing and generosity toward others?

2. What can you do about this attitude?

If You Have Bitter Jealousy
Daily Reading: James 3:13–4:12

I decided to look this passage up in the commentary, and found a very helpful word there. It has to do with our jealousy over our ideas and opinions. Here is what it says:

True wisdom displays itself in a *good life*, particularly in "gentleness" to the opinions and even the faults of one's

neighbors. If anyone forgets this and is so absorbed in a sense of the sole correctness of his own opinions and a resulting sense of superiority as to feel bitter jealousy of his rivals and *selfish ambition* to be recognized as an exclusive leader, then when such a man claims *wisdom*, he is a liar.*
(Burton Scott Easton, *The Interpreter's Bible.*)

That set me thinking of the many times I have held on to my own opinions and have put down in my heart the opinions of others. Have we not all done this to one degree or another—to our own hurt?

Christian fellowship is certainly marred if not destroyed when we entertain this jealous regard for our own rightness. It is merely a way of raising ourselves above others, making ourselves feel better about us at someone else's expense.

And what is the cure? Such jealousy of being considered "the leaders," the "knowing one," "the right one," must be sacrificed by becoming "the wrong one" in our own hearts—and before others! Part of the reason for talking about our needs, our wrongness, our sins—is so that this fierce, jealous pride which is in all of us can be crucified. And there are no people on earth better at harboring this kind of pride than Christians!

I hope that this week's theme is doing something tremendous for you. For my own part, one of the most freeing and happy experiences in my whole life was the discovery (or the revelation, to be more exact) of how jealous I was. Far from being a negative downer, it brought me inner freedom to rejoice in newfound forgiveness! And so can it with you, as you allow the Holy Spirit to reveal places where you are jealously guarding your "rightness" over others. When we give it up, Jesus stands to bless and heal us in new depths, and that has to be wonderful!

A Prayer: Thank you, Father, for the wisdom from above, which is first pure, then peaceable, gentle, open to reason, full of mercy and good fruits without uncertainty or insincerity. Thank you for showing me the way to seek and find more and more of that wisdom, by giving up my "rightness" and my opinions which seek to set me above others. Help me to choose your wisdom today. In Jesus' Name. Amen.

1. Where have you recognized that you have jealously guarded your rightness over others?

2. Read James 4:1-2. How does jealousy lead to division and conflicts?

It Was Out of Envy
Daily Reading: Matthew 27:1–23

It is good to read again these painful words about the suffering and pain our Lord endured for us. And it is good to see this week's "sin" for what it is and where it leads: "For he (that is, Pilate) knew that it was out of envy that they (the religious leaders) had delivered him up" (v. 18). That is where our jealousies and envyings end up—at the cross of Jesus. "He bore our own sins in his body on the tree," says 1 Peter 2:24. It was our jealousies and our envyings, as well as that of the religious leaders of his time, that he carried to the cross.

As we complete this week of thinking about the hidden, often unrecognized sin, this is a good place to leave it. The leaders of Jesus' day did not know the motives they were coming from—even though Pilate, a pagan, knew it! And that, perhaps, is the most important thing we need to carry away from this week's Bible studies and readings: that our jealousies are often hidden even from us, and something in us does not want to see them or admit that they are there. We would much prefer a spiritual short-cut which would avoid thinking, talking, or praying about jealousy, for it is perhaps the most degrading (to us) of all sins.

And that is where it serves a useful function in dealing with our pride—the first of the Deadly Sins. For to admit jealousy, to ourselves, to God, to others, is humiliating, and the humiliation is a part of the healing! Blessed is the child of God who learns and accepts this lesson! Short-cuts which avoid the crossing out of our pride will not really eradicate this problem—merely gloss over it and seek to deny it.

The healthiest thing, emotionally and spiritually, we can do is to be as honest with ourselves as we can, and to pray for more light and more grace, until we have seen all that God wants us to see. For there is nothing there which his love and grace will not cover. Our pride will be the only casualty!

Remember that Paul said, "Whatever things were gain for me, I count as loss for Christ." And any modicum of our pride that we can save—to keep ourselves looking good in our own eyes or the eyes of others, keeps Jesus out of that place. For he dwells with the humble and contrite heart.

So be of good cheer as you go on in your walk with Jesus. He knows all about you and loves you. You do not have to play games with him.

His mercy, grace, and forgiveness spell life, healing, and hope for all who stand before the cross and say, "God be merciful to me, a sinner."

A Prayer: Lord Jesus Christ, Son of God, have mercy on me, a sinner. Amen. (The Jesus Prayer)

1. The leaders of Jesus' day did not know the motives they were coming from even though Pilate, a pagan, knew it.

(a) How are you recognizing more clearly the motives that control you?

(b) What are some of the motives that control you?

Chapter Review

Jealousy springs from a bitter root, and its fruits are also bitter. It was the first sin, as Lucifer, the archangel of light, rebelled against God out of jealousy (Isaiah 14:14). We see it in the first temptation as Adam and Eve were tempted to be "like God, knowing good and evil" (Genesis 3:5). Satan even accused God of jealousy!

But as much as we may deplore jealousy in others, are we aware of its hidden movements in ourselves? This week's devotions have focused on this hidden sin that cannot bear appearing in the light. To admit jealousy to ourselves, to God, to others, is humiliating because jealousy seems like such an ugly sin. The humiliation of exposing and confessing this "second rate" sin is part of the healing. Our jealousy and envyings end up—at the cross of Jesus.

1. After this week of reading and pondering on the subject of jealousy, where are you freer to face, admit, and confess your sin of jealousy?

"WON'T SOMEBODY LOVE ME?"
IDOLS ARE NOT JUST MADE OF MARBLE

"I am the Lord
your God who
brought you out of
the land of Egypt,
out of the house of
bondage—You
shall have no other
Gods before me."

Exodus 20:23

SIXTEEN

Covetousness is Idolatry
Daily Reading: Colossians 3:1–11

The words are old-fashioned and out of use. "Who is an idolator any more in our advanced society?" we might say. After all, we do not carve out images and pray and make sacrifices to them. So why this emphasis on idolatry? Put it on the "back burner" for a few moments, and let's talk about the other old-fashioned word, "covetousness." That may strike a little nearer home, for after all, we've learned the Ten Commandments (haven't we?) and duly recited the words, "Thou shalt not covet." Covetousness, the dictionary tells us, is the state of having an inordinate desire for that which belongs to another. Whatever you or I love with an inordinate, unlawful desire to own for ourselves, is covetousness. And whatever we love to that extent is, in practical terms, putting it in the place of God, who is alone to be the center of our affections. And that is idolatry.

If you have not acquainted yourself with this truth, it might be well to go over it several times, to let it saturate your thoughts. For all of us are, at times, guilty of putting other goals, other things—and other people—and most of all ourselves before God, and therefore need to heed this word of St. Paul: "Put to death what is earthly in you: immorality, impurity, passion," (and we can certainly assent to the need for all that) "evil desire," (all desire that is not of God) "and covetousness, which is idolatry. On account of these the wrath of God is coming." We cannot expect a holy God to wink at our continuance in any known sin or disobedience. He is holy and righteous, and calls us to lives of obedience and faithfulness.

Ask the Holy Spirit this week to show you places where idols lurk, where you have put something or someone in the place where only God should be. For if you are doing this, your object is to be loved or to be fulfilled by another. You are looking for fulfillment from the creature rather than the Creator.

A Prayer: O divine Master, grant that I may not so much seek to be consoled as to console, to be understood as to understand, to be loved as to love. For it is in giving that we receive, it is in pardoning that we are pardoned, and it is in dying that we are born to eternal life. Amen. *(Francis of Assisi)*

1. Where are you seeking fulfillment from anyone or anything rather than God?

Solomon's Folly

Daily Reading: 1 Kings 11:1–13

Solomon's ruin is traced in two steps in this passage. First of all, he took many wives, princesses of neighboring countries, in order to insure peace with those kingdoms. It was a case of human wisdom overriding the express command of God (v. 2). The second step in Solomon's ruin was that indeed the influence of his wives did turn his heart away from wholly following the Lord, "And so he did for all his foreign wives, who burned incense and sacrificed to their gods."

The poet Alexander Pope has a little quatrain which speaks to the danger here:

Vice is a monster of so frightful mien,
As to be hated needs but to be seen;
Yet seen too oft, familiar with her face,
We first endure, then pity, then embrace.
(*Essay on Man*, 1733-1734.)

The lesson for us here is that we can turn away from God in easy, almost unconscious steps. There was a time, in the beginning of his reign, that Solomon's heart was toward the Lord. His prayer is recorded in 1 Kings 3, and it was in essence a prayer for "an understanding mind to govern" the people wisely. God was pleased with what he had asked, and said to him, "Because you have asked this, and have not asked for yourself long life or riches or the life of your enemies, but asked for yourself understanding to discern what is right, behold, I now do according to your word. Behold I give you a wise and discerning mind. . . . I give you also what you have not asked, both riches and honor. . . ."

With that promising start, and the continuing blessing of God, Solomon became "the wisest man of his age." But he allowed human reason to discount the simple command of God, and thus became foolish. His lesson can be important for us, for God is still in the business of hearing and answering prayer! And he still honors the prayer which seeks his will instead of our own. Thus we can be furnished and equipped for every need. But if we, like Solomon, out of a desire to be loved, to be at peace, to enlarge our circle of friendship, begin to excuse and make light of that which we know to be wrong, we are on slippery ground. From having his heart wholly toward the Lord, making excuses for the idol worship of his foreign wives, Solomon ended up entering into the same sin— that of idolatry. When we excuse sin in others around us because we do not want the conflict of standing for the truth we know and love, we can become soft, our consciences become blurred, and that which we first endure, we can eventually "pity, then embrace." Then our clear witness for Jesus Christ is blunted and made ineffectual by our idolatry with the other person or persons involved.

A Prayer. Save us, O Lord, from being hard and right in our relationship with others, yet preserve us from making easy compromises with evil out of a desire to keep a relationship with another person. Give us wisdom in all our relationships, that they may be purified by thy presence and more and more conformed to thy holy will. In Jesus' Name. Amen.

1. Where, like Solomon, do you allow your human reason to discount the simple command of God?

2. Where do you excuse others in order to avoid conflict?

A Mother's Idolatry and Its Fruit
Daily Reading: Genesis 27

The Bible is unblinking in the portraits it gives us of its "heroes." There is no glossing over of the faults and failings of these people, and we can believe that these things were written for our instruction and for our good! Rebekah had a favorite son. So, apparently, did Isaac, though that does not seem to figure so largely in the story. But Rebekah definitely preferred Jacob. Not content to let God raise him above his brother, if that should be his will, Rebekah instigated this little deception which would end up in Jacob stealing the blessing of his older brother. (Although they were twins, Esau was first-born, which in those days gave him a distinct advantage when the father bestowed his paternal blessing.)

The result was that Isaac was deceived and gave the primo-genital blessing to the second-born, Jacob. But that was not the end of the story. "Now Esau hated Jacob because of the blessing with which his father had blessed him," and planned to kill him in revenge. Again Rebekah intervened, fearing that she would lose both her sons if one should kill the other.

The point for us is that her interference and her obvious preference of one over the other did much to cause friction, hatred, and alienation between the brothers. They had their own responsibility in it, of course, but Rebekah's hand was definitely soiled with her sin of idolatry and control. Like so many well-meaning parents, her "help" often did more harm than good, because it came out of wrong motives! God would intervene and redeem the situation, but we cannot presume upon God. We must allow the Holy Spirit to show us where, like Rebekah, we try to manipulate our families for our own selfish purposes. Once we begin to see it, we can confess it, give it up, and begin to trust God in a new and more fulfilling way. After all, he loves our children more than we, and with a love that is clean and free from personal interest. He knows what is best, and our own scheming and manipulating only add confusion, pain and delay in the working out of his purpose. Rebekah's example should warn us all!

A Prayer. O God our Father, help us always to remember that your love is greater than ours. And help us never to do anything to grieve your fatherly heart never to do anything to turn to bitterness the brotherly love which ought to be the mark of every human relationship. Help us to accept nothing but your guidance, to serve nothing but your will; to seek nothing but your glory; through Jesus Christ our Lord. Amen.
(Adapted from William Barclay)

1. In what ways do you recognize that you try to manipulate your family for your own selfish purpose?

2. What steps can you take to release your family to God's will for them, rather than playing God in their lives?

A Father's Idolatry and Its Fruit
Daily Reading: Genesis 37

Yesterday we thought about Rebekah's interference in her children's lives, growing out of her idolatry with her son, Jacob. Today's scripture concerns Jacob himself, who seems not to have learned from his experience of younger days (which we read about yesterday). His preference for his son, Joseph, led to bitter enmity and jealousy between Joseph and his older brothers. And the Bible clearly says that the reason Jacob loved Joseph so much was that he was the son of "his old age." He was also the son of Rachel, the wife whom Jacob loved in the beginning. But in loving Joseph, Jacob was really "loving himself," and the attitude Joseph had toward his brothers shows the bad result of such favoritism. "Joseph brought an ill report of them (his brothers) to their father" (v. 2b).

Most parents find that one or two of their children "please" them more than others. This can come about from a whole spectrum of emotional reasons—often having nothing to do with the child, but with what is still unresolved in the parent. Some of you who read these lines may have felt yourself among the unfavored and many have spent years striving fruitlessly to gain that preferred place. Others may have basked in the favored position. But in Joseph's case, God allowed great and prolonged suffering to come in order to mature him and cleanse him from the effect of Jacob's idolatry. And Jacob's suffering with the loss of Joseph can be seen in the light of God's allowance—for his love for Joseph was sinful and selfish. It had no life nor good in it, either for himself or for Joseph. And so the years of grief and loss were allowed to cut across that love, until, in God's mercy and wisdom, the relationship could be renewed on a different basis.

All our relationships are tinged and burdened with self. God, in his mercy and patience, deals with them one by one. Sometimes we wince in pain as a relationship is severed, or seems to be severed, by death or by some other circumstance. But if we will trust that God is in charge, and that he can both destroy and create, we can relax, letting all our relationships grow, mature, change, and be healed in Christ. It is one of the areas of greatest need for all of us, and only the healing power of Jesus can make of our relationships what they are meant to be.

A Prayer: Continue, Lord Jesus, to show us your light in all our relationships; that we can see where we need to free others to be them selves; that we can, by grace, be to them what we are called and meant to be; and that we can love them with your love, which passes knowledge. Amen.

1. This week as we've been concentrating on idolatry, what relationships of yours are you seeing as "tinged with self"?

2. How can you cooperate and "let these relationships grow, mature and be healed in Christ"?

Idolatry Avoiding Truth
Daily Reading: 2 Timothy 3

Today's reading divides itself into two sections. The first half of the chapter paints a bleak picture of "the last days," (which the writer understood to include the time in which he lived). The second half of the chapter is positive—and we'll look at that shortly.

In that first half we have a description of people who "hold a form of religion but deny the power of it" (v. 5). They are not very attractive, these "lovers of self . . . lovers of pleasures rather than of God." Their sins apparently disfigured them.

It reminds one of *The Portrait of Dorian Gray* by Oscar Wilde. In that story a young man gives himself increasingly to a life of self-pleasing, seeking to satisfy his flesh and caring not who was hurt in the process. And a strange thing about it was that he continued to look young, strong, and healthy, while a certain portrait of himself (which he kept carefully hidden) grew increasingly grotesque, its face showing the downward progress of its owner toward complete disintegration and ruin. In the closing scene of the motion picture, he destroys the picture, and takes on all the accumulated grotesqueness before he dies.

If we could see our souls and what avoiding truth, or denying the power of God in our lives, does to them, we might be more willing to undergo the momentary pain or discipline of having them healed. Our Christian experience is an experience in self-denial (to some extent), and as such offers us an opportunity to let truth re-form us inwardly and outwardly. The outward we can see and rejoice in. The inward may be more clearly seen by others. In any case, these are humble, small steps at not denying the power of the faith we profess.

Jesus Christ is our present help, and we find it out as we go daily to him in our need. We are putting the idolatry of self-love aside in favor of reality and obedience to the Holy Spirit.

The second half of this chapter is a very encouraging word. True, there are imposters and deceivers in the world, going on "from bad to worse." But we do not have to be distracted by them. "As for you, continue in what you have learned and have firmly believed, knowing from whom you learned it. . . ." As we walk on together, we encourage one another by our honesty, and our openness to talk about where we are and the needs we have. When we honestly confess our disobediences and sins together, we can all go again and again to the Fountain of life and cleansing, and go on our way rejoicing. We do not have to let self-love have the last word. Not as long as Jesus lives!

A Prayer: Lord, so often you astonish us by granting requests which were only half-formed enriching our experience in unexpected ways, reminding us of factors we have over-looked. However you answer our prayers, may the outcome be that we love you more, understand your purpose better, and believe in you with greater confidence. Through Jesus Christ our Lord. Amen.

(Adapted from Contemporary Prayers for Public Worship, ed. Caryl Micklem)

1. List the places in your life where you have had a positive experience of self-denial, and an opportunity to let truth re-form you.

"A Cell of Soft Selfishness"
Daily Reading: 1 Samuel 2:22–31 and 4:1–18

Eli was confronted by "a man of God" with a difficult message to deliver to him. Eli had failed God because he honored "thy sons above me." Although in many ways Eli had done well, he had failed in this critical point.

One writer says:

> . . . There is always a difference between sentimentality in the handling of children and the sound preparation which is necessary for a life of service. So often the home is nothing but a *cell of soft selfishness*. (itals. mine.) Children do not learn within it the meaning of sacrifice and devotion and service. Parents in their struggle to make their children better off fail to make them better. *Unconsciously* they betray their own true ambitions. Anyone connected with education quickly recognizes how many children are spoiled by their parents' inverted pride. Materialistic standards of success control too many parental hopes, and consequently bring ruin upon distinguished family traditions. Eli was weak when he allowed Hophni and Phinehas to defame their office. He was content with the preferment their position gave them, instead of demanding from them any adequate discharge of their responsibilities. (John C. Schroeder, *The Interpreter's Bible*, Vol. 2)

Our story today goes on to describe the sad and tragic end, both of Eli and his two wicked sons. But the important thing for us is to ask ourselves what we are really conveying to our children—by our lives, our conversation, the things we really love and live for. Our children pick up what we are much more than they do what we say. And that is something for us to ponder.

It would be a very unhappy thing to have pronounced over our lives, that we honored our children above God. Yet the temptation lurks within us all, and must be watched. For here we can easily be deceived and misled, thinking that we are being loving and good.

A Prayer: O God our Father, we thank you for our families; for the joy and blessing we have in these ties that bind us together. But we know, too, that we often forget that you are the Weigher of motives and of the inmost heart. Deliver us from making idols of those we love. In Jesus' Name. Amen.

1. What are you conveying to your children (if you are a parent) or to others around you, by your life, your conversation, and the things you really love and live for?

2. How can we be delivered from making idols of those we love?

Idolatry and Insincerity
Daily Reading: Galatians 2

Today's reading should encourage all of us who have a problem with wanting people to approve of us. This chapter gives us a little insight into the spiritual struggles of two of the most distinguished Christians of all time—St. Peter and St. Paul. Peter (or Cephas, as Paul calls him here) had not fully overcome the desire to be approved. Although he and the other apostles had clearly stated that God did not require Gentiles to become Jews in order to be Christians, there were some in the Church who did not fully agree with this, fearing that the traditions of the Jews would be lost. Peter was having a wonderful time of fellowship with Gentile Christians, eating with them (which was an offense to Jews). Then certain men came from Jerusalem, and Peter, wanting to have *their* approval too, withdrew from eating at the table with Gentiles, "And with him the rest of the Jews acted insincerely, so that even Barnabas was carried away by their insincerity" (v. 13).

Think about that in the situations we meet today. We want to be loved and accepted by everyone. Are we guilty of putting an insincere face on in order to be accepted? Are we sometimes guilty of saying behind someone's back what we would not say to their face? Or do we avoid doing or saying certain things in the presence of someone we know might not approve? These are some suggestions to start you prayerfully thinking about how your idolatry (your desire to be loved) leads you into insincerity.

It goes without saying that to give up idolatry does not mean that we become rude, blunt, hurtful, dumping our feelings out on others under the guise of being sincere! But too many Christians play-act with other Christians instead of developing real relationships.

A Prayer: Father, I thank you for the example of Paul in courageously standing for a principle when others were making false compromises. I thank you for his honesty and love in confronting Peter to his face rather than speaking behind his back. May I have the grace to be steadfast, honest, and sincere, without being self-righteous and holier-than-thou. And may I have more regard for your approval than for that of any human being. In Jesus' Name. Amen.

1. Where are you seeing that your desire to be loved leads you into insincerity?

2. How can you stop "play acting" and develop real relationships?

Chapter Review

"I am the Lord your God who brought you out of the land of Egypt, out of the house of bondage. You shall have no other gods before me." (Exodus 20:23)

Idolatry is the worship of something or someone in place of God. Anything we place before obedience to and worship of God is an idol—another person, status, material possessions, family, our own "spirituality," or many other things. We pin our affections on these persons or things because of what they can do for us. Thus ultimately, idolatry is an expression of self-love. Yet God commands us to have no other gods before him.

Idolatry is a persistent sin, often disguised as noble and worthy, growing out of the very depths of our fallen nature inherited from Adam and Eve. We often mistake it for true love and resist when God begins to deal with our idolatry.

1. In what instances have you pleased others, thereby improving their opinion of you in order that you might be loved, honored, and adored by them?

2. In what ways do you prefer other people or things to God's will in your life?

SELF-RIGHTEOUSNESS
WHAT'S WRONG WITH BEING RIGHT?

"I tell you there
will be more joy
in heaven over
one sinner who
repents than
over ninety-nine
righteous persons
who need no
repentance."

Luke 15:7

SEVENTEEN

What's Wrong with Being Right?

Daily Reading: Luke 18:9–14; Luke 15:1–7

"I tell you there will be more joy in heaven over one sinner who repents than over ninety-nine righteous persons who need no repentance. " (Luke 15:7)

I'm not sure we have ever grasped the full impact of that statement. Of course we know that our Lord was not condoning sin or approving of it. But the way he says it, it sounds like there is a limited amount of joy in heaven over "righteous persons who need no repentance." And that's startling isn't it?

What is he talking about, really? Is it not that disposition within your heart and mine, which, although we may do our duty as we see it, and refrain from doing wrong, takes pride in our rightness, and fails to see the large areas of neglect or to take into account the wrong motives in what we do?

Take the first: the large areas of neglect. Jesus told a parable once about servants who worked all day, and came in only to be told by their master to prepare his meal before their own. Then he applies it directly to us, and says, "So you also, when you have done all that is commanded you, say, 'We are unworthy servants, we have only done what was our duty'" (Luke 17:10). That puts all our goodness and righteousness in a different light, and should take some of the starch out of it!

Then take the second: our wrong motives for right actions. Have you ever looked back on some "good decision" you had made (a really good and right thing for your life) only to find that you had hidden agendas that you didn't talk about or perhaps did not even realize yourself, unconscious expectations, ambition, pride and so on, intermingled with your desire to do what was good and right? Many of us have seen such, and like Martin Luther, have discovered that there is the taint of self and sin in our most holy acts. So, we need something beyond our righteousness. We need a Savior. We need the righteousness which only he can provide. Otherwise we are stuck with our little, puny "right acts," and they don't seem to make heaven very happy. But when we do what we can, make the right decisions as best we can, but then realize that "We are unworthy servants, and have only done our duty," we can still take the place of the one who said, "God have mercy on me, a sinner." And that is the place where the joy, the peace and the "well done" can be felt in our hearts. it is the secret of the saints, and the stumbling block of the Pharisee spirit.

A Prayer: O Lord, have mercy on me for I am weak; remember, Lord, how short my time is, remember that I am but flesh. My days are as grass, as a flower of the field for the wind goeth over me, and I am gone. By all that is dear to thee, all that we should plead, and before and beyond all things by thyself, by thyself, O Lord, and by thy Christ: Lord, have mercy on me, the chief of sinners.
O Lord, let thy mercy rejoice against thy judgment in my sin. O Lord, hear, O Lord, forgive, O Lord, hearken and do; do and defer not for thine own sake; defer not, O Lord my God.
(Abridged from *The Private Devotions of Bishop Lancelot Andrewes, 1555–1626*).

1. Where have you taken pride in your "rightness"?

2. Where has your self-righteousness put others down?

Whatever Was Gain to Me

Daily Reading: Philippians 3:1–14

This passage is one to which we return again and again, because it touches so pointedly on one of our big problems as Christians: our pride in accomplishment. Of course, the world says we should be proud, that we should compete with one another for top place, and gives us many excuses for taking pride in our family lineage, our education, our looks, our position, our accomplishments, and our children.

But read this passage again. What does Paul say? He has many reasons for being proud, in a worldly sense. He could boast of his good family lineage, of his good education, of his moral accomplishments, and of his religious zeal and fidelity. But when he met Jesus face to face on the Damascus Road, those things seemed to fall away into nothingness. He was confronted by a holiness so pure that nothing he had seemed pure any more. He was confronted by a love so intense that his own seemed pale and of no consequence. He was confronted by a life so full and free that he lost interest in holding on to anything he had counted as a plus or a gain in the past. "if I can only have this!" was what his heart cried out.

This same Jesus confronted you in your life at some crucial point. For each of us, that point differs. It may be very dramatic for some of us, and for others, it may be simply a gradual awakening to the great spiritual realities and an inner desire to respond to Jesus' love. Whatever it is, we all come to him knowing that we need him, that we are not adequate in ourselves, and that we are *wrong*. The Holy Spirit convicts and convinces us that we are sinners and need a Savior. Where then is there any need or use of building up our old pride of place, family, name, achievements, education, etc.? Paul says it all: "Whatever things were gain for me (read, "my self life") those I counted as loss for the sake of Christ" (v. 7). That was true for him and is true for us. Whenever we build up *self*, we take away from Jesus and his place in our lives. Staying needy is a way of staying close to him.

> I need thee every hour,
> In joy or pain,
> Come quickly and abide,
> Or life is vain.
> I need thee, O I need thee,
> Every hour I need thee;
> O bless me now, my Savior,
> I come to thee.   *(Annie S. Hawks, 1835–1918)*

1. In what ways have you competed with others by taking pride in your family, education, looks, accomplishment, children, or position?

2. What circumstance(s) in your life do you believe the Lord has allowed so that you would remain needy?

The Way of a Fool
Daily Reading: Proverbs 30:11–14; Proverbs 12:15–19

The Book of Proverbs is an amazing collection of wisdom, often pointed, sharp, and incisive, and not infrequently witty. It was intended to teach those who love the Lord the wisdom of walking upright before him and the folly of following the way of "the world, the flesh and the devil."

Today's reading, especially verse fifteen of chapter twelve hits right home in this week's theme of self-righteousness.

"The way of a fool," says the proverbist, "is right in his own eyes." Ouch! "But a wise man listens to advice." Now the writer knows that we don't want to be fools and that all of us would like to be wise men and women! So he contrasts the way of the fool and the way of the wise. And that's where the crunch comes. For *usually* we think our way is right! My opinions, my convictions, my way of doing things, my methods, my ideas are they not dearer than dear to us?

What can be done? Perhaps the key word here is *listen.* The wise man *listens* to advice. The writer of these lines remembers that on retreat once, one of the leaders asked him, "Do you listen to your wife?" (And his wife often offered words of advice, counsel, and wisdom.) His answer had to be, truthfully, "Sometimes." But he made what seemed a good decision. He would go home from the retreat and begin to really *listen* to her, to hear what God might say to him through her. And then he made a fateful decision. He would listen, but he would not *tell* her that he had decided to listen. That might give her too much encouragement and "power" over him. And so it happened. He had hardly been home an hour when his wife said something that he did not agree with. And he thought, "I am so glad I didn't tell her that I was going to listen to her." And he would have been saved a lot of grief and trouble had he been willing to heed and follow her good counsel!

The word for all of us is, "Listen!" Listen to what others are saying, even if you don't like what they say—or, perhaps better, *especially* if you don't like what they are saying! It could be the sharp two-edged sword of the Spirit of truth, separating the darkness of your way ("right in your own eyes") from the light of truth ("good advice"). We can trust God to keep us from harm as we hear and heed good advice. Our biggest problem will come with forcing ourselves to listen to our heart and spirit, so that we can get beyond the pain, hurt pride, rightness—into a new freedom and joy.

Do you not think the writer of these Proverbs knew how hard it is, and what a reward awaits us when we will really listen to good advice? Giving up our treasured rightness may be the hardest task set before us as followers of the Lowly One. For that rightness keeps us high, hard, and superior to others. When we humble ourselves to *listen*, he can increase in us and that is all joy!

A Prayer: O send out thy light and thy truth, and let them lead us; let them bring us into the ways that are pleasing in thy sight. When we do not see the way, help us to be quiet in spirit and listen, and to remember that we are the children of thy love, So amid all the changes and choices of life, may we ever grow in our trust and faith in thee, through Jesus Christ our Lord Amen. (Adapted)

1. What opinions and convictions have you been holding on to tenaciously?

2. Whom do you find it difficult to listen to when you are convinced that your way is best?

3. What reward awaits you when you really listen to good advice?

When Evidence is Ignored
Daily Reading: Jeremiah 2:20–37

The prophet Jeremiah pictures Judah as a woman running after lovers, faithless and without principle. It is a graphic and sordid picture of spiritual infidelity and apostasy. Yet, he says, in the midst of it all, she says, "I am innocent; surely his anger has turned from me." And God says, "Behold, I will bring you to judgment for saying, 'I have not sinned'" (v. 35).

There is a spiritual principle here which we very much need to see. Even greater in God's eyes than all her sins of unfaithfulness was her refusal to see that she had sinned and her refusal to acknowledge it. "I will bring you to judgment for saying, 'I have not sinned.'" There is an echo here of the words of 1 John 1:8, "if we say we have no sin, we deceive ourselves and the truth is not in us." And these words of Jeremiah are echoed in the words of our Lord to the Pharisees, "If you were blind, you would have no guilt; but now that you say, 'we see' your guilt remains" (John 9:41). What he is saying is that their very assertion of spiritual superiority keeps them from getting rid of their guilt before God; they are *locked in* by their self-proclaimed rightness.

A word of warning needs to be said here about the reactions that may come up in us from time to time. If you find yourself getting angry, or bored, or unhappy about too much concentration on sin—remember that you are in a special time of training by the Holy Spirit. The old Adam may protest and seek ways of making yourself feel better *in order to escape the conviction of the Holy Spirit* by which God would bring you into a new place of wholeness and freedom. Do not rob yourself of this blessing by listening to the voice of self. All of us, especially good, right people need this immersion into the truth of how far we fall short of the glory of God in all our goodness. It is a truth so nearly lost to much of the body of Christ (yet so old that the Bible and the hymnals are full of it) that it sounds strange, like some new teaching. Don't believe that it is new. Our old nature does not want to die; it wants to be justified. But seeing it in its self-righteous pretenses is one way of nailing it to the cross.

A Prayer: Plenteous grace with thee is found,
   Grace to cover all my sin;
   Let the healing streams abound
   Make and keep me pure within
   Thou of life the fountain art;
   Freely let me take of thee ;
   Spring thou up within my heart;
   Rise to all eternity.
                    (Charles Wesley 1707–1768)

1. Where (just like Judah) have you been saying (or thinking): "I'm right" or "I'm innocent"?

2. When have you attempted to make yourself feel better in order that you might avoid the conviction of the Holy Spirit?

A Warning of Love
Daily Reading: Matthew 23:1–28

I read seven "Woes" to the scribes and Pharisees in this powerful chapter. In six of them Jesus calls them "hypocrites," and in one, he addresses them as "blind guides." At one time in my Christian life I had trouble seeing the love of Jesus, or the kind of love which I thought Jesus usually showed, in this passage. It seemed to me that he was loving to everyone but the Pharisees.

Then one day the Lord showed me something. First, he showed me that I was a Pharisee in my heart—trying to build up rightness and taking pride in the fact that I had a good number of "right deeds" on my record! The second thing he showed me was that these thunderous words to the Pharisees were actually warnings of love. He *did* love the Pharisees, and was trying to break through their hard shells of self-righteousness! What a revelation that was!

Perhaps you have had the experience of seeing some particularly "right" person in their adamant shell which could not be penetrated. Words, threats, pleas, cajoling—all useless. They were enclosed in their rightness. (Such people can be very difficult and hard to live with!) A particular former parishioner comes to mind as I write this: a man from a European background, who had worked his way up in a company to a comfortable job, and who had subdued his wife and all those around him by his incorrigible rightness. He was correct in all his religious and political views, and never lost the opportunity to express them with great force. He was a man of honesty and moral integrity. But all who knew him regarded his wife as a saint for having lived with him for forty or more years, and his children, as they grew older, tried to get away from his influence as much as possible. It would be very easy to sit in judgment on such a person, if one did not see how very much we are like him in many ways. Wherever we allow our opinions and ideas to become strong, lordly, and domineering over others—there we become encased in self-righteousness.

Jesus did love the Pharisee. Jesus *does* love us, even if we are at the moment stuck in our rightness. But his hard, sharp words come against that rightness in an effort to break through and release another kind of life, another dimension of life. Paul describes it beautifully in Galatians 5:22: "But the fruit of the Spirit is love, joy, peace, patience, kindness, goodness, faithfulness, gentleness, self-control; against such there is no law!"

Need we say more?

A Prayer: Lord Jesus Christ, it is the fruit of the Spirit which I crave in my inmost soul. Deliver me from every tinge of self-righteous hardness, that this marvelous fruit may grow and mature in me, to the honor and glory of your great Name. Amen.

1. What opinions and ideas have you allowed to be strong and domineering over others?

2. In what respects are you like the Pharisees?

3. How do you recognize the Lord's strong words to the Pharisees as words of love?

Unless Your Righteousness Exceeds...
Daily Reading: Matthew 5:1–20

Are we getting the point? Is it beginning to get clear, that the Christian life is not that hard, striving after perfection, "I've got to be right at all costs" kind of life? It is a joyful, living "up and down" experience of real people who are aware that they haven't arrived, yet are glad to be on the way!

The Pharisee is a good study of a religious type, and if you asked the average person outside the church to describe a Christian, you would probably get a pretty good portrait of a Pharisee. Scholars tell us that the main characteristic of Pharisees was their legalistic rigorism. They were rigidly right! Their outward behavior was what they depended on to make them right with God, and they were serious about it. The second characteristic was their respect for the traditions of the elders and their conformity to conventions passed down to them from the past. Thus they were disturbed by a teacher like Jesus, who *seemed* to be saying things in a new way, not based on careful scholarship or quoting from the ancient teachers. Can you see how their righteousness was open to

Jesus' charge that it was insufficient? Yet they were, in many ways, the most religious people of their day. Their whole bent was to keep themselves right, legalistically and ritually, with God.

Obviously Jesus is not saying that it is right to ignore the law. He very vigorously says that he is upholding the law. What he is looking for in the children of the kingdom is a heart attitude which knows that no amount of right behavior will do—that a new spirit and new life are required. He promised the Holy Spirit would come and make his home in those who loved him. And that promise he fulfilled on Pentecost (Acts 2) and continues to fulfill in the hearts and souls of every believer in him.

So our righteousness is of a different quality, a different type—not just more of the same. Even the Pharisees could have this righteousness when they began to see their real need and abandoned their efforts to build up merits and prideful achievements, and considered themselves good candidates for God's mercy. "God be merciful to me, a sinner," is still the prayer which brings that righteousness which exceeds that of the scribes and Pharisees, and clothes us with it.

Dressed in his righteousness alone,

Faultless to stand before his throne!

1. Where are you beginning to see your real need to abandon your efforts to build up your own merits and achievements?

He Came for the Unrighteous
Daily Reading: Matthew 9:1–13

There are few verses in Scripture more encouraging than this one: "Go and learn what this means, 'I desire mercy, and not sacrifice.' For I came not to call the righteous, but sinners."

In that simple statement Jesus declares that he came for those who are wrong and know it. He knew that his coming would be meaningless to those who were satisfied with their own righteousness. If men think they are good enough in themselves, and if they have no awareness of sin and need, they do not seek and they do not find the Savior. It is the sick who go to the physician. It is the wounded who seek healing.

The joyful news is that we can face who we are, what we are, what we have done, what we have left undone—all without condemnation—because our need calls down God's mercy. Our wrongness pleads his righteousness. Our inadequacy to make it on our own without him evokes his plenitude of grace, strength, and help in time of need.

Someone has said that unless we recognize our pain and bring it to speech, we are doomed to live without hope. Painless people are hopeless people. What does that say to us who know our pain, our failure, our need? It means that we experience hope, for we meet him who touches us at the very point of our pain. There is a gospel song which says, "He touched me and made me whole." And that is true for every one of us who allow him to be to us the Savior he came to be. He touches our memories of bad things that have happened to us, and heals them. He touches our guilt and gives us forgiveness. He touches our traumas and frees us from them. Not once only, but in many times and places do we need that healing touch.

Perhaps more than we can know, he touches us in our attitudes, and step by step heals and brings us into change and greater wholeness. Is this happening to you? It can. He is victor! He is able! He is willing! He came for us—the wrong ones!

A Prayer: Thanks be to thee, my Lord Jesus Christ,
For all the benefits thou hast won for me,

For all the pains and insults thou hast borne for me.
O most merciful Redeemer, Friend, and Brother,
May I know thee more clearly,
Love thee more dearly,
And follow thee more nearly:
Day by Day.
              (St. Richard of Chichester, c. 1197–1253)

1. "He touches us in our attitudes and step by step heals and brings us into change and greater wholeness." Where is this happening in your life?

Chapter Review

Jesus told the parable of the Pharisee and the tax gatherer to those "who trusted in themselves that they were righteous . . . ." The Pharisee spirit is especially contagious among "religious" people, and we always stand in grave danger of trusting in ourselves, that we are righteous. It is easy to begin to mistake good behavior and "right" acts for righteousness. "I came not to call the righteous, but sinners" (Matthew 9:13). Let this week's Bible study confront you in "the self-righteousness department."

1. What qualities or activities are you proud of?

2. Do you believe you are accepted by God on the basis of what you have done for him? Why?

WHO ME, ANGRY?
A WARNING LIGHT—DON'T IGNORE IT!

*Be angry but do
not sin; do not let
the sun go down
on your anger,
and give no
opportunity to the devil.*

Ephesians 4:26-27

EIGHTEEN

Be Angry But Sin Not
Daily Reading: Ephesians 4:22–32

If there is one stereotype that we Christians hold onto about Christians above all others, I think it would be this: Good Christians don't get angry. Is that how you feel, or how you have felt in the past?

From time to time one meets a Christian who absolutely denies ever getting angry. He or she does not raise their voice, lose the "reasonable" tone, etc. Being in perfect control of the emotions seems to be the height of such a person's image of what a Christian should be.

It comes, then, as something of a shock, to read these words of Paul to the Ephesians. "Be angry." Is he telling us that it is good to be angry? In a sense, perhaps so. It is good to be angry at sin! It is good to have righteous anger at a situation that calls for it. But that does not seem to be what the apostle is saying here, at least not in a primary sense. Is he telling us that from time to time we are angry, will be angry? This I think is the primary meaning which can be most helpful to us. We all get angry. Christian or non-Christian, there is still enough of the old self in us to be hurt, to be resentful, to be irritated by something in others or in a situation around us. And then we are face to face with reality: We are angry. What shall we do about it? The most deadly and dangerous thing to do is to push it down and pretend it isn't there. For then, like a root fire, it travels underground, seeking some outlet. And often it will burst forth in unexpected situations or on some unsuspecting target—when we over-react because we haven't dealt with our anger back when it happened. The apostle's instructions are very clear: Don't let the sun go down on your wrath. And what does that mean? Don't harbor it, nurse it, clasp it to you like some precious possession you can't let go of. Deal with it. And usually the most healthful way is to deal with it right when it is happening *with* the other person. If that is not possible, we can deal with it as soon as possible. But there is a clue to giving up anger: to have it really go, we have to look at where we have been wrong—even in the smallest degree. Only the Holy Spirit can show that to us. When we have once seen wrongness on our part, the anger can quickly evaporate, we can forgive and be forgiven and the anger no longer controls the situation. It really does work, and these devotions are meant to help us deal with our anger more honestly and wholesomely.

A Prayer: I thank you, Father, that I don't have to pretend to be what I am not, that you love me and accept me as I am— imperfect, still often proud, hurt, and angry when I should be beyond that. Yet you call me to live in this honest and open way, and I pray that you will help me deal with hurts and angers as they happen, so that Jesus Christ might be formed more fully in me. In his Name. Amen.

1. Where have you harbored or nursed anger?

2. In the situations where you have nursed anger, where can you see your wrongness?

The Anger of Man
Daily Reading: James 1:19–27

There are two important points in today's reading about anger. One is that we have some control over it. "Let every man be slow to anger." Did you ever feel yourself *about* to get angry, and know that you had some choice to refuse it or to give in to it? There are times when we can consciously feel that brief moment of choice. With practice, the apostle seems to be saying, we can enlarge that moment. We can choose not to fly off the handle. For some of us that will be a much harder battle than for others! In *The Royal Way of the Cross*, Chapter forty-two, Fenelon says, "A heated imagination, vehement feeling, a world of argument, and a flow of words are really useless. The practical thing is to act in a spirit of detachment, doing what one can by God's light, and being content with such success as he gives" (p. 133). This is what James is talking about when he counsels us to be slow to anger.

The second important point in today's reading is also touched on in the quotation from Fenelon. Our anger does not accomplish what we wish. It may intimidate, it may get some immediate result—but the long-term result is nil, because "The anger of man does not work [read *accomplish*] the righteousness of God." When we hold on to our anger and refuse to give it up, we are seeking to control and shape some person or situation by it. Our anger gives us power (we think). As long as we stay angry, we have that inner feeling of power. But in truth it does not achieve any worthwhile goal.

The solution to the problem of anger is hinted at here in today's Bible reading: "Let every man be quick to hear." Ah, there it is again! We are called to listen to the other, and not just to our own hurt, anger, and emotions. Hearing can be a key to releasing and giving up the anger which otherwise becomes a wedge and barrier in our close relationships. Jesus Christ often speaks to us through other people's words. And if we have an ear to hear, it is surprising what he will say to us to our joy and blessing!

A Prayer: Almighty Father, King of Heaven, give me grace each day to seek, above all other things, thy Kingdom to seek it in peace and in turmoil, in sickness and in health, in temptations and in persecutions, in times of calm and times of tribulation, in times of danger and in times of safety; to seek it in the world, in the Church, and in myself, for the sake of him, the King of Love, even Christ our Lord. Amen.

(William Portsmouth)

1. How have you sought to use anger to give you power—or to get your own way?

2. List the places recently where you have been able to "listen" to others and not just to your own hurt?

Putting Off the Old Man
Daily Reading: Colossians 3

Several generations ago a famous preacher preached a sermon entitled *The Expulsive Power of a Great Affection.* His theme was that when we really begin to be possessed by a great love for God, that love expels from our hearts many negative, hurtful things. Perhaps in your own experience you have found this to be true, especially when you first awakened to a new faith in and love for Jesus.

But that first blush of rapture which many Christians feel in their early days of awakening has a tendency to fade. We are not exactly sure how or when it happens, but little by little the old nature reasserts itself. And this is a critical point in the spiritual pilgrimage of any person. What seemed to be effortless and almost automatic now becomes harder and less exciting.

It was to such a situation as this that Paul wrote our lesson today. The Colossians had believed the gospel, and had found newness of life in their faith in him. But life went on, and things were not always "peachy-keen and hunky-dory." There were problems to be faced, inward and outward, hence the practical, down-to-earth instructions in this chapter about interpersonal relationships in the home and in the church. Conflicts had arisen and would arise. And they had to be dealt with in harmony with all that the Colossians had believed and had previously experienced.

Put to death the earthly . . . put off the old nature . . . and put on the new nature. Put on . . . compassion, kindness, lowliness, meekness, and patience and if anyone has a complaint against another, *forgive* each other. And above all, put on love. These extracts sum up both the promise and the challenge of our life in Christ. We have a new nature, given us by the Lord himself, who quickened our spirits by his Holy Spirit, and who dwells within us. Yet we have to put away the anger, malice, slander, and foul talk and falsehood—all of which belong to our old nature which "you have put off . . . with its practices!"

It's a very down-to-earth picture of *our* lives, and it challenges us to live up to the life God has given us. The simple means remain for us to use, and this chapter really describes our life in a helpful and encouraging way.

Our discipleship is a learning process. Today is one more step along the way of a pilgrimage. Jesus is with us as we go, showing, teaching, counseling, encouraging, correcting, warning, chastising, and forgiving. His love is over us and we need not fear to do battle with the old self—putting it off in preference to the "Great Affection" which God has poured into our hearts by the Holy Spirit—our love for Jesus Christ and our love for one another!

A Prayer: Father, let the word of Christ dwell in me richly, and give me a thankful heart! Whatever I do, in word or deed let me do everything in the name of the Lord Jesus, giving thanks to thee, Father, through him. Amen.

1. How do you forgive another person?

2. How do you put away anger, malice, etc., without being unreal?

The Wrath of God
Daily Reading: John 3:16–36

We are thinking about anger this week—the fact of it and what we can do with it and about it. Today's reading takes us to one of the most beloved chapters in the Bible, John 3. Perhaps more people have memorized John 3:16 than any other verse in the entire Bible, and if you haven't learned it yet, it is well worth tucking away in your storehouse of memory.

But as we come to the end of this chapter, where the evangelist so earnestly presents the claims of Jesus Christ for our absolute and unwavering trust, he makes a very strong statement. "He who believes in the Son has (present tense, present reality, Hallelujah!) eternal life! He who does not obey the Son shall not see life, but the *wrath of God* rests on him" (John 3:36).

One writer expresses it this way:

The ordinary Christian teaching about God needs infinite stiffening. . . . The sterner side of God is quite as prominent, even in the New Testament, as the more humane side; it is only that preachers have fallen into a way of dwelling on the latter to the exclusion of the former, whence the sickly one-sidedness of our current religion. . . . Men have come to think of God as a weak and indulgent parent, who will not be hard on them in any case, who will think more of their happiness than of their perfection, and give them the things which they want or think they want . . . and veneration is drowned in a sickly flood of talk about divine love. (Percy Gardner, "The Practical Basis of Christian Belief," *The Interpreters' Bible*.)

One of the reasons we have become so unreal about our own anger and negative emotions is that we have pictured God in these unreal terms. But seeing him in both his wrath and his mercy, we can see the appropriateness of allowing our own full range of human emotions their legitimate place. We do not have to become repressed, artificially "good" people. At times we may even have some of his righteous wrath within us! At any rate, we do not need to be afraid of *feeling*. It is a part of our created nature. God's wrath is not inconsistent with his love. His wrath is against that which destroys, warps, and distorts his creation, which he made in free untrammeled love. Abiding in his wrath only means refusing to give up that which hurts and destroys!

A Prayer: O God our Father, who even in thy wrath thinkest upon mercy: we thank thee for what thou art and for what thou hast made us to be. We thank thee that thy Son Jesus Christ has revealed to us perfect God and perfect man. So give us grace to become more and more like him in thought, word and deed through the same Jesus Christ thy Son our Lord, who with thee and the Holy Spirit ever livest one God, world without end. Amen.

1. The devotion for today talks about not having to become repressed, artificially "good people." Take a look at your own life. Where have you chosen to be repressed and artificially "good"?

2. How can you change?

Jonah's Anger with God
Daily Reading: Jonah 4

Jonah is a delightful, thoroughly human character, and in spite of his stubbornness (or perhaps because of it) we can feel a real kinship with him. Perhaps we have all been given assignments which were so thoroughly distasteful and repugnant to us that we would have taken almost any means to avoid carrying them out. At any rate, Jonah took what seemed an effective means to escape his unpleasant mission of announcing Nineveh's doom. Not that he minded Nineveh meeting its doom! On the contrary, he would welcome it. But he didn't like going there to warn them that it was coming!

Then after God prepared the unusual transportation back to shore, and Jonah decided to be obedient and carry his message to Nineveh, he expected at least the consolation of seeing the "big show." What he had not counted on was that the king and people of Nineveh took him seriously, truly repented and began to change. Jonah was embarrassed. He felt like a fool. He had not suggested any *ifs* or *maybes*—just that Nineveh would be destroyed in forty days. And now God's graciousness was at work, sparing the city!

Chapter four of this remarkable book is a gem, because it shows a man at his petty worst in conversation (honest conversation, we might add) with his Creator. And it shows God talking back in very reasonable tones, almost like a patient parent talking to a naughty child. The encouraging thing about that is this: God knew Jonah's heart. Although stubborn and petty, he loved God and God is training him, even as he sends him on his mission. God is always training us for greater understandings and always pushing us beyond where we would comfortably like to stay in our inward life and thoughts. And Jonah knew God well enough to know that he could voice his ugly, accusative, angry feelings to him. If we are angry at God (and it does happen) and if we do not deal with it, we will make others the scapegoat for that anger.

Today's reading says that it is safe to face our anger at every level, because God is merciful and gives us that freedom as his children. Sooner or later we will have to see, as Jonah did, that our anger is wrong. Only God is right!

A Prayer: Father, help me to take to heart the lesson of Jonah. If there is anger toward you, may I no longer hide it, but face it knowing that there is healing and forgiveness in Jesus. Cleanse me from secret faults, O God, and renew a right spirit in me So may no other sun go down on any wrath buried within me, that I may be a clear channel of thy love. Through Jesus Christ our Lord. Amen.

1. Why do you think Jonah was so angry?

2. Where are you like him?

Moses' Righteous Anger
Daily Reading: Exodus 32:7–35

You can imagine how Moses must have felt! After forty days alone with the Lord on Mount Sinai, he returned with the precious treasure of the Ten Commandments in "the writing of God, graven upon the tables," only to hear as he and his attendant Joshua neared the camp, the noise of riotous partying. "And as soon as he came near the camp and saw the calf and the dancing, Moses' anger burned hot, and he threw the tables out of his hands and broke them at the foot of the mountain"(v. 19).

There are times and there are circumstances which demand righteous anger. If we have so bound ourselves into some false image of the people we think we should be that we cannot express that anger, everyone is the poorer for it. Of course there is a danger that we will get some unrighteous anger mixed up with it, for we are not pure and totally sanctified. But God will use the righteous anger to cut through the easy evasions and excuses which otherwise would prevent his word from getting through to another person. Genuine love calls for this anger in the face of persistent and destructive wrong!

We can see how Moses loved the people of Israel as he prays for them (vv. 31-32). "Alas, this people have sinned a great sin; they have made themselves gods of gold. But now, if thou wilt, forgive their sin—and if not, blot me out, I pray thee, out of thy book which thou hast written."

Never allow yourself to think that anger and love cannot live in the same heart. Forget that false idol of the placid, calm, understanding person who always speaks in reasonable terms. Learn to be real with the people around you, for in that very reality God can do a mighty work.

A Prayer: O God, help me to respond to the circumstances and the people in my life in greater freedom and reality, not hiding myself from hurtful things, but facing them with Jesus Christ and his grace. I thank you that you are teaching, training, and healing me for a more abundant life in him. Amen

1. With whom are you truly real?

2. How can you learn to be real with the people around you?

Sharp Contention !
Daily Reading: Acts 15:22–41

"And there arose a sharp contention, so that they separated from each other; Barnabas took Mark with him and sailed away to Cyprus, but Paul chose Silas and departed, being commended by the brethren to the grace of the Lord."
(vv. 39-40)

The Bible is remarkably frank in the pictures it gives us of the heroes of faith. We learn about David's sin of adultery, we see his simpering idolatry with his son, Absalom, which almost cost David the kingdom; we see Jacob doting over the two sons of his favorite wife, and fostering jealousy in his other ten sons. And here we see two great men locked in open controversy.

Mark had left Paul and Barnabas in Pamphylia, "and had not gone with them to the work" (v. 38). In other words, Mark had "jumped ship" so to speak—probably because it was harder than he had expected! Barnabas had actually been Paul's "sponsor" as we read in Acts 11:25. He had gone to

Tarsus to find Paul and had brought him back to Antioch. He was the senior member of the Barnabas-Paul team on their first missionary journey.

But Paul obviously had a fiery disposition, and could be quite volatile. And the feeling was strong enough that the two men decided it was impossible to continue on together. Barnabas and Mark went their way, and Paul and Silas became a new team of missionaries. They were later reconciled, and even Mark was again accepted by Paul (2 Timothy 4:11).

The important thing here is to see that they were free to be real. They did not have some preconceived idea of what it meant to be "Christian." They loved the Lord, but they were also still real people. We need to see the same freedom is ours today—not to justify our sin, but to appropriate the fullness of our life in Christ. It is safe to be real!

A Prayer: Lord, help me to face my real feelings in all situations and to trust you to help me work through them, believing that it is safe to be real in Jesus' Name, Amen.

1. How are you facing your real feelings about anyone with whom you differ?

2. How can you allow God to help you work through these feelings?

Chapter Review

The ability to get angry is a part of our God-given emotional structure. One of the things we need to learn is that repressing or denying anger leads to a depressing of all emotions. Anger is potentially destructive, especially if it is indulged as a method of controlling others. But anger can be constructive as a warning of something wrong in ourselves or others that needs changing. To nourish anger and hold on to it brings about division and separation between ourselves and others. Let God show you the truth about your anger (both recognized and unrecognized) and what to do with it.

1. As you review this past week, list the circumstances that made you angry.

2. What do you do when you get angry?

3. What are God's instructions about anger? (See Colossians 3:8)

WHY DOESN'T SOMEONE UNDERSTAND?
SELF-PITY—A PERENNIAL COMFORT BLANKET

*O Lord thou hast
searched me and
known me! Thou
knowest mine
down-sitting and
mine up-rising:
thou understandest
my thoughts
afar off.*

Psalm 139:1-2 (KJV)

NINETEEN

Lord, Do You Not Care?
Daily Reading: Luke 10:38–42; John 5:1–9

This week we will be looking at some aspects of the insidious sin of self-pity. Self-pity doesn't seem like a sin. It does not even seem like something we can avoid when we indulge in it. But let us look at what the Bible illuminates on this problem, and ask the Holy Spirit to make us sensitive to it, both in ourselves and in others.

Mary and Martha and their brother, Lazarus, seem to have been special friends of Jesus. In John 11 we are told, "Now Jesus loved Martha and her sister and Lazarus" (v. 5). So we can infer from this that there was a continuing relationship and friendship between these three people and the Master.

It was Martha's honor and privilege (and I'm sure, her joy) to be hostess to Jesus when he came to Bethany. Whether their home was large or small, it did not matter. They loved him, he loved them, and their home was a welcome place for him who had no place of his own.

When Jesus came, doubtless others came with him. We can infer that by the verse which says, "But Martha was distracted with much serving." All of the twelve? We do not know. But Martha's reaction was to pity herself, and she broke all rules of etiquette by complaining to the guest about how much she had to do! Mary was not doing her part!

Have you ever felt that way when your friends found other things to do and you were left to do some humdrum chore alone? Perhaps it was not so much that you *minded* doing it— as you hated having to do it alone! Self-pity!

The lame man by the pool of Bethesda was in the same frame of mind. Asked if he wanted to be well, he made his plaint of self-pity because no one would help him into the pool at the critical moment.

Self-pity is a way of comforting ourselves when things don't go the way we want them. It grows out of our feeling that we have a right to better conditions or a fairer shake.

But it is a very different thing than pity or mercy for others. For it saps our energy, it cuts off our relationships with others, it tells us a lie that we are a victim and can do nothing about such circumstances, and it justifies us in our self-concern. Christians have a better way.

But often the first thing to be done in dealing with any problem situation is to recognize and confess to the Lord that we are in self-pity, and then look for a solution to the problem. Self-pity speaks so loudly that we can't hear much else with our inner hearing until we give it up!

A Prayer: Lord, I thank you that I do not have to live in bondage to self-pity. However long I may have indulged in it or howsoever frequently I may have entertained it, I can be free. By the grace and merit of Jesus, I can put off the garment of sadness, and put on the garment of praise. And so, Father, I would clothe myself in such a garment! All praise and thanks to you, All-worthy One. In Jesus' Name, Amen.

1. How do Martha's actions indicate she's in self-pity?

2. What were the results of self-pity in the man by the pool?

The Sad Story of a Sulking King
Daily Reading: 1 Kings 21

You would think, would you not, that being king was enough for anyone. Even being king of a small country like Israel would be quite a satisfying position. But Ahab was used to getting his own way. One way or another, he usually prevailed. And now he had run into a man who wouldn't budge. It was not that Naboth was nasty about it. He simply said, "I will not give you the inheritance of my father." His home was more important to him than the king's approval!

It would be easier to judge Ahab for his childish behavior if we did not remember when we have done similar things. Oh, to be sure, most of us have learned to hide these feelings from others (or think we have). But alone, or inside our hearts, do we not, in a sense, turn our faces to the wall and refuse to eat? At any rate, we sulk in self-pity all too easily.

Jezebel gave the wrong kind of help. She gave him pity and justification for his feeling. What we need when we get into such a mood is not someone to sympathize with us and tell us how right we are, but someone who will speak to our childishness and sin, help us see and feel how wrong we are. That is a friend indeed!

It makes no difference how successful we may have become in our work, or how important or dignified we may appear to others—we are all susceptible to the temptation to withdraw, to sulk, to feel sorry for ourselves when things really go against us. We may cover it up with anger and not even know that the root is self-pity.

The remedy? Start with what you know about yourself and about Jesus Christ. Do you see anything in him that suggested that he ever wasted a moment in pitying himself? Yet who would have been more justified in so doing? Look at yourself. Do you really think you would be happy, even if you got your way in the particular incident, or if you won your particular point? Would there not be something that should come up to dissatisfy you shortly again? If that is so, why waste time indulging this debilitating sin! Be done with it!

There is a beautiful anthem by Johannes Brahms with some particularly appropriate words to our theme. They read:

Why brood all day in sorrow!
Tomorrow will bring thee God's help benign
And grace sublime in mercy.

The Remorse of Judas
Daily Reading: Matthew 27:1–10

The Gospels almost let Judas disappear after his heinous deed of betrayal. We lose sight of him during the awful events of the arrest, trial, and crucifixion of the Lord. And then, almost as an afterthought, some of the Gospel writers (and Luke in Acts) tell us of the bad end to which Judas came.

But Judas was not the only one who denied Jesus. True, he went voluntarily to the authorities and *offered* to betray him, but Peter, the chief of the Twelve, also denied Jesus under pressure—denied even knowing him.

The glimpse we have of Judas after his act of betrayal and the glimpses we have of Peter following his triple denial of the Lord stand in sharp contrast. Both were "sorry" they had failed. But Peter's sorrow was repentance, and one gets the feeling that Judas' sorrow was that things had worked out so badly, and he didn't know what to do about it. Remorse is a kind of pitying of ourselves when we do not really want to take responsibility for what we have done and when we are too haughty to admit our wrong and find forgiveness. Pride can be a terrible master, and a lot of people suffer from remorse as a choice because they do not want to face their essential wrongness and humble themselves before God in repentance. Self-punishment is tied up with this—being angry at oneself and sorry for oneself at the same time. Who has not experienced it!

Judas "punished" himself by hanging himself. But I do not believe he ever gave up his self-pity. "It wasn't my fault," perhaps he said. "I didn't think it was going to turn out this way." (Have you ever done something hurtful to another person while you were angry or jealous, and then regretful doing it?) Remorse, says the dictionary: "prolonged and insistent self-reproach, and often intense suffering for consequences that cannot be escaped." Repentance, on the other hand, is defined as "an awareness of one's shortcomings morally or spiritually, and a change of heart." One is self-oriented, self-centered, while the other is faith-oriented and full of hope. Whenever we talk or think about any wrong, we have the option of going as Peter went rather than the route which Judas took.

A Prayer: Thank you, Father, for Jesus! Thank you for sending him to this earth, to set us free from having to wallow in the bondage of vain regret. And now, because he died for me, and because his blood avails to cleanse me from all sin, I can be free to live in joy and hope! Hallelujah! Do help me to live in the positive assurance that, unworthy though, I am through my many sins, I have a Savior! Amen.

1. There is a big difference between remorse and repentance. What is it?

2. Where are you currently living in remorse?

3. Where are you currently living in repentance?

Why Cast Down, O My Soul?
Daily Reading: Psalm 42

Alexander Maclaren, the great nineteenth-century English Baptist preacher, says about Psalm 42, "The whole psalm reads like the sob of a wounded heart. The writer of it is shut out from the Temple of his God, from the holy soil of his native land. One can see him sitting solitary yonder in the lonely wilderness. . . . with a longing, wistful gaze, yearning across the narrow valley and the rushing stream that lay between him and the land of God's chosen people, and his eye resting perhaps on the mountain top that looked down upon Jerusalem. . . . He was depressed because he was shut out from the tokens of God's presence [the Temple]; and because he was depressed, he shut himself out from the reality of the Presence." (Alexander Maclaren, *Psalms for Sighs*.)

The key is in the last sentence. Because the psalmist was depressed, he shut himself out from the Presence of God. That in my own experience and that in the experience of many others I have known is exactly what we do. We allow our *feelings* to act as though they were the final word, and assume that they are telling us the truth about God. Thus we deny ourselves the very power which could and would bring us out of our depression and into the sunlight of God.

The psalmist has grown wise in his walk with God. He acknowledges his longing, thirsting questioning, and his sadness. "My tears have been my food night and day. . . ." But three times in this psalm and the one following he repeats the refrain, "Why are you cast down, O my soul? And why are you disquieted within me? Hope in God; for I shall again praise him, my help and my God."

One of the biggest things about self-pity when we find ourselves in it is to begin to take steps to get out of it. By its very nature it makes us sluggish, almost enjoying its hopelessness and despair. But we can, by the grace and power of Jesus Christ, get up and do something about it. We can sing a hymn; we can praise God out loud. We can begin to memorize some scripture or some great poem or other thought. We can take authority over Satan in the Name of Jesus and begin to do battle against the thoughts and feelings he is giving us. If we find that there is sin unconfessed, making us guilty, we can confess it and accept forgiveness. Too many times we leave our confessions short, without going the final step of accepting the cleansing and forgiveness which is ours when we repent. Then we can set our faces to go on with Jesus as obediently as we can, no matter what. Such an attitude will go far in dispelling the debilitating wasteful condition of self-pity!

A Prayer: Father, I thank you for the light of truth. I thank you for Jesus Christ and his all-sufficient blood to cleanse me from every sin. I thank you for the Holy Spirit who dwells within me, and for the fruit of the Spirit, which is joy, love, and peace. I thank you that my feelings, though they are often affected by many circumstances, do not have to rule me, because I belong to you. Thank you, Father, for my new life in Jesus. Amen.

1. How can you take steps out of self-pity?

2. What specific steps do you need to begin to take in your life now?

Tell the People to Go Forward
Daily Reading: Exodus 14:5–31

One of the things that may invite self-pity in us is our feeling of helplessness against "overwhelming odds." It may be that the housework seems just too much to handle. Or the children! Heaven knows that a mother with small children has her hands full day and night, and she may sometimes be tempted to feel it's just too much. A man may feel that his work and its demands are more than he can handle, and then have to face the problems of bills and financial needs at home as well.

Before we get too involved in thinking about such things, let us remember the plight of the people of Israel as they stood before the Red Sea, with Pharaoh and his troops bearing down on them from behind. They went into fear, panic, self-pity, accusation, and anger! And Moses again went to the Lord, and laid his case before him. God's answer was, "Why cry to me? Tell the people to go forward!" But where was forward? It was through the impossible. It was right into the Red Sea.

The way to deal with many things that befall and beset us is to use this same principle. God's word to us still is, "Go forward."

Go forward in believing more simply that God has the answer to your needs, that he knows where you are, and that he is able and willing to help you!

Go forward in letting God show you how he would have you grow and change. Too many Christians want to stay in spiritual kindergarten, playing in the school yard. Our

Christian life is meant to be a time of growing and changing—not just settling down with a few new things to believe and the hope of going to heaven when we die. Eternal life has already begun, and we are on the way to what we shall be! Think of it. Go forward in that attitude of wanting to be done with childish things of your past and going into greater maturity.

Go forward in losing your all-consuming concern with yourself, and begin to learn to serve others. That must have been quite a sight, those hundreds of thousands of people, young and old, marching into the impassable Red Sea. Some would need more help than others. There was much for all to do.

And there still is. There are people to be served, to be loved, to be cared for. There are whole areas of our relationships which God would have us bring into greater conformity to his will.

The Holy Spirit will show you, he will still lead you on to greater growth.

Don't stagnate! Go forward!

A Prayer: Father, I thank you for the call to go forward, and not to remain behind locked in old unproductive patterns and ways. I thank you for those who are encouraging and helping me, and for the gentle, strong urging of the Holy Spirit. Continue the work you have begun in me, and bring it to your desired completion in your own time and way. In Jesus' Name. Amen.

1. What circumstances in your life are overwhelming to you now?

2. How can you go forward?

When Feelings Talk
Daily Reading: 1 Kings 19:1–18

The psalms are full of honest expressions of feelings. Where other books in the Bible may tell us how other people have reacted to God or how we should respond to the gospel, the Psalms actually express the response—for the psalmist and for us.

Psalm 77 describes a time when the psalmist was feeling low. Remembering back when things seemed better, it seemed to him that God must have forgotten his people, or that he would never again be favorable to them.

Self-pity is often like that. It may start as a kind of harmless reverie, and them build upon itself until it has a full-grown case for hopelessness and accusation against the goodness and mercy of God. When we get into that state, we are very much in danger of losing our will and determination to be obedient that we know is right.

The psalmist has the solution for these talking feelings, as far as his own experience was concerned. First, he "came to himself" so to speak, and said, "I say, 'It is my grief.'" Grief was talking, as it is apt to do when it is present, in hopeless, self-pitying terms. But then he goes on, "I will remember . . . call too mind . . . meditate on all thy work." Remembering the things that God has done for us in the past is a helpful way of fighting present despondency.

Martyn Lloyd-Jones, a contemporary English preacher says in his very helpful book, *Spiritual Depression*, "There is nothing that is quite so variable about us as our feelings. We are very variable creatures, and our feelings are, of everything that belongs to us, the most variable of all." And these negative feelings of self-pity and grief can be very powerful in pulling

Why Doesn't Someone Understand? • 249

us away from our straight course. The writer of the Letter to the Hebrews had the right idea when he spoke of running the race set before us, "looking unto Jesus, the author and finisher of our faith." Although the psalmist did not know Jesus, he knew God, and could think on him and what wonders he had wrought in the past. We have even more reason for encouragement, and greater reason to think upon, call to mind, meditate on what he has done for us. The truth should deal with what these feeling tell us, so that feelings give way to the reality of God and his promises, presence, and purpose in our lives.

A Prayer: Thank you, Father, for giving me feelings, for life would surely be dull without them. Thank you for the good feelings when we are blessed with a sense of your presence, and for the reality of that presence when we cannot feel it. You are training us through these ups and downs to hold onto that reality, and to walk calmly forward in unshaken trust in you. In Jesus' Name. Amen.

What Are You Doing Here?
Daily Reading: 1 Kings 19:1–18

Surely this is one of the most humorously encouraging stories in the Old Testament. Elijah, the great hero, has stood faithful against all odds, and finally challenged the queen and her prophets of Baal, exposing them as frauds. What a feat! You would think after God's answer by fire on Carmel that Elijah would be ready for all comers.

But then Jezebel sent word, promising to do the same to him as he had done to her prophets, and Elijah got scared. He began to run, and ended up miles and miles away from the capital city, weary, discouraged, and full of self-pity. "Lord, take away my life, for I am no better than my fathers" (v. 4). Exhausted, he went to sleep, and when he awoke there was food ready for him. Strengthened, he continued his journey all the way to Horeb.

There in a cave the Lord spoke to him. "What are you doing here?" And Elijah rehearsed his tale of woe, and spoke of how unfair it was that he was left alone to defend God's honor. God commanded him to go outside, and there he witnessed a great strong wind, breaking the mountains in pieces; then an earthquake, and finally a fire—all the pictures of untrammeled power! "But the Lord was not in . . . the wind . . . the earthquake . . . the fire," And then came "A still small voice." The Voice asked him, "What are you doing here?" And Elijah repeated his complaint. But God showed him that there was much to be done, and the situation was not as bad as Elijah had described it—seven thousand people had not bowed their knee to Baal.

Remember those words the next time you find yourself feeling that things are not fair, feeling sorry for yourself, feeling a little hopeless about things. "Go, return," was God's message. Elijah had to go back to where duty and "the action" lay. And so do we. But not in our own strength. Not with our self-generated cheerfulness. We are to go in his strength. He is the answer to this condition of self-pity about which we have been thinking this week. No self-pity can remain when we get up and go on our way to carry out his word. His is the power which overcomes the world, outside us and within us. Looking to him we can find strength and renewal for this and every day.

Listen to the still small voice and obey!

A Prayer. Almighty and most merciful God, grant to us the knowledge that you are greater than our needs, always more ready to hear than we are to pray, and confirm us in our desire to keep steady in our commitment to do your will, not regarding the dis-couragements which others may offer us or those which rise in our own hearts. May we listen and ever obey, for Jesus' sake. Amen.

1. Where have you had a sense of unfairness, or felt sorry for yourself this week?

2. What should you do about it?

Week Review

"O Lord, thou hast searched me and known me! Thou knowest mine down-sitting and mine up-rising. Thou understandest my thoughts afar off." (Psalm 139: 1-2, KJV)

We know what an "uprising" of thought is, when we rise up to our full height to explain, defend, or express ourselves! But do you recognize your inner "downsittings"? Self-pity is such a one. When we feel that no one understands, that it isn't worth going on, we are "down-sitting." Then we are tempted to comfort ourselves with self-pity.

This week we have asked the Lord to expose our self-pity areas and how this emotion can be a tool of Satan to hinder us in our Christian battle.

1. If self-pity is a way of comforting ourselves when things don't go the way we want, or when we haven't had a fair shake, we need to know when we are in self-pity. How can you tell when you are in self-pity?

2. What do you turn to when you get stuck in self-pity? (T.V., food, fantasy, etc.?)

THE FINE ART OF GETTING EVEN
VINDICTIVENESS BEARS BITTER FRUIT!

*Beloved, never
avenge yourselves,
but leave it to the
wrath of God,
for it is written,
"Vengeance is mine,
I will repay," says
the Lord.*

Romans 12:19

TWENTY

Never Avenge Yourselves

Daily Reading: Romans 12:14–21

This week's theme confronts us with a very common trait in all of us—the desire to "even the score," to pay others back for wrongs or hurts we have received. Webster defines vengeance as "Punishment inflicted in return for an injury or an offense; retribution; often passionate or unrestrained revenge." It comes from the same Latin root as vindictiveness, vindicate, to claim, defend, avenge. The very words have both thoughts imbedded in them: to claim what is rightfully ours and to punish or to get revenge. No wonder, then, that it is universally present in the human heart, no matter how spiritual we may think ourselves, or how loving we may have become.

That part of this week's theme is extremely important. We Christians know that it is wrong to seek revenge; that it is wrong to foster hatred and bitterness, and it is completely antithetical and contrary to the spirit of Jesus. So far, so good. But what happens practically, experientially, and emotionally when someone really hurts us is that what comes up in us is the strong desire to strike back—verbally or otherwise! And no one is more merciless than the person who perceives himself or herself as a helpless victim!

We are then faced with a dilemma. We should not be vindictive. "Beloved, never avenge yourselves, but leave it to the wrath of God; for it is written, 'Vengeance is mine, I will repay, says the Lord'" (Romans 12:19). There are two important words here: If we seek to avenge ourselves (claim what is rightfully ours in retribution) we usurp the place which belongs only to God. "Vengeance is mine," says the Lord. He has never delivered it over to us, and we have no right to take it in our hands, no matter what we feel! That is a big order, and something we need to take to heart seriously whenever the desire rises up within us. The second thing is his promise, "I will repay," says the Lord. Do you believe it? Do you really believe that God's justice will ultimately prevail, and that you do not have to worry about the other person going unpunished for his or her wrong? Can you leave it to him to do what is right and fair? In other words, do you believe, really believe, in the justice of a loving God? If so, then by his grace and with the power of the Holy Spirit you will be able to release the person who has wronged you from your personal demand that he or she get what is coming to them. You can leave him or her to God, and then be free of the controlling compulsion to straighten things out and get even.

A Prayer: Father! Help me to recognize the forces within myself which would demand and seek vengeance when I feel that I have been wronged. As I become aware of them, help me by grace to leave them on the altar of sacrifice, knowing how much I have wronged thee, and how greatly I have been forgiven. Then let me face those who have hurt me without bitterness or desire to get even, and show a Christ-like spirit toward them. I can only do this with thy help, which I ask in the Name of Jesus Christ my Lord. Amen.

1. Where do you have a strong desire to strike back?

2. In what ways do you see yourself as a helpless victim?

The Revenge of Potiphar's Wife
Daily Reading: Genesis 39

Thinking about vindictiveness, we turn to one of the classic examples of it in the Bible. In this lesson, we see how easily feelings can change from attraction to hate when self-will is crossed and pride is injured.

The story is too familiar to need repeating again, so let us think in terms that apply to our situation today.

Have I felt humiliated or rejected by someone close to me? Is my response, like Potiphar's wife, (more respectably, of course) to act in such a way that the person will be hurt?

Our reaction to such humiliation or rejection may be a definite withdrawal, ignoring, shunning of the other person. Or we may find ourselves saying or thinking very unkind things about her or him. Gossip surely has in it the element of unconscious vindictiveness as well as of jealousy. And if we would allow our hurts and slights to come to the surface, deal with them at the cross of Jesus Christ, forgiving and seeking forgiveness, gossip would surely stop. Nothing can so quickly mar and destroy true fellowship as backbiting and gossip.

Potiphar's wife disappears from our story, so we cannot know what befell her eventually. We have to leave that in God's hidden operations, as we have to leave much of the "unfairness" of life in his hands, trusting him to work according to his nature and his wisdom. But we do see Joseph, punished wrongly, yet letting it all mold and meld him into a more merciful and forgiving person. God was in it, using even this wrong to shape and mold Joseph for his special role in salvation history. So nothing was and nothing is lost, as long as we keep looking to God in every situation, no matter how unfair it seems, and no matter how people may look as though they are "getting away with it."

A Prayer: Lord Jesus, everywhere and always inspire us to refuse the evil and choose the good; and we beseech thee, give us grace never to judge our neighbor rashly, whilst one by one we ourselves endeavor to learn and perform thy will, for thine own Name's sake, Amen. (Christina G. Rossetti, 1830)

1. Where (like Potiphar's wife) in your life have you been hurt or rejected by someone and you've wanted to act in such a way that that person will be hurt?

2. Rather than be hurt by unfair treatment, Joseph allowed the wrong punishment to mold and meld him into a more merciful and forgiving person. Where do you need to stop fighting the circumstances of your life and give up anger and vindictiveness?

The Revenge of Ahab
Daily Reading: 1 Kings 22

"There is yet one man by whom we may inquire of the Lord, Micaiah the son of Imah; but I hate him, for he never prophesies good concerning me, but evil." (v. 8)

Ahab had all the prophets money could buy! They were ready at a moment's notice to prophesy whatever the king wished. They were skilled in flattery and in making it sound pious and holy. So when the king of Israel wanted to have spiritual confirmation before setting out on what could be a dangerous undertaking (going to battle against Ramoth-Gilead), Ahab just sent for his court prophets, who easily detected what he wanted and accommodated him accordingly.

It is all too easy to fall into the same pattern of telling people what they like to hear in order to gain their approval, or to have them tell us what we like to hear! It is a kind of quid pro quo: you tell me I'm O.K., and I'll tell you you're O.K. But at what cost! At the cost of a relationship with depth and meaning. It is a thin veneer of a relationship which cannot bear any real weight when trouble comes and real feelings come out!

Ahab was not a man who liked to hear anything bad about himself. He was like the saying on the coffee mug a friend gave me some years ago. It pictured two frogs standing with their arms across each others shoulders, and underneath it said, "You can always tell a smart man: His views are the same as yours!" That is especially true when people's views about us confirm what we want to think about ourselves!

Vindictiveness came into play immediately in this story when Micaiah was called. One thing about Micaiah: he would tell what he thought was the truth even to the king! But no sooner had he done so (prophesying that if Ahab returned from the battle alive that the Lord had not spoken by him) than the king ordered Micaiah thrown into a dungeon.

One wonders as we read this story if our reaction is all that different inside when people tell us unwelcome truth! What comes up, unless we really flee to Jesus and pray for grace to hear, is a desire to silence the speaker and discount the message.

Ahab took his revenge on the prophet, for after all, he was king. But in the end, how much wiser he would have been to sacrifice his pride, hear what the man of God was saying and change his course. His story would have ended differently.

Thanks be to God that we can put down and refuse to live out the desires that spring up in us when people say unwelcome things to us! We can "agree with our adversary quickly," (as Jesus told us) and move into a chastened, more realistic, and more wholesome view of ourselves, and find acceptance and love which we might never have realized otherwise.

A Prayer: Thank you, Father, for those who speak to me, even when I wish they would not! I pray for a hearing ear and a listening heart so that I will be able to respond as Jesus would have me respond, not demanding constant approval of everything I do or say, but treasuring honest relationships which can grow and mature in you. This is your gift of grace to me, and I thank you for it. In Jesus' Name. Amen.

1. In what relationships have you sought to gain approval by telling people what you think they want to hear?

2. What people in your life have you desired to silence or ignore in order to discount their message of truth?

God's Vengeance
Daily Reading: Ezekiel 25

A lot of Christians fret over the unfair things of life. We may openly or secretly (unconsciously) carry great anger at God for many years because of some wrong that was done to us or something in our lives which we felt was unfair. This can be a great hindrance to growth in our discipleship and a block in our spiritual maturity. Sometimes people carry bitterness toward wrongs inflicted on them in childhood and bitterness toward those who inflicted them to such an extent that they are spiritually stunted and physically sickened by it.

Today's chapter may seem strange at first, for it is a direct Word of the Lord to four nations, neighbors of Israel: The Ammonites, Moabites, Edomites and the Philistines—and to each of them God promises fearful vengeance for past specific wrongs done against his people.

What does that say to you and me? Does it not reassure us again that we can leave all in God's hands, and give up the bitterness which may have poisoned the stream of our lives up to now? God's mill grinds slowly, but grinds exceeding fine, as the old saying goes. But knowing this, do we dare go on demanding "the pound of flesh" from those who have wronged us? Do we not rather act wisely by forsaking wrath and leaving it with God?

Yea, when their wrath against us fiercely rose
The swelling tide had o'er us spread its wave,
The raging stream had then become our grave,
The surging flood, in proudly swelling roll
Most surely then had overwhelmed our soul.

Blest be the Lord, who made us not their prey:
As from the snare a bird escapeth free,
Their net is rent and so escaped are we,
Our only help is in God's holy Name,
Who made the earth and all the heavenly frame.
    (The Psalter, 1912, from Psalm 124)

A Prayer: Have mercy on us, O Lord, and teach us to be merciful for Jesus' sake. Amen.

1. What are the places in your life that you consider you have been treated unfairly?

2. How have you dealt or are you dealing with these feelings?

Silencing Truth
Daily Reading: Mark 6:7–29

John the Baptist was like Elijah of old—fearless in his confrontation with corruption mixed with power. He did not hesitate to "call a spade a spade" and hold the standards of God up to all—high and low alike. Herod, the king had unlawfully married his brother's wife, after divorcing his own. Heedless of his own safety, John cried out against this, and Herodias "had a grudge against him and wanted to kill him" (v. 19). As we have seen this week already, it was always dangerous to be a true prophet, for those in power did not take lightly to unwelcome truth, and the prophet's only protection was God himself. In John the Baptist's case, Herodias finally succeeded in her wicked plan to silence him, when Herod, drunk and swollen with vanity, promised Salome, Herodias' daughter "whatever you ask me, . . . even half my kingdom." At her mother's bidding, Salome asked for the head of John.

It is good to look at this story in two aspects: that of the person who is determined to get even and that of the person who has risked much for the sake of truth.

When a person "speaks truth" to another, we cannot always be sure that the motive is unmixed, pure love. John loved God and was intensely committed to proclaiming a message that cut the diseased growth of Israel to the very ground, so that a healthy, wholesome nation might rise up. His message was "The Kingdom of heaven is at hand: Repent!" It was not an easy-going reassuring message. It stirred hearts deeply, and some went to be baptized by him in the Jordan, confessing their sins. Others mocked and waited to see him get into trouble. But whatever the motive or whatever the mixture of motives may be in the person who dares to speak truth to us, he or she is taking a risk. Even the very relationship itself may be risked. Parents instinctively feel this about their children as they grow older, and often refrain from speaking words which could turn their children into the right way out of fear of losing the relationship. Husbands and wives often make silent pacts (unspoken) with one another, not to confront the other in special, sensitive areas, for fear of retaliation by the other. When one speaks freely, we need to examine our motives before God, and see that we are no better than (indeed, greater sinners than) the person to whom we are speaking. From the standpoint of the speaker, that is an important prerequisite for effective truth speaking.

But when another is speaking to us, we have no right to demand of them scrutiny of their motives, etc. We owe it to God, to the other person, and to ourselves, to listen and fight the desire in us to retaliate. Only in this way can we move beyond the knee-jerk, reflexive "get even" syndrome and let God use other people—even with their impure, mixed motives—to correct and bless us.

A Prayer: O God of grace and truth, I say that I love the truth, yet there is that in me, which hates to hear it when it corrects or challenges me. Forgive my haughtiness in reacting badly when another person points out something wrong that I have said, or done, or some wrong attitude I have displayed.

*Let my love of truth and desire to change and grow in Christ
be greater than my self-love which smarts and wants to strike
back! And let Jesus be the Victor in me. Spirit of Truth prevail
in me! Amen.*

1. Herodias held a grudge against John because of the truth he
had spoken to her. In what ways are you vindictive when
someone says something to you that you do not like to hear?

A New Commandment

Daily Reading: 1 Thessalonians 5

Jesus gave us "a new commandment," on the very night of
his betrayal and arrest. That commandment is "Love one
another as I have loved you." Here in today's reading Paul
says it in a little different way. He talks about esteeming those
who labor among us and "over us" in the Lord; those who
"admonish" us; to be at peace among ourselves; admonishing
the idle, encouraging the weak and faint-hearted, patient with
all. Then he talks about our attitude toward those who actually do us evil. "See that none of you repays evil for evil, but
always seek to do good to one another and to all" (v. 15).
Earlier this week we have thought about our reactions to
admonition. Admonition is defined as "friendly reproof;
counseling against a fault or oversight; warning."

Then we are carried beyond that friendly counsel, to a situation
where someone does "evil" to us. We live in an evil world,
and there are times when everyone of us experiences what the
apostle is talking about here. People do bad things to other
people. People say false and unkind things about other people.
People do evil to one another. Have we not all experienced it?

If we are not prepared to handle such a situation, we are living in some kind of unreality about human nature and its effects.

But what can we do? When you find yourself the target of unfair, false, and malicious charges, whisperings, gossip and slander, what do you do? If you do not let it drive you to your knees before Jesus Christ, it can (1) make you bitter and vindictive, (2) destroy your peace of heart and conscience, and (3) impair your health—either or all of these! So when evil is done to us, real, malicious evil, flee to the cross. Gaze there upon One who when reviled did not revile back; who did not open his mouth to his accusers, and who prayed for them, "Father, forgive them, for they know not what they do." How can we stay long at that cross, and see the "sorrow and love" that came streaming down to us in all our unworthiness, and then get up and desire to wreak vengeance upon those who for reasons we do not understand (and which they do not fully understand) seek to do us harm? Our safety, our defense, and our hope is in Jesus and who he is; in God, our mighty fortress. We do not have to repay evil. For once we have started on that course, and allowed the bitter poison to seep through our souls, what more do we than those whom we call "evil"? Has not the devil won the victory by enticing us to stoop to the same level? God forbid! Let those who seek to follow Christ flee unto him for succor and comfort, and leave the judgment with God!

A Prayer: Bless O Lord, all our relations, friends, and all who have been kind to us, all who love us, and care for our good. Turn the hearts of those who love us not, and think evil of us. Kill in us all the seeds of envy and ill will; and help us by cultivating within us the love of our neighbor, to improve in the love of thee ; through Jesus Christ our Lord. Amen. (Adapted)

1. What do you do when you find yourself the target of unfair or false charges, gossip, or slander?

2. How can the Lord cultivate within you love of your neighbor?

Counted Worthy

Daily Reading: Acts 5:12–42

Then they left the presence of the council, rejoicing that they were counted worthy to suffer dishonor for the Name. (v. 41)

The apostles were arrested for teaching and healing and thrown into prison, but were released by an angel, and instructed to again stand and teach in the temple. Seized a second time, they were carried before the Council, and after declaring that "We must obey God rather than men," were beaten, charged not to speak in the name of Jesus and released.

They then had a choice. They could become cowardly, bitter, resentful that they could not follow God without such a price being extracted. Or, they could do what they did: "They left the presence of the council, rejoicing that they were counted worthy to suffer dishonor for the Name" (v. 41).

As we finish this week's thoughts about our innate, human desire to get even, let this lesson carry our minds and hearts to a higher plane. There is something noble here which should appeal to every one of us. God's honor is at stake, and some are called to "suffer dishonor for the Name." Not everyone. Not even every Christian. But some are called to bear that burden, carry that part of the cross for the sake of the body of Christ. The apostles counted it an honor. Do we?

Speaking personally, when it has happened to me, I have had a hard time fighting self-pity, resentment, and the desire to get even with those who were perpetrating the injury! Yet, it seems to me, we are all called to be willing to go this way should God choose to lead us in it.

You cannot be a Christian without paying a price. The world is still hostile to the things of God, for the world spirit is antithetical to the spirit of God. So those who follow Jesus will suffer some degree and some form of rejection and persecution. It may be slight, or it may be severe. But there is grace for whatever degree is laid upon us. But above all, we must not allow it to harden us into self-righteousness! If there is one thing above all that is unbecoming to a child of God it is this rigid, Pharisaical spirit of superior rightness over those who are not Christians, or those who are not "of our kind."

The apostles were free to be themselves, to go about their lives as God was leading them, because they were not waiting to see the judgment of God fall on their enemies, and they were not comparing their own rightness with the other people's wrongness.

A Prayer: Thank you, Father, for the grace to bear whatever in your wisdom and will comes into our lives. Grant us to love the unlovely, to speak and act according to your will as best we can understand it, and to leave the results with you. And save us from the scourge of self-righteous judgment of those who do us wrong. For we are not worthy of the great love you have shown us, and we are ever dependent on your mercy and grace. In Jesus' Name. Amen.

1. How do you fight self-pity, resentment, and the desire to get even with those who have hurt you?

2. How can you daily stop comparing your rightness with other people's wrongness?

Chapter Review

A cliche says: "Don't get mad—get even!" How many of us follow such advice? Vindictiveness is often a subconscious process, waiting for an opportunity to "even the score." Wives and husbands may refuse to argue a point, but rather wait to even the score when the other is in a vulnerable position. Humor is often used as a weapon of vindictiveness.

It may even be that we wait self-righteously for another to fall or be exposed as wrong. Our feelings in such a case betray that the sin of vindictiveness lurks in our hearts.

God alone is safely able to avenge. When we take it on ourselves, we continue the see-saw of "who is going to win?" Ask God to teach you more about vindictiveness and learn how it operates in your life.

1. What process is necessary before we can treat our "enemy" in the way described in Romans 12:20?

2. After considering the subject of vindictiveness, do you see more clearly in what circumstances you become vindictive? What are they?

EVERY DAY IS A NEW BEGINNING
THE CROSS BEFORE US AND THE PAST BEHIND US!

Many are the
afflictions of the
righteous; but the
LORD delivers him
out of them all.

Psalm 34:19

TWENTY-ONE

Delivered!
Daily Reading: Psalm 34

I sought the Lord, and he answered me, and delivered me from all my fears. (v. 4)

This entire psalm is a psalm of testimony and hope. David is able to trust the Lord today because of what God has done in the past.

As we move along, if we are like most people, we need from time to time a real sense of beginning again. Any task can become wearisome, especially one which calls for discipline and self-denial. And so it is with this task which we have undertaken in the belief that God will help us.

First of all, remember his help in the past. Remember, whenever you are tempted to grow discouraged, those blessed moments when light and hope pierced through, and you *knew* that God was on your side helping you. We all have them, but it is easy to forget. Perhaps they are like the seed down by the roadside, and the birds of the air (the frets and cares and concerns of the day) come in and pluck them away to keep them from taking root. Remembering, giving thanks and rejoicing in God's delivering help can make a powerful weapon against discouragement. This is what the Lord's Supper, Holy Communion, does for us. It focuses our eyes on that time when God in Christ poured out his life for us. Who can be hopeless in the face of such limitless love?

Second, "forgetting those things that lie behind," take today as a new and fresh start. Past failures, mistakes, disobediences are past. But today is a new opportunity to go further in our walk of faith and obedience. Today is God's gift, in which he beckons us onward in our life in him. "Look to him and be radiant" (v. 5) so your face shall never be ashamed. He has delivered us in the past, and he will free us in this present.

A Prayer: Father, it is nothing but self-centered forgetfulness that could keep me from remembering all you have done in the past. Thank you for reminding me of your faithfulness, and by grace enable me to live this day faithfully. In Jesus' Name, Amen.

1. What are your best weapons against discouragement?

2. During the last nine weeks, list the places where you have seen God's special help.

Do Not Rejoice in Success!
Daily Reading: Luke 10:1–20

"Nevertheless, do not rejoice in this, that the spirits are subject to you; but rejoice that your names are written in heaven." (v. 20)

This may at first seem to be a strange scripture to put into our thoughts, when we are moving along toward a goal we believe to be good and right for us. After all, success is one of the goals that pulls us forward, is it not?

But Jesus knows the danger of success! He knows its potential temptation and its brevity. If we work simply for some longed-for goal, once we reach it we may become momentarily dizzied by it. It has happened to many. We see it sometimes in public figures who allow the adulation of the crowd to blind them to the realities of life. Becoming intoxicated with adulation, they become addicted to it, and live only for more and more approval. And it has the power to destroy, literally to take the soul out of a person. On a less dramatic scale we may have seen it or felt it in our own lives. This distinction has, alas, happened to successful spiritual leaders at times, who allowed their God-given success to "go to their head" and plunged forward disastrously to their own ruin and the scandalizing of those who followed them.

Jesus is saying that some things are so much more important that we should make them the object of our rejoicing. If we are more keenly aware of him, if we are more sensitive to the needs and hurts of others, if we are living in the peace which passes understanding, knowing that our "names are written in heaven," then our rejoicing is grounded in him and what he is doing. It is cause enough for rejoicing. And it is a rejoicing that can go on and on, as *we* grow in the grace and knowledge of our Savior.

A Prayer: Success and beauty—how often have I longed for them or gloried in them! But Lord, I would rejoice in your beauty and pray for more beauty of spirit. I would rejoice in the victory you have won for me in your sacrificial life and death, and praise you for ever and ever. Amen.

1. Do you see places in your life where you are motivated by desire for success or adulation? What are they?

Job's Rightness
Daily Reading: Job 1:1–5, 6:22–30

"Turn now, my vindication is at stake. Is there any wrong on my tongue?" (v. 29b and 30a)

Job is the picture of a man whose whole soul desired to be right before the Lord. He made it his care and concern always to do the right thing. "He feared God and turned away from evil" (1:1). And God blessed him with sons and daughters and with great wealth. So far, so good.

But then a cloud enters the picture, and God allows Satan permission to test Job. As we read this sometimes difficult book, we may be astonished and even dismayed to think how much calamity befell this good and right man. How easy it is to identify with him as he utters his complaints against his "comforters" and even against God, who seemed so far away and so uncaring!

Through these pages, one thing comes out very clearly. Job was thoroughly convinced of his rightness, and could hear no suggestion of wrongness in himself. His righteousness was the deepest core of his being.

We must read this story against the backdrop of all that we have come to know about God and about ourselves. We must remember that God had a purpose in allowing this evil to come upon his servant, not because he is unkind, or because he had forgotten Job in his trouble. Rather, his purpose overarched all that was happening, a purpose that even Satan did not understand!

It is intended to show all of us that our hope and trust must not be in what we are able to achieve. Such a burden is too much for us. We need a lighter yoke and an easier burden. Our rightness is too heavy a load to carry. So God invites us to put it down, to strive for something more worthy and more attainable. To strive to know ourselves better, to seek the grace to accept ourselves as needy, weak mortal creatures is a task far more worthy than that of trying to stay right, defend our rightness in all circumstances and to make it the badge of our honor.

Hear this in the right way: We need the freedom to fail! Failure is not the worst thing in the world. It may even be necessary to break the hard crust of spiritual superiority we Christians build up around ourselves. if we humble ourselves,

God will not have to break us. But if we insist on living by our rightness, thinking we are too good, too strong, too loyal and true to fail—we may be in for a rude awakening!

Job's lesson was not for him alone. It was for us all.

A Prayer: Help me, Lord, to get my priorities straight to seek to be more open and willing to "be wrong" than to be proved right and superior. And give me grace to do this graciously, in Jesus' Name. Amen.

1. What steps can you take to lay down the heavy load of "your rightness"?

2. In practical day-to-day matters, how can you become more open and willing to "be wrong"?

Job's New Self-Knowledge
Daily Reading: Job 42

"But now my eye sees thee; therefore I despise myself and repent in dust and ashes." (v. 5b-6)

There came a moment in this long and painful encounter between Job and his friends when God himself entered the conversation. There comes a moment in our lives, when we have done with all the self-explanatory comebacks, all the protests of innocence and rightness, and we suddenly see the futility of it all! Why do we need to defend our rightness in any given situation when we know that we are so far from what we should be and, by grace, can become? Once we have truly seen ourselves against God's perfect example, Jesus

Christ, why do we have to uphold our honor and integrity (and pride) by insisting that we could not possibly be wrong, no matter what others may be saying to us?

How many arguments in families might be suddenly concluded if one or the other would say, "Wait a minute! I don't want to carry this on, defending myself and accusing you (even by implication). I am wrong. I want to hear, really hear what you are trying to say to me, and I'm afraid my self-righteousness has made me hard of hearing!" Do you think that would bring most arguments to an end?

Job was thoroughly and absolutely convinced that there was no wrong in him. God had allowed these terrible things to happen, and at one point God asks, "Will you even put me in the wrong? Will you condemn me that you may be justified?" (40:8). Yes, that is exactly what we are willing to do, that is the length we are willing to go once we get set on the track of not being wrong! Just think how your thoughts run when in your mind you accuse God of doing or allowing unloving things to happen to you or those you love.

But when that moment of self-knowledge came, and Job suddenly knew something he had not known before, he was ready to lay down his arguments, and simply to humble himself before the Lord. And his knowledge of himself increased his knowledge of the Lord. He was closer to God than he had been before.

This is surely one of the most basic and least understood truths of our whole Christian experience. It is the way to joy and peace.

A Prayer: Lord Jesus, when you were accused, you did not open your mouth in defense. Yet, when I feel accused, I have a multitude of words in my own defense, I see the folly of that, and how it robs me of much peace, how it damages my relationships with others. So teach me, Lord, the secret of how to meet every accusation fair or unfair, as you would have me do. Amen.

1. List the circumstances in which you have defended yourself (if only in your mind) and accused someone else this week.

2. Job's knowledge of himself increased his knowledge of the Lord. Where is this knowledge taking place in your life?

David's New Beginning

Daily Reading: Psalm 51

Restore to me the joy of thy salvation, and uphold me with a willing spirit. (v. 12)

At the beginning of this psalm are these words: "A Psalm of David, when Nathan the prophet came to him, after he had gone in to Bathsheba."

That tells us immediately that these timeless words grew out of the most shameful episode in David's life. He had lusted after the beautiful Bathsheba, committed adultery with her, and then, when he found that she was carrying his child, plotted to have her husband killed in battle, to cover up his previous sin. Not a very pretty picture of the man who is called "a man after God's own heart."

Yet it can be, and should be, a great encouragement to us. Not an encouragement to sin, of course! But an encouragement to see God's justice and mercy at work in the life of a man whose heart truly was "toward God." The Bible does not cover up the flaws in the lives of its heroes, and that is meant to help us see them as people of flesh and blood, prone to all the temptations and pitfalls that we experience. In their failures as well as their successes we are being encouraged never to let a failure or a relapse become the occasion of giving up.

Many of us do not realize when we are being tempted into sin that the adversary's real intent is to paralyze us and make us totally hopeless about ourselves. The momentary reward or pleasure we derive from the sin is scant reward for the devastating sense of condemnation, guilt, and despair which follow. What we need to do is what David did here. We need to go humbled and chastened before the throne of a holy God, confess whatever it is that needs confessing, take responsibility for what we have done, accept the forgiveness of our heavenly Father, forgive ourselves, and rise up to go on in his strength. We are ever in need of these new beginnings, because we have not reached perfection or perfect likeness to Jesus Christ.

But the thing to underscore is that there is a new beginning. We move from conviction of sin, the desire to be cleansed "through and through," pray for a new heart and a right spirit, and then, with our mouths filled with gratitude, we can "show forth" his praise.

Every day is a fresh beginning;
Listen, my soul, to the glad refrain,
And, spite of old sorrow and older sinning,
And puzzles forecasted and possible pain,
Take heart with the day, and begin again!
(Susan Coolidge)

A Prayer: O Lord, let us neither be pulled up with any vain confidence in ourselves nor cast down by any lack of trust in thee, but keep us in thankful dependence upon thy mercy and help. When we are alienated from thee and lose our way, recall us quickly to thy paths; and when in shame or fear we would flee from thee, let thy love lay hold on us—the love that stooped to the manger and suffered on the cross for us—for our hope is in thy merciful kindness; through Jesus Christ our Lord. Amen.

1. When have you let failure or relapse become the occasion of giving up?

2. Every day is a fresh beginning! Where do you need to realize that and begin again?

Restored
Daily Reading: Luke 18:9–14 and 1 John 2:1–2

This is a familiar parable, and the main object of it was to show that the Pharisee's "rightness" kept him from the blessing God would have given him. His rightness was a barrier between him and God.

But let us look at the other character in this little story—the tax gatherer. We all know that tax gatherers were perhaps the most despised people of that time. They were collaborators with the hated Roman overlords, and under the system of the time, they were free to impose as much tax "as the traffic would bear." In other words, they could charge the people whatever they could get away with, and then they had to pay only a certain amount (allotted by some calculation of the Romans) into the emperor's treasury. The rest they could keep for themselves, and most of them became wealthy. But the Jews considered their wealth blood money. So when Jesus chose a tax gatherer for this story, he reached down to the bottom of the social scale in order to make his point, just as in using the Pharisee, he reached to the top of the religious-piety scale.

But this man—the tax gatherer—went away from the temple with a new beginning. "He went down to his home justified," says our Lord. There is something very touching and exciting about those words. For if this man, whose whole way of life was a stench in the nostrils of his people, could have a new beginning we need not despair!

The passage from John underscores this tremendous reality, saying "if anyone does sin, we have an advocate with the Father, Jesus Christ the Righteous." So there it is again, the offer of the Lord held out to us in our repeated neediness to a new beginning. So let the theme of the week become a reality in your life: nothing can or should deter you from your onward way with Jesus. No amount of failure is any reason for not getting up and going on today.

Since the Lord waits to be gracious, why should we not accept his grace and go forward? Every day is a new beginning!

He who would valiant be
'Gainst all disaster,
Let him in constancy
Follow the Master.
There's no discouragement
Shall make him once relent
His first avowed intent
To be a pilgrim.
    (John Bunyan, 1684, alt. English Hymnal Version)

A Prayer: O God, by whom the meek are guided in judgment, and light riseth up in darkness for the godly; Grant us, in all our doubts and uncertainties, the grace to ask what thou wouldest have us to do, that the Spirit of Wisdom may save us from, all false choices, and that in thy light we may see light, and in thy straight path may not stumble; through Jesus Christ our Lord, Amen.

(Book of Common Prayer)

1. Like the Pharisee, whose rightness kept him from the blessing of God, is there any "rightness" you are hanging onto that might prevent you from a new beginning with God today?

2. "He went down to his home justified." How can you, like the tax gatherer, do that today?

Do Not Lose Heart
Daily Reading: Luke 18:1–8

And he told them a parable to the effect that they ought always to pray and not lose heart. (v. 1)

Every day is a new beginning! That they ought . . . not lose heart." Are these not the same thing? Jesus invites us to a way of living which is so new, so radically different, so simple, yet for us at times, so difficult that we need such encouragements! And so he told this simple little story about a poor widow and a judge so crooked that he "neither feared God nor regarded man." Yet the judge was the widow's only hope of vindication. And so she kept coming back, pleading, demanding, praying, urging, pestering—until the judge could stand it no longer. Her persistence won out!

Jesus, in his characteristic fashion, had taken a human picture and made it divine. If a human judge, so unjust as this man, would yield finally to the pleas of this widow, he is saying how much more will your heavenly Father, true, just, and merciful as he is, yield to your persistent prayer.

Transfer this, then, to the rest of our lives: to our stumbling, our failures, our disappointments in ourselves. If we take these to him, with the same persistence, can we doubt that he will bring us through? Our problem, both in our prayers and in all our spiritual disciplines, is that we are apt to give up when we should be doggedly pressing through. Many places give us this same principle: "The kingdom of heaven suffers violence, and violent men take it by force" (Matthew 11:12). In other words, the eager press into the kingdom, forcing themselves beyond the usual, the comfortable, the easy conformity to their old lives. It is this that will bring results: our willingness to go through the barriers of our old habits of thought, feeling, and action. This persistence we offer to God as evidence of our desire to be done with our old ways. He has promised and he will faithfully fulfill his promise, to give us all the grace and help we need. So, thank God for the new beginnings we have today! There is only one thing that can defeat us: if we let down and give up. Otherwise, if, like Paul, we "press toward the mark," we are sure of finding that newness of life in which he calls us to walk.

A Prayer: Thank you, Father, for this encouraging word not to lose heart. Thank you for being near, even closer than breathing. You know my need even before I do, and you still call me to press on toward the mark. With your help, I will. In Jesus' Name. Amen.

1. Why do you not need to be afraid of failing? How can this make you more free?

2. In what areas of your life do you need to be more persistent and persevering?

3. How can you do that?

Chapter Review

Many of us do not allow for failure in our self-expectation, so we are confounded and angry when failure comes.

The psalmist knew reality (and himself) well enough to know that he would not always be "in victory." But his faith in God was based on experiencing trouble and deliverance, need and help. "This poor man cried and the Lord heard him and saved him out of all his troubles."

Paul the apostle knew the sting of failure. In Romans 7, he discusses the dilemma of wanting to do good but failing to do so. It is not to excuse our sin or our spiritual laxness to face this truth, and to learn to live with the certain knowledge that failure is not the end.

Jesus taught us to pray, "Forgive us our debts as we forgive our debtors" (Matthew 6:12). What are these "debts" he speaks of if they are not continuing failure to be all that we should be and were created to be? If there were no failure, there would be no need for forgiveness!

Through our failure we learn more deeply who we are as creatures and sinners, and we learn the tremendous help God gives to those who in their failures cry out to him. We do not have to be afraid of failing. All we need to do is to go one step at a time—forward! Every day is a new beginning.

1. What have you learned about others through their failures? (Read Jeremiah 17:5 and 6 before you write your answer.)

2. What have you learned about yourself through your failures? (Read Jeremiah 17:9.)

3. What have you learned about God in your failures?

FEAR: FAITH IN THE WRONG PERSON—YOU!

"FACE THE THING YOU FEAR THE MOST
AND THE DEATH OF FEAR IS CERTAIN."

*For God hath
not given us the
spirit of fear;
but of power and
of love, and of a
sound mind.*

2 Timothy 1:7 (KJV)

TWENTY-TWO

No Spirit of Fear
Daily Reading: 2 Timothy 1

For God did not give us a spirit of timidity, but a spirit of power and love and self-control. (v. 7)

The King James version translates that verse like this: "For God hath not given us the spirit of fear, but of power and love and of a sound mind."

Fear takes many forms. It may be a warning signal which we receive inwardly and react to by simply not venturing forth or trying the thing which seems fearful. Many people bind themselves into a terrible bondage with such fear, perhaps not even realizing that they are slaves to it. One woman always planned her trips or vacations around the fact that under no circumstances would she fly. This automatically ruled out any part of the world where, for practical reasons, flying would be the only means of getting there. Another hid her talent for singing "under a bushel" because she always got stage fright when she started to sing. Instead of pressing through the possibility of loss of pride if she should make a mistake, she refused to sing, and missed the blessing of the gift God had given her. Then someone *insisted* that she must sing out of obedience to God! The result was dramatic, and not only was she blessed, but many others, too.

What form does your fear take? The apostle says we were not given a spirit of timidity. Are you aware that shyness is a form of fear, and that it is not glorifying to God? How many of us who are "shy by nature" stop to think about the fact that we are protecting raging egos?

Pray this week for the Lord to bring up the areas of fear that you are being run and ruled by. He has given us the "spirit of power and love and self-control." It is up to us to claim the gift and develop it. We can overcome fear, instead of being overcome by it. Courage is not the absence of fear. It is learning to look fear in the face and going on in spite of it. Let's seek that kind of victory over every area where fear still lurks!

A Prayer: We bring thee, Father, our daily work, our hopes and dreams, and every experience, of our lives. Whatsoever our hand findeth to do, let us do it in faith and prayer, that we may fulfill thy gracious design. Through Jesus Christ our Lord. Amen.

(James Ferguson)

1. What are some of your present fears?

2. What form does your fear take?

Fear of Others
Daily Reading: John 20:19–31

. . . The doors being shut where the disciples were, for fear of the Jews, Jesus came and stood among them and said to them, "Peace be with you." (v. 19)

If any group ever had legitimate cause to be afraid, the disciples were the group. Their Leader had been crucified, dying the death of the lowest criminal. And since they were known to be associated with him, believing and preaching the same message that he had taught, there was no reason for them to suppose that they would be allowed to get away with it. So they gathered secretly behind closed doors, "for fear of the Jews."

The wonderful thing in this story is that those closed doors did not keep Jesus out! "The doors being shut . . . Jesus came and stood among them." That should encourage us to know that, even when we retreat behind closed doors, Jesus can still get in and speak his healing and reassuring word to us. He did not tell them that they would have no opposition and trouble. He had already warned them over and over again that in this world they would suffer persecution. But now, in their fear, he speaks his word of peace. And that is important.

Is our fear of what others will do or how they will react to us, or what they might say about us, as well-founded as was the disciples' fear of the Jews? In all the difficulty that you or I may have experienced as followers of Jesus, have we faced a danger as great as that? I doubt it! Why then, let fear of others shut us in, make cripples of us, keep us from enjoying and growing in our faithwalk with Jesus Christ? Whatever ridicule or disapproval we might incur will do us no real harm. In fact, if we let it, it may very well be used by God to help us look at some things about ourselves that are not very pretty. When people say negative things about us, there is often some truth hidden in the chaff of their prickly words!

As you learn to be honest and to speak the truth in love to those close to you, you will find that, though the truth may hurt, it will also heal and free. And you will also find that your sensitive reaction to criticism (even implied criticism) is but the reaction of a wounded pride. Knowing that, you can tell the Lord you are sorry for being prideful and ask him to continue to work a real change in your heart.

Never fear what others can do to you. They are not your final judge nor your final hope.

A Prayer: Set free, O Lord, the souls of thy servants from all restlessness and anxiety. Give us that peace and power which flow from thee. Keep us in all perplexity and distress that upheld by thy strength; and stayed on the rock of thy faithfulness, we may abide in thee now and evermore. Amen. (S. F. Fox)

1. What reactions of other people do you especially fear?

2. How can you be set free from this fear?

Whom Shall I Fear?

Daily Reading: Psalm 27

The LORD is the stronghold of my life; of whom shall I be afraid? (v. 1b)

This is one of the most beautiful psalms in the entire Psalter. If you have never learned it by heart, it might be a good thing for you to attempt. What assurance and blessing there is in its phrases: Though a host encamp against me, my heart shall not fear." "He will hide me in his shelter (or pavilion) in the day of trouble." "When my father and mother forsake me, the LORD will take me up!" And many more.

David makes it clear that his reason for confidence in the face of those who threaten him is not his own strength or bravery. It is because "The LORD is the stronghold of my life." He has progressed far enough in his relationship of trust and faith to be able to say this. Have we? Or do we still try in our own strength to meet those situations which threaten our security, our peace of mind, or the lives and welfare of those we love?

Luther, the great Reformer, said it like this: Did we in our own strength confide Our striving would be losing.

Like David, he is saying that his strength is not his own, but is the Lord within. And that same strength is ours, can be ours, is meant to be ours! Whatever trouble is allowed to come upon us, we are not meant to sink down under it in craven fear and self-pity, saying "Oh, I'm just not able to stand this!" We are meant to fall down upon our knees and say, "The Lord is the stronghold of my life: Of whom shall I be afraid?" And if there is still fear there we must confess it, because it is an accusation against the goodness, the power and the love and care of our heavenly Father! Fear is saying "I am the only stronghold of my life, and I'm not strong enough." Of course you aren't! No one is! But God is and God has promised to those who love and follow him that he will give us grace and strength sufficient for every need! Not just some needs, but every need. "Of whom shall I be afraid?" "Wait for the LORD, and let your heart take courage; yea, wait for the LORD" (v. 14).

A Prayer: May the strength of God pilot us. May the power of God preserve us. May the wisdom of God instruct us. May the hand of God protect us. May the way of God direct us. May the shield of God defend us. May the host of God guard us against the snares of evil and the temptations of the world. May Christ be with us, Christ before us, Christ in us, Christ over us. May thy salvation, O Lord, be always ours, this day and for evermore. Amen. (St. Patrick's Breastplate, AD 389–461)

1. How, in your life, have you allowed fear to come upon you?

2. The psalmist says, "Wait for the LORD and let your heart take courage." How can you practice this?

Fear of Death
Daily Reading: Hebrews 2

Since therefore the children share in flesh and blood, he himself likewise partook of the same nature, that through death he might destroy him who has the power of death, that is, the devil, and deliver all those who through fear of death were subject to lifelong bondage. (vv. 14-15)

John Wesley was brought up in a strict, devout home. His father was a clergyman of the Church of England, and his mother, Susanna, was the daughter of a clergyman, and was herself well trained in spiritual things. But John was always plagued by an old harassment—the fear of dying. After his experience which has since been termed "the Aldersgate experience," in which he felt his heart "strangely warmed," and a new faith in Christ and Christ alone had arisen in his heart, he noticed one thing in particular. When the old fear of death came back, he hurled in the enemy's face the fact that he trusted in Christ and his redemptive work for his salvation, and he found that the fear departed!

Most of us have an underlying fear of death—of being no more, of being cut off from loved ones and the joys we have known in the world. Much of the raucous noise and so-called music of the world is a kind of desperate din to drive away such thoughts or feelings.

Christians have never been taught to take death lightly, or to pretend that it is a good friend. Our text today clearly says that it is the devil who has the power of death. In other words, death is not a part of God's good creation, but is something that sin brought into our experience, and something which had to be dealt with by God himself. And this he has done in Jesus—taking death itself as the weapon against it—Jesus allowed death to do all that it could, and yet prevailed. No wonder Christians have flocked to the church on Easter to celebrate his victory!

He shows us the way to handle the fear of death: by voluntarily laying down our lives to God. If we allow God to do with us as he chooses, and learn to give up insisting on our own way, we will find that our fear of what the future holds—even of death itself—will lessen. Jesus, long before the cross, said, "I came not to do my own will, but the will of my Father who sent me." If we will practice doing his will, our morbid fear of what is going to happen to us will fade, and we will begin to taste the freedom from that bondage which he offers us even now.

A Prayer: O Lord Jesus Christ, who when thou hadst conquered death didst bless those who have not seen thee and yet have believed; forgive us who, like thy disciples, are slow of heart to believe, and pour into our hearts the joy of faith unspeakable and full of glory; that being risen with thee in heart and mind, we may seek those things which are above, where thou sittest on the right hand of God, and livest and reignest with the Father and the Holy Spirit, world without end. Amen. (Fredrick B. McNutt)

1. How has the fear of death been a problem to you?

2. In what way does Christ show us how to handle the fear of death?

Be Not Anxious
Daily Reading: Matthew 6:19–34

*"Therefore I tell you, do not be anxious about your life,
what you shall eat, or what you shall drink, nor about your
body, what you shall put on. . . . Do not be anxious about
tomorrow, for tomorrow will be anxious for itself."*
(vv. 26 and 34a)

Jesus would not have told us, "Do not be anxious," if it
were not possible to achieve this state of life. He recognizes
and mentions the source of so much of our anxiety: security,
clothing, the future. What would you add to those as the
sources of your own anxiety?

The foundation of freedom from such anxiety is the knowledge
of who God is and our relationship to him. The Father, says
Jesus, clothes the lilies of the field more gorgeously than
Solomon himself was ever clothed. He feeds the birds of the
air and not one of them falls to the ground without the
Father's care. Knowing that this God is our heavenly Father
should enable us to relax and trust him to make it possible for
us to earn all that we need for ourselves and our families. If
we put into practice the law of faith which Jesus is teaching
us, we will find that it brings results. Over and over again he
bids us believe, trust, believe, trust—be living in God. God's
supply is greater than our need, and our little horizons need
enlarging to take in the plenitude of God's supply.

But there is a condition, if you will—a provision which God
has laid down for our spiritual life and growth: "Seek first his
kingdom and righteousness." God will not become a cosmic
genie, to be pulled out of Aladdin's lamp every time we want
something for ourselves. It doesn't work that way, for that

would mean spiritual death rather than life. If we get our priorities straight, and really begin to long for and seek God's will and rule (his kingdom) in ourselves first of all, "all these things will be yours as well." So there is no room for worry, no cause for anxiety.

A very famous Christian, the late beloved Corrie Ten Boom, had been imprisoned in the notorious Nazi prison camp at Ravensbruck. She had witnessed the death of her aged father shortly after he was arrested for helping Jews escape from the Nazis, and she witnessed the death of her sister, Betsy, shortly before she, Corrie, was miraculously released from prison through a "clerical error." Corrie had a favorite phrase which you can make your own. "There is no panic in heaven; only plans."

We really do not have to continue living in anxiety. The peace of God which passes all understanding can become ours, as we allow God to lead us into deeper trust and greater obedience to his will for us.

A Prayer. O God, what is before us, we know not whether we shall live or die, but this we know: that all things are ordered and sure. Everything is ordered with unerring wisdom and unbounded love by thee, our God, Who art love. Grant us in all things to see thy hand. Through Jesus Christ our Lord. Amen.

(Rev. C. Simeon, 1759)

1. What are the sources of your anxiety?

2. How can the peace of God be yours daily?

Fear of Humiliation
Daily Reading: Exodus 4:1–17

But Moses said to the Lord, "Oh, my Lord, I am not eloquent, either heretofore or since thou hast spoken to thy servant; but I am slow of speech and of tongue." (v. 10)

It looks like Moses feared public speaking, and was very self-conscious about his speaking ability. Many a brave person, who would stand and fight physically quavers before the possibility of standing up before a group to say something.

All of us have some fear of humiliation. As we are thinking this week about the various aspects of our fear, this needs to be seen as one of the sneaky ones that may control us more than we know. Most of us will "walk a mile" to avoid a situation that is designed to humiliate us.

Yet humiliation is one of the chief ways God deals with our pride. Do we see pride as the first of the deadly sins, as the Church has taught it to be all through the centuries? Do we see pride as the root of arrogance which seeks to raise us above others (even secretly) and ultimately above God? For pride never willingly bows. It never truly gives up. It may yield the point, lose a battle now and then, but basically continues to rise above it all. That is its nature.

Humiliations crucify pride. Can you not think of things that happened in your own life that were excruciatingly painful at the time because they were so humiliating to your dignity or your good image? And later on, when the humbling has taken its effect, we can look back on such incidents and laugh. That is a healthy kind of laughing, for it is at ourselves, and pride has suffered a good blow in the process!

Our fear of humiliation will grow less as we learn not to take ourselves so seriously. Moses needed to trust God that he would give him the ability to say what was needed. I know a minister who stutters rather badly, but who has the ability to speak quite fluently when preaching. God is able!

Ask the Lord to show you where your fear of embarrassment is protecting some hidden mountain of pride. Remember that the "mountains and hills" must be brought low, and the valleys exalted to prepare the way of the Lord.

A Prayer: O Lord Jesus Christ, who didst humble thyself to become man, and to be born into the world for our salvation, teach us the grace of humility; root out of our hearts all pride and haughtiness, and so fashion us after thy holy likeness in this world, that in the world to come we may be made like unto thee; for thine own name and mercies' sake. Amen.

(Bishop Walsham How, d. 1823)

1. What are some of the things that happened in your own life that have been excruciatingly painful to your pride?

2. How can you learn not to take yourself so seriously?

When I am Afraid

Daily Reading: Psalm 56

When I am afraid, I put my trust in thee. (v. 3)

This is a tremendous little verse! It frees us up to admit and acknowledge that we are afraid. So many of us grew up with the idea that it was cowardly to admit fear, and we learned to hide our fear as well as we could on most occasions. How much healthier it is to have it out in the open. The psalmist says, "When (not if) I am afraid, I put my trust in thee."

When we are afraid, fear is a fact, and should not be denied. To repress it is simply to bury it to do deadly work within—and how many of us have suffered unduly because we put more strain on our bodies and emotional systems than God had meant them to carry, just because we were too proud and stubborn to get our fear out in the light.

A little child is sometimes afraid in the dark. He may wake up and see shadows moving like menacing figures, and feel terror-stricken. And then he makes the decision to go for help—to his parents' bed. And soon the fear is no more. Are we not like that? Admitting and confessing our fear to our heavenly Father can be a step into freedom that is nothing short of miraculous.

All this week we have been thinking about various forms of fear. But remember the basic truth: Fear is faith in the wrong person!—*You*! Self-trust is misplaced trust and is bound to fail us sooner or later.

A man faced a serious operation—open heart surgery. For the most part, he seemed to be calm and peaceful as the time for the surgery approached. But his wife, who knew him, watched for little signs of fear—and when they came, she would gently insist that he ought to confess his fear to the Lord. Reluctantly, sometimes after bravely insisting that he was not afraid, he would make his prayer. And two things would always happen: he would become inwardly aware that he had been afraid, and the fear would leave!

So do not be afraid or ashamed to admit the presence of fear. Confess it to God, talk it over with someone you can trust, and ask God to free you from it. For God did not give us the spirit of fear, but of power and love and self-control. By the grace of God through Jesus Christ, we can choose to put our trust in him. And making that choice frees the Holy Spirit to bring us the peace which passes understanding.

A Prayer: O Lord, this is all our desire—to walk along the path of life that thou hast appointed us, when as Jesus our Lord would walk along it, in steadfastness of faith, in meekness of spirit, in lowliness of heart, in gentleness of love. Let not the cares of this life press on us too heavily; but lighten our burdens, that we may follow thy way in quietness, filled with thankfulness for thy mercy, and rendering acceptable service unto thee; through Jesus Christ our Lord. Amen.

(Maria Hare, 1798, abridged)

1. What fear have you been ashamed to admit?

2. To what people are you free enough to confess your fears?

Chapter Review

Fear is unbelief. It responds to a situation as though God were absent from it or powerless to do anything about it. There is a healthy fear, by which we are taught to avoid danger, to respond to emergencies, and to exert extra strength.

But Jesus tells us to "fear not." He reminds us that even the sparrow's fall is not without the Father's care, and that even the hairs of our head are numbered. Trust can replace fear.

The psalmist says, "When I am afraid, I will trust in thee" (Psalm 56:3). This means that we have a choice. We do not have to be afraid. Fears come up within us, but "God hath not given us the spirit of fear, but of power (his power), and of love (living in his love) and of a sound mind (seeing reality rather than our fear fantasies)." Learning to face our fears and deal with them is one of the important life lessons for us all.

1. From what other fears have you been freed?

2. "The fear of the Lord is the beginning of wisdom." How does this fear counteract other fears?

3. How does getting our fears out into the light help us to see them for what they are?

PLAYING GOD—
THE SIN OF CONTROL
LETTING GO IS A FIGHT TO THE FINISH!

*Commit thy way
unto the LORD;
trust also in him;
and he shall bring
it to pass.*

Psalm 37:5 (KJV)

The Martha Complex

Daily Reading: John 11:1–44

Martha seems to have been a person who tried to be in control of her own life, and there was at least one other incident recorded in Scripture that confirms this characteristic. In the tenth chapter of St. Luke's Gospel, Jesus had been a guest in Martha and Mary's house. Martha, wanting to make sure everything was in order, and wanting to be a "good hostess," had been very busy around the house while Mary simply sat down at Jesus' feet to hear his teachings. When Martha complained that Mary was not helping, Jesus spoke to her sin and said that only one thing was needful and that Mary had made the right choice.

In today's reading we find Martha displaying her control in another way. Her brother, Lazarus, who was a special friend of Jesus, had been very ill. While he was sick, and while Mary and Martha and the others were very concerned for him, word had been sent to Jesus to come quickly. One can imagine that Martha had a big hand in this. She had faith that if Jesus would come and say the word, her brother would live. Mary had such faith, too, but the picture of Martha suggests that she may have been the one to take action to get Jesus there as quickly as possible. But he did not come when they sent for him! He delayed two days longer, and in the meantime, Lazarus died. Now word comes that Jesus is arriving, at last— late, as Martha sees things! And so she hastens out to meet him and to rebuke him for his failure to come when needed.

"Lord, if you had been here, my brother would not have died!" she blurted out accusingly. Wouldn't it have been too bad—for Martha, for Lazarus, and for everyone, if she had been able to write this story her own way! As it happened, this becomes the precursor of the Resurrection, and the occasion of some of the most beautiful words of truth and promise our Lord ever spoke. Are you not glad that Martha was not allowed to control the situation?

Think about this before you hasten to get into control of situations in your own life, thinking that if things do not go the way you think they should that all will be lost! Giving up control is giving God permission to be God! A small courtesy on our part!

A Prayer: Father, this day open my eyes to the ways in which I seek to control my own life and the lives of others. Help me to yield up all areas of my life to your direction. In Jesus' Name. Amen.

1. How did Martha try to control Jesus? What did he do about it?

2. Can you think of ways you try to control God? How?

Peter's Rebuke
Daily Reading: Matthew 16:13–28

But he turned and said to Peter, "Get behind me, Satan! You are a hindrance to me, for you are not on the side of God, but of men." (v. 23)

We are thinking all this week about our drive and tendency to try to control people and events around us. We do not think of it as trying to play God, but that is exactly what we are doing when we try to "stay in charge" of everything. We may think our motives are pure and good. Certainly, you cannot fault Peter's desire to see Jesus kept safe from the impending threat in Jerusalem. He loved Jesus. He wanted to see his ministry grow and enlarge, so that many, many others could find the same truth, the same help, the same hope that he and his fellow disciples had found listening to Jesus and following him. He believed Jesus had a great future, and he was ready to do everything he could to insure that nothing should stand in the way.

Can you imagine his shock and pain when Jesus turned to him with that stinging rebuke: "Get behind me, Satan! You are a hindrance to me, for you are not on the side of God, but of men"? Maybe Peter took it in his stride. The Gospel discreetly omits any mention of his reaction. But it does give us the follow-up words of Jesus, charting a course for himself and all who would follow him that would make the would-be follower think about what was involved!

Let this incident sink into your own heart, reminding you of the times when perhaps you thought you were moving from noblest motives to direct and shape someone else in the role or the direction you thought best. Parents, particularly, need to be wary of motives in directing their children into certain ways in order to make their lot better. It is easy to try to live through our children, and we may think we are doing them a good service when in fact, we are not "on the side of God, but of men." Far better it is to pray for them, advise them to seek God's direction, and free them to be themselves inasmuch as we are able.

Control is a particularly difficult problem to tackle, because it usually comes disguised as such a worthy thing. But Jesus cut through all that Peter thought, recognizing the subtle voice of the tempter in his words, and despising them heartily, in spite of Peter's conscious motives. Once we accept the idea that it is wrong to try to control others, we can ask God to show us where our control competes with his rightful place in the lives of those we love. It does not mean that we should not be honest and offer counsel. But it does mean that we must allow others to obey God for themselves, free of our desire to make their lives conform to all our ideas.

A Prayer: Thank you, Father, for the freedom to choose your way. Thank you for those who have taught and trained us, but left us free to make choices and to learn what it means to obey you. Give me grace to discern my own tendency to control others and enable me to refuse to play God in their lives, so that you, Lord Jesus, may rule and guide. In Jesus' Name. Amen.

1. Where do you recognize your drive and tendency to control people and events around you?

2. Matthew 16:22-23. How do you try to protect others from painful situations?

Misplaced Concern
Daily Reading: Matthew 12:38–50

While he was still speaking to the people, behold, his mother and his brothers stood outside, asking to speak to him. (v. 46)

This little incident is tucked into the ongoing story of Jesus' ministry, and it seems obviously intended to convey that wonderful reply which he made: "'Who are my mother and who are my brothers?' And stretching out his hand toward his disciples, he said, 'Here are my mother and my brothers! For whoever does the will of my Father in heaven is my brother, and sister, and mother.'" What a wonderful way for him to express his closeness to all who seek to follow the will of God! We are family—a part of God's family! Paul says it another way in Ephesians 2:19, "So then you are no longer strangers, and sojourners, but you are fellow citizens with the saints and members of the household of God."

Having said that, let us look back at the picture of Mary, the mother of Jesus, and her other sons. It seems that they were concerned for the welfare and safety of Jesus. Mary, of course, had stored up many a thing in her heart concerning this special Son of hers since the visit of the shepherds many years before. And no doubt, she had often recalled those words of the aged Simeon when she and Joseph took Jesus into the temple: "Behold, this child is set for the fall and rising of many in Israel, and for a sign that is spoken against (and a sword will pierce through your own soul also), that thoughts out of many hearts may be revealed" (Luke 2:34-35). We know from other passages that his brothers did not believe in him at first (John 7:5). So we can imagine that they, like some of his friends (mentioned in Mark 3:21) thought he was beside himself! And so the family comes to reason with him perhaps, possibly to try to steer him away from what they thought would be a disastrous and dangerous outcome if he did not change his direction. We can sympathize with their concern, but we can also see their wrongness. How like Peter it seems they must have been, seeking to turn Jesus from the very course God had set out for him to follow!

God's will does not always correspond to our best human wisdom and insight! We must remember that fact when we drive to control the situations around us, when we feel compelled to try to control others whom we love. We are responsible as parents to speak the truth to our children, but there comes a time when we must leave them to follow the light of their own hearts, even when we are convinced that such a course is wrong!

Mary would come to see how it all fit together. She would suffer the sword piercing through her own heart. And the Christian world has long stood with her in her sorrow at seeing her beloved Son condemned and crucified. But we have a little glimpse of Mary and his brethren after the Resurrection. In Acts 1, as the disciples gathered in the Upper Room to wait for the promised coming of the Holy Spirit, we are told that they "with one accord devoted themselves to prayer, together with the women and Mary the mother of Jesus, and with his brothers." So we know that they had come to see the folly and uselessness of their misplaced concern.

A Prayer: Lord, you know my concerns for those I love and for the situations in my life. You know, too, that sometimes I feel compelled to reach out and control people or situations. But I know that such efforts are really efforts to play God, and I am sorry for them and want to give them up. So I ask for your abundant grace to change, and trust you more. In Jesus' Name. Amen.

1. Where must you allow people to follow the light of their own hearts even though you are convinced they are wrong?

You Know Not What You Are Asking

Daily Reading: Matthew 20:17–34

"You know not what you are asking. Are you able to drink the cup I am to drink?" (v. 22)

Mrs. Zebedee's prayers were much like some of ours. And her concern was something we can all identify with. She wanted the best for her sons, and she thought that the best was naturally the highest. How many of us push our children in ways that are unfruitful and harmful for them because of some mistaken idea of what will make them happy. Too many young people have been "set up" with the idea that the best thing in the world is to make more money than their parents did! Or that education and more education is the answer that will bring life's fulfillment!

We are thinking about "control" this week as something we all need to become aware of in ourselves, so that we can "back off" and let God be God.

Of course Mrs. Zebedee was right in praying for her children. She may not have known fully who Jesus was, but she went to him with her concern. We, too, can go to him with our concerns—large and small—and pour them out before him. But sometimes we may be told that we do not know what we are asking. The thing we ask for may come with a lot of baggage we had not counted on. And that is why it is better to turn it over to the Lord and let him choose what is best, rather than trying to instruct him as to how things ought to go in the lives of those we love. Remember that little song we sang at Christmastime as young children? It went like this:

As for me, my little brain Isn't very bright,

Choose for me, old Santa Claus What you think is right!

Apply that to all the situations in your life at this point, and turn those situations over to the Lord, asking him (and giving him permission) to do what he knows is right and best. That kind of prayer cannot fail!

A Prayer: O God, the God of all goodness and grace, who art worthy of a greater love that we can either give or understand: Fill our hearts, we beseech thee, with such love toward thee that nothing may seem too hard for us to do or to suffer in obedience to thy will: so that we may become daily more like thee, and dwell more and more in the light of thy presence; through Jesus Christ our Lord. Amen.

(Farnham Hostel, adapted)

1. Where have you been pushing for the highest or the best for you (and yours)?

2. How can you "back off" and let God be God in these areas?

The Man Who Trusts in Man
Daily Reading: Jeremiah 17:1–18

Thus says the LORD, "Cursed is the man who trusts in man and makes flesh his arm, whose heart turns away from the LORD." (v. 5) "Blessed is the man who trusts in the LORD, whose trust is in the LORD." (v. 7)

It is interesting that the inspired prophet puts these two verses in a juxtaposition, as though to underscore the difference between these two ways of life. The first man, whose trust is in "man" is like a desert shrub, dwelling in dried up "salt land." Not a very pretty picture, and especially powerful in a land where water was always at a premium. Then comes the second part—the picture of the one whose trust is in the Lord. Like a tree growing by an unfailing stream, its roots go out generously, and when the heat of the day comes, there is still plenty of moisture to keep it in leaf and fruit. A beautiful picture of an oasis and one of the Bible's favorite pictures of a life that is rooted and grounded in God.

What a sad and pitiable life is that which sees no farther than the wits and wisdom of mankind. If you have known people who live that kind of life, you know very well how limited and cramped a life it is. We need largeness, the vastness of God's bounty in order to become the people we were intended to be. And if we let our hearts "turn away from the Lord," we are inevitably choosing the way of cursing, because God cannot bless disobedience and sin.

What we may not realize, however, is that we all too easily trust in ourselves our own wisdom, our ideas, our opinions, and then we blame God when things do not turn out well. It is better by far to begin to see that our sight is limited, our wisdom is but partial, and we need the wideness and height of God's point of view applied to every situation of our lives. Our control, our feeble attempt to guide and direct everything around us (and everyone around us) by our insights and opinions can only turn out sadly. For, in very truth, when we do such things, we are trusting in man, and usurping God's place.

With the prophet we can say, "Thou art my refuge in the day of evil." Nothing can befall us except by the permission of our heavenly Father, and he sees the end as well as the beginning. If we keep our hearts toward him, we can move through every circumstance with grace enough, and with our "leaves and fruit" still showing that we are in touch with the springs of living water.

A Prayer: O Lord, never allow us to think that we can stand by ourselves, and not need thee. Amen.`
(John Donne, 1573–1631)

1. Where this week have you been trusting in your own wisdom, ideas, or opinions?

2. What can you do about this?

See If There Be Any Hurtful Way in Me
Daily Reading: Psalm 139

And see if there be any wicked way in me, and lead me in the way everlasting. (v. 24)

The marginal note tells us that the Hebrew word which is translated "wicked" in this verse means "hurtful," "Search me, O Lord . . . and see if there be any hurtful way in me." That is a prayer we can all afford to pray frequently.

The thing we are hopefully seeing, as the Lord continues to show us the wrongness of our control, is that without knowing it there can be hurtful ways in us. We may think that what we want for others is for their good, but actually may be coming out of a lot of unrecognized, buried garbage in us. As we grow more trustful in allowing others to react honestly to us, we will find that much of what we thought was good was in fact self-expression, self in control for its own purposes. And when self directs our way, we can be very hurtful to others.

The late Corrie Ten Boom, whom we mentioned last week, used to say, "Corrie Ten Boom without Jesus is a menace to the world." And she meant it. She had come to distrust her own way. And we should pray for that same healthy distrust. Yesterday's reading said that the heart is deceitful above all things and desperately wicked. Today the psalmist prays "Search me, O God, and know my heart!" If we allow God to search and try us, there will be pain. The dross of the hidden self will be burned up. Not all at once, but as we continue praying this prayer.

A very devout and pious mother whom I know wreaks sorrow and pain on all those in her family. She is never wrong. She is spiritually superior. She does not say, "I am sorry." Christians should not sin, and she considers herself blameless in that area. So others avoid her, and her family continues to suffer from her blindness of heart.

By allowing others to be truthful with us, by praying that God will search and try our hearts, by continually praying against our desire to play God in other peoples' lives, we can be freed from such debilitating and hurtful blindness of soul.

"See if there be any hurtful way in me, and lead me in the way everlasting!"

A Prayer: May it be so, Lord. Amen.

1. What have you begun to see in you, that you previously thought was good, that you now see as hurtful?

2. How can you face this reality and still go on living with purpose and joy?

Fret Not
Daily Reading: Psalm 37

"Fret not yourself." The dictionary gives the meaning of "fret" in these words: "1. To eat away; gnaw; also, to wear away; rub; chafe; 2. To make by gnawing or wearing away a substance; as, to fret a hole in cloth; 3. To roughen, agitate, or disturb; to ripple; 4. To tease; irritate; vex; worry."

"Fret not yourself." Do not wear away, agitate, disturb, irritate, vex, or worry yourself. What a sensible and needed word of advice!

Why is it safe to "fret not"? Why can we relax in such a world as this, with all of its temptations, dangers, its opportunities for disaster—is it sensible at all not to fret and worry about what might happen?

Jesus said, "Take no thought. . . ." "Sufficient unto the day is the evil thereof." He seemed to think it was sensible to fret not.

The prophet says, "Thou wilt keep him in perfect peace whose mind is stayed on thee , because he trusteth in thee " (Isaiah 26:3). He seemed to think it was sensible to fret not.

St. Paul said, "The fruit of the Spirit is love, joy, peace. . . ." He seemed to think it is sensible to fret not.

It is safe, then, to let go of the desire and demand to stay in control of our lives. It is safe to let God direct our way. It is safe to refuse to fret over those who seem to be "getting away" with sin, rebellion, wickedness, and evil. God assures us that he is still on the throne of the universe, and that he will deal with each situation in his own judgment and mercy.

So we can believe, trust, relax, and go on with our lives. Let the peace of God, the fruit of the Holy Spirit in your life, relieve you of the burden and irritation of fretting over wrong and from the impossible burden of trying to make it all right!

A Prayer:
  Drop thy still dews of quietness
  Till all our strivings cease.
  Take from our souls the strain and stress
  And let our ordered lives confess
  The beauty of thy peace.
                    (J. G. Whittier)

1. Why is it safe to "fret not"?

2. How can you believe, trust, relax, and go on with life?

Week Review

Control is the attempt to play God by managing our own lives and by manipulating others. Even tiny children try to control their environment and manipulate their parents. It is a part of our very nature. Yet God is God, and warns us that we cannot usurp his place. Our attempts to play God, unless checked and repented of, can play havoc with loved ones, and bring tragic and heart-breaking results.

1. After reading, thinking, and praying about your control all this week, read Matthew 20:21-22. How do you seek to control or manipulate people for their own good?

2. What can you do to allow God to deeply change you in this area?

PRESSING TOWARD THE GOAL
HE CONSTANTLY DRAWS US ON!

One thing I do,
forgetting what
lies behind and
straining forward
to what lies ahead,
I press on toward
the goal. . . .

Philippians 3:13

TWENTY-FOUR

Tell the People to Go Forward
Daily Reading: Exodus 14:10–31

The Lord said to Moses, "Why do you cry to me? Tell the people of Israel to go forward." (v. 15)

The people of Israel were setting out on a long and difficult journey. It was a journey from slavery to freedom. On that journey they would suffer setbacks, disappointments, and above all, they would suffer from their own lack of commitment to the journey. In that, they are not unlike us. We have set out on a journey, too. Our journey, like theirs, is from slavery to freedom. From slavery to old, unproductive habits of eating, disorderly habits in the use of our time, wasteful habits in the use of opportunities to be better followers of Jesus. And though we may deplore those habits, they are deeply ingrained, and have a strong hold on us. We will not get free from them without a determination to persevere.

Many of the Israelites were ready to give up, give in, and go back to Egypt, when they saw the powerful, cruel army of Pharaoh bearing down on them. They were painfully aware of their weakness and the strength of the enemy. But what they needed was to remember the strength of God. He says, "My strength is perfected in weakness" (2 Corinthians 12:9). As long as they thought only of their own weakness and the power of the enemy, they were stymied in their fear. But the Word of the Lord came, rebuking them even for spending time crying to the Lord. "Tell the people of Israel to go forward."

And that is the word for us. What a gift it is to have people in our lives willing to move forward with us! We can be a great help and encouragement to one another in this long, arduous journey. Remember, slavery is hard to break. It is one thing for the slave to escape, for the real slavery is inside. As long as Israel felt like, thought like, and acted like a slave, he was still a slave no matter where he was.

Our goal is to be free from the tyranny of inner slavery to help us become the persons we were created to be in Christ. What does it matter if it takes longer than we like? What does it matter if there is hard work, pain, tears, and failure involved in the journey? The important thing is that we are on our way to freedom—the freedom for which Jesus came, for which he gave his life, and which he offers to us if we are willing to persevere. Don't lose sight of the goal!

A Prayer. Father, I thank you for calling me out of bondage to myself, my sick and unfruitful thoughts and ways, into a better, higher, nobler way. I thank you for leading me this far, and pray for grace to persevere until I reach the journey's end— whatever it is you have planned for me. In Jesus' Name. Amen.

1. What do you believe to be your specific areas of slavery (misuse of the computer, unproductive habits of eating, disorderly habits with time and opportunities, etc.)? Be specific!

2. What steps can you take to begin to come to freedom in these areas?

Across the Jordan
Daily Reading: Joshua 3

The priests who bore the ark of the covenant of the Lord stood on dry ground in the midst of the Jordan, until all the nation finished passing over the Jordan. (v. 17)

Today's Bible reading from Joshua takes us a full forty years beyond yesterday's reading and shows the new generation of Israelites on the threshold of the Promised Land. But only a few of those who had started out would be allowed to enter this new land—such was the price of their stubborn unfaithfulness!

The Jordan symbolizes an impossible barrier to the fulfillment of their dream. The land which God had given their forefathers lay just across the Jordan, but there were no bridges or superhighways spanning its muddy waters. And, in addition, they arrived just when the river was at a floodtide! Can you picture the helplessness of the people—with thousands of people, men, women, and children, plus cattle and other belongings, standing at the brink of a deep, fast-flowing stream? It would be enough to discourage the stoutest heart!

Does it remind you of things in your own life that seem to come across your path just when the goal is in sight—sometimes impossible things which you have no power in yourself to conquer? That is what the Jordan has represented to Christians over the centuries.

This, however, is just where faith and faithfulness come in! We serve a God who can handle a situation like this. He can take any impossible situation, and open a way through it for us. He has done so for millions, and will do so for us. What we need is to use the tiny bit of faith we have when we confront such an impossible situation—believing that God will work for us exceedingly, abundantly above all that we can think or ask! He longs for our good even more than we do ourselves, and can only do us good, not evil, all the days of our lives.

Legend tells us that the priests carried the ark down into the stream, and that they carried it until the water came up to their very noses, before God caused the waters to part. Sometimes we have to be willing to wade into an impossible situation with nothing but our faith that God will bring us through. If we hold back, protecting ourselves, fearful of being wrong, we may miss the blessing altogether.

God is faithful to do his part, but he does expect us to exercise our "faith muscles" in trusting him and moving on toward the Promised Land. Are you moving faithfully, trusting him for the impossible?

A Prayer. Father, I do choose to trust you in my present situation. I choose to believe that you are in my life for good and that you will never fail nor forsake me. Give me grace to go on with you, trusting you more, obeying you more faithfully, loving you more. In Jesus' Name. Amen.

1. What seemingly impossible barrier lies in front of you right now?

2. How can you move faithfully on trusting him in this impossible situation?

What Do These Stones Mean?
Daily Reading: Joshua 4

And he said to the people of Israel, "When your children ask their fathers in time to come, 'What do these stones mean?' then you shall let your children know, 'Israel passed over this Jordan on dry ground'. . . . that you may fear the LORD your God for ever." (vv. 21-22, 24b)

Those were not just ordinary stones. They were stones gathered from the bottom of the deep river. They were stones with a story. Every one of us is called at times to go through deep waters. It may be the sorrow and grief of losing someone close to us. It may be the hurt of rejection by someone we have loved. Whatever it is, it was a time of trial, stress, and of proving that God is a keeper of his Word. For he has promised never to leave nor forsake us. "When you pass through the waters, I will be with you," he says; "And when you pass through the rivers they will not sweep over you" (Isaiah 43).

It is important, as we go through such times, to gather "stones of remembrance." That is what Israel was doing in this chapter—building a monument of sorts from the smooth stones from the depths of the impossible Jordan. When people (especially their children) asked questions about those stones, they would tell their story, and the very stones would speak.

You and I have words that can encourage and strengthen the faith of others if we will gather our stones of remembrance out of the depths of the impossibilities of our lives. Who but God could bring us through such difficulties? And it is right, then, that our monuments of praise should glorify him and encourage others to find him their very present help in time of trouble.

One of the beautiful things about fellowship in the body of faith is that we have the opportunity to share and encourage others who are facing some of the same struggles and temptations we have gone through. None of us arrives at the same place at the same time, so there is ample opportunity to reach out with an encouraging word, as well as receiving encouragement from others in our times of need. And God gets the honor and glory, for it is his Spirit who has brought us together, and who is the bond of our fellowship.

Make much of the testimony which God gives you in those hard places. There is life and strength in such testimony for others.

A Prayer: Thank you, Father, for the remembrance of your saving help. Thank you for the privilege of encouraging others along their way. By your grace we will continue to keep a faithful witness so that others, "Who have not passed this way before" can look up, believe, and rejoice in your wonderful power. In Jesus' Name. Amen.

1. Where have others sharing their lives with you helped and encouraged you to go on?

2. Like the children of Israel, who gathered "stones of remembrance," what can you specifically remember about God's faithfulness to you?

A Company of Believers
Daily Reading: Malachi 3:6–18

*Then those who feared the LORD spoke with one another;
the LORD heeded and heard them, and a book of remembrance
was written of those who feared the LORD and thought on
his name. (v. 16)*

The particular thought that interests us in this passage is the almost incidental statement that "those who feared the LORD spoke with one another."

The people were in an environment where many of their neighbors did not fear nor revere God. It was important, then, that those who sought to walk with God should "speak with one another." They belonged together, and their fellowship was important.

This is the last book of the Old Testament, and you can see almost a forecast and foretaste of those little fellowships which made up the early church. Living in a hostile world, they gathered together to encourage, correct, teach, and build one another up in their common faith in Jesus and their commitment to him.

Small groups and your family can be an opportunity to taste the blessing of fellowship with others who are thinking on spiritual things, trying to be open with one another, and who are concerned with building one another up in their common faith in Christ and commitment to him.

For the fellowship of the Spirit is essential if you are going to go on in your walk with Jesus, growing more and more in likeness to him, and putting self with all its demands in its proper place. Most of us find we cannot do it alone.

A recent TV program on bodily health asked the question: how do you motivate yourself to do exercise? There were a variety of answers, but one of the most common was, "I go to a group" or "I attend a class." Motivation is a prime concern for spiritual as well as physical health. It is not the one who begins the race, but the one who completes it who is crowned as victor.

So seek the Lord's will for you, and talk it over with a friend or family member as to what the Spirit is guiding you to do to keep motivation high in going on in your life of disciplined freedom in Christ.

"Those who feared the LORD spoke with one another." That need is in us all, and the Lord has provision for meeting it if we are open to his guidance. May he guide your thoughts and decisions this week as to where you will go from here.

A Prayer: Holy Spirit, you are able to see and know our needs far better than ourselves. Vouchsafe to guide and direct our thoughts that we may find and follow your wise and blessed will. In Jesus' Name. Amen.

1. In what way have these devotions been an encouragement, a correction, and a place to grow for you?

2. What will you do to maintain continued growth?

Care in Building
Daily Reading: 1 Corinthians 3:10–23

If the work which any man has built on the foundation survives, he will receive a reward. (v. 14)

All this week our thoughts are turning to what lies ahead of us in our Christian walk. We have started out on a course, and have continued along a way intended to bring new order, discipline, and freedom in our lives. We have paid a certain price to come this far—and we have come to know ourselves well enough to know that there will be a cost to going on! No victory without its price!

But has it not been your experience that the blessing far outweighed the cost? Has not God often surprised you with his graciousness and overflowing blessing? What he asks of us is really very little compared to what he is willing to give us.

Paul is speaking here of the spiritual foundation of the Church, of our lives as Christians. He makes it abundantly clear that there is only one foundation, and that is Jesus Christ. Anything else will cave in under us, sooner or later.

And we have all had the tremendous blessing of knowing that truth, so that we could, quite simply and without any fanfare, place our faith in him, take him as our one and only hope for life and for the life to come. Once we have done that, with all that we are and all that we have, our lives are then positioned on that solid, trustworthy foundation. But the foundation is not the whole house. A structure of living must go on the foundation. It is the role of the foundation to support and sustain that which is built upon it. And therein lies our challenge.

Paul talks about two different types of material being used: the first was "good" material—gold, silver, precious stones. A building erected of such materials would stand the test. Then there was the "cheap" material—hay, wood, straw—material that would be consumed in the fires of testing, to the loss of the builder. He is saying that the choice of materials is up to us.

Gold of obedience, silver of sacrifice, precious stones of thankfulness—these materials will stand. But the hay, wood, and straw of self-desire, self-deceit, self-will—will profit nothing. These devotions challenged us to sort out the difference daily, and weekly. What kind of material is going into our lives? Will it bring joy or will it bring sorrow?

A Prayer: Father, I thank you for the sure foundation Jesus Christ, on which I can build my life day by day. I thank you for your supply of grace which enables me to make hard choices against easy indulgences. I thank you for those you have given to help and encourage me to let each day's building be something that will bring joy instead of sorrow. In Jesus' Name. Amen.

1. In the last several weeks, how has God surprised you with his graciousness and overflowing blessing?

2. In what new ways have you learned afresh the blessing of obedience?

I Do Not Run Aimlessly
Daily Reading: 1 Corinthians 9:19–27

Well, I do not run aimlessly, I do not box as one beating the air; but I pommel my body and subdue it, lest after preaching to others I myself should be disqualified. (vv. 26-27)

Running aimlessly. The very picture of it is a sad one, of someone who does not know what to do, or what direction to go. Yet in our Christian lives, are we not often guilty of doing just that: running aimlessly? running about with no real goals or purpose, darting from one "duty" to another, letting our lives be used up without really deciding what course of action we should be on?

These devotions have attempted to cut across that aimlessness. They have come into our lives with a challenge to let Jesus increase in us and to let self decrease. Like Paul, we may have found the struggle intense at times. He speaks of "pommeling" his body to subdue it. Just what that may have meant, we do not know, but it does indicate a manful struggle against the body's demands.

Paul was no amateur Christian. By the time he penned these words, he was a veteran of many a spiritual battle, and had undergone what would appear to be heroic hardships for the sake of Jesus Christ. Yet he can fall back on none of these. He still must stay alert and persevere, "lest having preached to others, I myself should be disqualified." Knowing that, kept him on the battleline.

Our trouble with any discipline is that we want it to be over, so that we can "get back to normal." But it was the "normal" way of living that got us into trouble in the first place, and we need to see discipline—not as a short-term shot-in-the-arm, but as a different way of living. Discipline is meant to free us inwardly to become the constructive, creative, fulfilled people we were meant to be. Jesus gives us the discipline as a loving gift in order to free us for the life that is life indeed. As long as we cling to the idea that real living is undisciplined living we will fall back into our old patterns. And we know where those patterns lead—into despair, self-hate, bitterness, and depression. But if we accept discipline as the path of real freedom, we will see it as a long-term, permanent way of living which can bear much fruit.

A Prayer: Forgive me, Lord, for wanting the easy way instead of the good way. Forgive me for longing for those unproductive indulgences which bear no fruit for you, and bring only discontent and despair. Give me grace to stand against the demands of the flesh to be pampered and pleased, and to stand with you, Lord, in faithful obedience which is freedom indeed. In Jesus' Name. Amen.

1. What specific course(s) of action have you chosen in order to no longer "run aimlessly"?

2. Discipline is meant to free us inwardly to become the constructive, creative, fulfilled people we were meant to be. How are you experiencing this to be so?

Need of Endurance
Daily Reading: Hebrews 10:19–39

*For you have need of endurance, so that you may do the will
of God and receive what is promised. (v. 36)*

That is what we all need—endurance! Too many of us
Christians are what someone has termed "Dazzle Droopers."
We start out in a cloud of dust and a blaze of glory. But then,
for one reason or another, enthusiasm declines, and we droop
by the way.

Pray for the grace of endurance and the grace to keep on
keeping on. Jesus has called you to it. He has pioneered the
way in his own flesh, and has blazed a trail for us to follow.
He gives you the needed grace for each temptation, each trial,
each difficulty as it comes along. He renews his promise daily
to be with you always, even to the end of the age. The Holy
Spirit, the Comforter, dwells within you, to encourage and lift
up your spirit when you are feeling low, to correct you when
you would go astray, and to convict you of those sins and sin
areas where God is still at work purifying you to make you
wholly his. So you can see the need for endurance.

One of the saddest things we have to face is seeing people
make a good start with Jesus and then dropping by the way.
We can see and feel the promise of their new life in Christ, and
even see them tasting the first fruits of the Spirit. Then when
the flesh, the world, and the devil make their bids, and come
against these newborn souls with allurements, demands,
discouragements, or whatever weapons they can muster,
sometimes these newly awakened souls turn, get their eyes off
Jesus and the goal he has set for them, and become entangled
again in their old ways.

We need endurance. Only the steady, day by day plodding will get us to our goal. Do you have your goals in mind? Some goals are more intangible, some of them very practical like the goal of cleaning up one's room faithfully every day, of mowing the grass when it is needed and not just when it is convenient, etc. Enduring in the mundane application of our faith in Jesus will mean the difference between a life that goes nowhere and a life that has growth, change, and hope right at its very heart and core.

I pray for you the grace of endurance. Amen.

1. What long-range goals do you need to set for yourself?

2. How will you go about "reaching forward" to them?

Chapter Review

Goals are funny things. There are short-term goals and long-range goals. We might set such goals as: saving money for a trip, to gain or lose weight, to become more outgoing with others, to be on time, not to use the computer or cell phone after a certain hour of the evening, etc.

When it comes to assessing progress with goal keeping, we can be encouraged as we look back and challenged as we look forward. We all take a long time learning old habits—we don't break them and establish new ones in a few or even several months. Many of us need and require more help before trying to do it all on our own. Indeed Christianity is a social religion rather than a solitary one, and being a responsible member of the body of Christ involves receiving and giving help and encouragement.

The last twelve weeks of devotions began with a look at forgiving ourselves for not being perfect. We concluded with a study in patient perseverance "toward the goal." Disappointment with our past performance need not lead into despair. As we learn better what our old nature is in Adam, and how, even as regenerate believers in Christ, we are still subject to the subtle movings of self, we are better prepared to carry on a continuing batttle against it. The more we understand ourselves and life's battles, the more we benefit from these devotions and the truths they offer us. It's a lifetime experience. It doesn't matter how weak we are or how long it takes; with God's grace we will make it.

For additional life-changing devotional material, call us at
1-800-451-5006 or e-mail us at
customerservice@paracletepress.com

God bless you.

About Paraclete Press

WHO WE ARE

Paraclete Press is an ecumenical publisher of books and recordings on Christian spirituality. Our publishing represents a full expression of Christian belief and practice—from Catholic to Evangelical, from Protestant to Orthodox.

Paraclete Press is the publishing arm of the Community of Jesus, an ecumenical monastic community in the Benedictine tradition. As such, we are uniquely positioned in the marketplace without connection to a large corporation and with informal relationships to many branches and denominations of faith.

We like it best when people buy our books from booksellers, our partners in successfully reaching as wide an audience as possible.

WHAT WE ARE DOING
Books

Paraclete Press publishes books that show the richness and depth of what it means to be Christian. Although Benedictine spirituality is at the heart of all that we do, we publish books that reflect the Christian experience across many cultures, time periods, and houses of worship.

We publish books that nourish the vibrant life of the church and its people–books about spiritual practice, formation, history, ideas, and customs.

We have several different series of books within Paraclete Press, including the bestselling *Living Library* series of modernized classic texts; *A Voice from the Monastery*—giving voice to men and women monastics about what it means to live a spiritual life today; award winning literary faith fiction; and books that explore Judaism and Islam and discover how these faiths inform Christian thought and practice.

Recordings

From Gregorian chant to contemporary American choral works, our music recordings celebrate the richness of sacred choral music through the centuries. Paraclete is proud to distribute the recordings of the internationally acclaimed choir Gloriæ Dei Cantores, who have been praised for their "rapt and fathomless spiritual intensity" by *American Record Guide*, and the Gloriæ Dei Cantores Schola, which specializes in the study and performance of Gregorian chant. Paraclete is also the exclusive North American distributor of the Monastic Choir of St. Peter's Abbey in Solesmes, France, long considered to be a leading authority on Gregorian chant performance.

More Devotionals Available from Paraclete Press

You'll Never Walk Alone
A Daily Guide to Renewal
RONALD E. MINOR

176 pages, Trade Paper
ISBN: 1-55725-360-9
$13.95

For anyone who is struggling with feelings of loneliness or discouragement, this book provides a twelve-week path that will bring you a renewed vision for life! Longtime pastor and spiritual director Ron Minor digs deeply into the Scriptures to provide daily wisdom for such issues as dealing with loneliness, overcoming fear, and healing wounded relationships.

When the Road Seems Too Steep
A Daily Guide to Positive Change
RONALD E. MINOR

168 pages, Trade paper
ISBN: 1-55725-399-4
$13.95

This daily devotional provides a twelve-week journey toward the positive life change that Jesus promises. Weekly discussion topics include dying to our natural desires, living in the light of Christ, the joy resulting from repentance, and more.